Class
Culture
and
Education

for Winifred

Class
Culture
and
Education

HAROLD ENTWISTLE

METHUEN

First published in 1978 by Methuen and Co Ltd
11 New Fetter Lane, London EC4P 4EE
© 1977 Harold Entwistle

Printed in Great Britain at
the University Printing House
Cambridge.
Typeset by
Red Lion Setters,
Holborn, London.

ISBN 0 416 75710 3 (hardbound)
ISBN 0 416 75720 0 (paperback)

Contents

Introduction

This book examines a number of related concepts which are of importance to educational theory: equality, class, culture, work and leisure. Whilst an attempt is made to clarify these and resolve some of the conceptual ambiguities to which they are intrinsically prone, their interrelationship is also explored through discussion of some current educational problems, especially the problems posed for schools by the so-called culturally deprived. The debate about differential provision of schooling for different social groups is taken up through examination of the assumption that schools are middle-class institutions and the claims and counter-claims about the possibility of there being a common culture as the basis for a common curriculum in comprehensive schools. The concept of culture and, especially, the meaning of working-class culture requires examination in this context, as well as the thesis that any sub-culture constitutes an adequate or valid way of life.

Equality has been a subject of continuous discussion among educationists for at least half a century. It would seem that its meaning has been sufficiently clarified such that little more can be said about education and equality. It has even seemed, given the manifest inequalities which remain (and even intensify, some would argue) in advanced industrial societies, that the debate about equality in education does little to advance the establishment of just and equitable educational arrangements. Perhaps we ought to stop debating educational equality and attempt to fashion social concepts which might be sharper instruments of social reform. This, indeed, is the conclusion of the recent North American debate about educational inequality. However, the debate which led Jencks and others to conclude that social equality cannot be engineered through the schools is not without conceptual ambiguity itself, and it is necessary to look at the continuing discussion of educational equality in the context of this recent dismissal of schools as irrelevant to the achievement of social justice.

Earlier in this century, the debate about equality was conducted largely from the point of view of differences between individuals, the origins of these differences and the educational problems they appeared to create. Recent discussion has tended to focus on the problem of equality as one of diminishing the differences between groups. In particular, differences of access to privileged schooling and of achievement within schools have been related to the social-class backgrounds of students. However, the notion of social class (which, surprisingly, has received little attention from philosophers of education) seems also a blunt instrument for those in pursuit of educational and social reform. It is necessary to examine differing notions of social class and the relevance of these for educational theory. Taken together with the concept of equality, that of social class raises two important questions: (i) if we are committed to equality are we then committed to a classless society; (ii) if not, if we accept the inevitability of merited differences in status, power or economic reward, what do we have to say about those who remain underprivileged or deprived within any of these three categories? In particular, what sort of education is appropriate for those who find themselves in the lower strata with reference to status, power or the distribution of economic goods? Until recently, the notion that there were culturally disadvantaged or deprived children seemed too obvious to require close examination by educationists. Movements for social justice over two centuries derived their justification from the undoubted existence of underprivileged or disadvantaged groups. That there existed in schools children who were culturally deprived seemed axiomatic. Nor did the components of this deprivation seem anything but obvious. Deprived children were assumed to come from homes which were economically deficient and it seemed, despite obvious exceptions to the contrary, that economic deprivation correlated with cultural deprivation.

However, a number of sociologists of education now seem to be saying that deprivation can only have meaning as an economic notion. On this view, to speak of cultural deprivation is patronizing at best, at worst it is a device for schools' shrugging off their own limitations as instruments of working-class education. No doubt there are children in school whose housing, clothing and nutrition fall below standards considered minimal for a decent life in modern society. But, so the argument runs, these children come from homes in communities where there is life of such cultural richness and energy that it is probably culturally equal or superior to life amongst the middle class. On this view, the economically deprived can only be put at a cultural disadvantage by neglect of their culture in schools which are essentially middle-class institutions.

It is far from clear what social philosophy informs this polemic of those who argue that cultural deprivation is a myth. Aside from the logic of terms like deprived and disadvantaged, a good deal seems to hinge on the concept of culture which is taken to be educationally relevant. Although expressions like 'working-class culture' and 'middle-class culture' are in common use, teachers have usually assumed that the culture they were transmitting is classless. Thinking that their term of reference was to 'Western culture', they have been surprised to discover that the science, history, mathematics, geography, literature, art and craft which form the backbone of the curriculum have to be dismissed as mere middle-class culture or, by others (often educational conservatives) as a 'high culture' inappropriate for all except a gifted minority. But if teachers were mistaken about the universal reference within Western society of the cultural content of the traditional curriculum, a number of questions thrust themselves upon the attention of curriculum theorists. Some of these relate to questions we have already posed about the objectives of education as classless or class reinforcing. If the most important datum about any student is that relating to his present and likely future membership of a particular social class, what does this imply for the work of the schools? What would be adequate socio-philosophical reasons for schools transmitting different cultures to students from different social classes? What would be the cultural content of curricula aimed at different social classes, particularly in terms of notions like 'excellence' or 'the best'? Or, is there a sense in which the different classes might be well enough served by the transmission of a common culture? Would this, as English conservative educationists are apt to claim, inevitably be a diluted high culture, neither of use nor ornament to a majority of people, and a threat to the survival of Western civilization?

As well as having implications for an analysis of equality and class as educationally relevant ideas, this discussion of the cultural correlates of schooling cannot be divorced from two other human concerns — work and leisure. How is the problem of culture (and, indeed, the notions of equality and class) related to work and to leisure? It is a cliché that we should educate for leisure and this usually implies that students should be initiated into cultural activities which will help them to make profitable (perhaps creative) use of their spare time. But it has to be questioned how far this constitutes a satisfactory conception of leisure. How far is leisure itself a function of social class; has it any connection with the notion of equality? More than this, does it make any sense to dichotomize leisure and work? And still more fundamental, to what extent do the answers to this complex of educational problems we are discussing, deriving from notions like equality, class, culture and leisure, depend upon our having a clear notion of the role of work in individual life and in the dynamic of social and technological change?

In attempting to clarify these issues I have had the benefit of valuable initial comment and discussion from the following friends and colleagues: Arpi Hamalian, Bill Knitter, Geoff Fidler, Eric Hoyle, Ray Bolam, Keith Baker, Chris Sinha and Gordon Reddiford. Most of the book was written during a sabbatical year made possible by the generosity of my own university and the award of a Canada Council Leave Fellowship. I am also grateful for the hospitality of the University of Bristol and, especially, the School of Education which arranged a number of seminars on themes associated with my research.

1

Equality
and education

The case for equality

Debate about our educational arrangements usually takes the case
for equality to be axiomatic. If there is controversy about equality in
education it rarely questions the justice of making our educational
provision less inequitable. Discussion tends to focus either on the
conceptual ambiguity of the notion of equality when applied to
education, or upon the unlikelihood of our ever achieving what
seems an unquestioned social ideal. This imperative towards equality is epitomized by John Wilson (1966 : 35):

> By most criteria of similarity, men seem very much alike: and
> equalitarianism has gained ground over the centuries not so
> much because egalitarians have browbeaten people into accept-
> ing new criteria (when they could quite reasonably have been
> content with criteria which justified inequality) but rather
> because they have succeeded in *waking people up* to the general
> similarities of all men which could be recognised, with a slight
> mental effort, by existing criteria of similarity.

Although by no means so convinced as Wilson of this self-evidence of the case for equality, even educational conservatives are apt to recognize that egalitarians have made all the running in the educational debate (Bantock 1975a : 134). One of them has recently complained that 'the whole tenor of discourse in our society has moved away from discussing whether or not inequality is a desirable object' (Utley 1975 : 23). Indeed, the emotional climate favouring equality is such that conservatives find it necessary to exploit it. Bantock, for example, approvingly coins the notion of 'cultural equality' though, as he defines it, this seems completely unrelated to the received notion of equality as somehow concerned with identity or sameness. In the same volume of critical essays, although concluding that education is essentially a matter of personal relationships such that 'it is essentially the sort of thing to which the concept of equality does not apply', Lucas (1975 : 39-40, 60) nevertheless concludes that 'it is difficult to fight equality', a doctrine compounded of 'valid principles which can scarcely be gainsaid'.

Yet it really is surprising that egalitarians have been able to dictate the terms of the debate about equality. Whilst concluding that he himself is an egalitarian, the editor of a recent published debate on equality and education confessed to finding 'the arguments for equality [to be] extremely weak. That is to say, no kind of abstract ideas on the subject seemed strongly, overwhelmingly persuasive' (Vaizey 1975 : 115). Indeed, the assumption of the American Declaration of Independence that it is a self-evident truth that 'all men are created equal' can itself be taken as evidence of the weakness of the case for equality. To claim that something is self-evident implies that justification is not required: it may also conceal the fact that reasons for making such a claim are not easy to come by. R.S. Peters (1966 : 120-1) argues that the case for equality is mainly negative: that is, in the absence of demonstrably relevant grounds for treating people unequally, the presumption ought to be in favour of equality of treatment. But, since Aristotle, there has also been a presumption that whilst justice requires that equals should be treated equally, it also requires that unequals should be treated unequally. And experience continuously teaches that what Lord Bryce called 'the stubborn fact of Inequality' seems undeniable.

However, though the assumption that 'all men are created equal' seems easily capable of empirical falsification, this does not dispose of the doctrine of human equality which, historically, has functioned as a moral imperative deriving from a particular conception of man and of human relationships and, usually, prefacing a programme of political action aimed at amelioration of those manifest inequalities which are assumed to dehumanize individuals and disfigure societies.

It was the conventional wisdom of the past two decades that the combined effects of the affluent society and the welfare state had been the conquest of poverty and a significant redistribution of wealth towards the lower income groups. With reference to the United Kingdom, Vaizey concluded (1975 : 62): 'Within one country it seems that over the years the distribution of income and of wealth is growing more equal and that the richer a country is the more equal its distribution of income and wealth is likely to be.' The prevalence of this assumption within the United States is well documented by Parker (1974). In both countries educationists were led to conclude that inequality was now only a marginal problem (Bantock 1975a : 134; Vaizey 1975 : 20, 62). James Coleman (1973 : 137) concluded his review of Jencks's *Inequality* with the assumption that the problem of equality is unlikely to remain an abiding social concern:

> It should ... be pointed out that preoccupation with inequality of opportunity and inequality of result in society is probably only a current preoccupation that derives from structured inequalities of opportunity for certain groups like Blacks and women. When these are reduced, social attention will likely pass to other questions of social reconstruction such as how to increase the degree of responsibility of persons towards particular other persons.

However, on this formulation of the problem, it is by no means clear that equality is an issue which may soon be conveniently forgotten. Blacks and women comprise more than one-half of the American adult population. If this is a measure of the ground to be covered, our attention may be forced to pass to other questions only in the very long term. And in view of the conflicting evidence from other students of the American social scene[1] that inequalities persist, even become wider, not narrower, it is not clear that social

institutions *can* readily be restructured in order that the 'structured
inequalities of opportunity' for those groups can be 'reduced'.
Indeed, other sociologists and economists have argued that
inequality is endemic in the structure of advanced capitalist
societies. MacIntyre (1970 : 69) believes that 'the steady erosion of
welfare institutions, the continuous recreation of poverty is a part of
the truth about modern industrial societies'. Even Vaizey (somewhat in self-contradiction) writes of 'the evidence of academic
researchers and of government enquiries that there is a perennial
drift towards inequality, even within the public services which are
established on an ostensibly equalitarian basis ... society has a deep
movement towards inequality' (1975 : 48).

The case for inequality

This apparent tendency towards the continual renewal of inequality
in advanced industrial societies is usually taken to be a *malaise* of
capitalism.[2] However, cogent arguments are also adduced in
support of the view that it is inequality, not equality, which is
functional for a healthy society. On this view, inequality is not a
social *malaise* but a vital energy towards economic growth and social
well-being. It is, of course, part of conservative credo that competition (implying profit and loss — hence inequality) is the nerve of
industrial societies, ultimately benefiting everyone. Parkin (1973 :
117-8) summarizes this functional economic theory:

> ... inequality of reward is a necessary feature for any complex
> society, since it is a key mechanism for ensuring that talent is
> utilized in the most effective way ... Under conditions of equali-
> zation there would be a danger that key positions in a society
> would be filled by its less gifted members whilst the most
> talented languished in equally well rewarded but less socially
> significant positions.

And as Parkin goes on to demonstrate, inequality is taken to be
functionally necessary in those Eastern European states whose
official ideology is Marxist.

To this argument that inequality makes for economic efficiency is
sometimes added the conclusion that it is also sociologically
inevitable. Dahrendorf (1969 : 33-5), for example, argues that as

moral communities' societies require an unequal distribution of power: 'The origin of inequality is ... to be found in the existence in all human societies of norms of behaviour to which sanctions are attached ... There is inequality because there is law; if there is law, there must also be inequality among men.' Hence, '... because sanctions are necessary to enforce conformity in human conduct, there has to be inequality of rank among men ... the idea of a society in which all distinctions of rank between men are abolished transcends what is socially possible and has a place only in the sphere of poetic imagination.'[3] However, Dahrendorf also reminds us of Kant's aphorism that inequality is a 'rich source of much that is evil, but also of everything good'. He has in mind that the good which derives from inequality is the ultimate destruction of inequality: '... every system of social stratification generates protest against its principles and bears the seeds of its own suppression. But for others the good which is implicit in inequality lies in the possibility of raising the standard of living of the disadvantaged through the extra, efficient efforts of those who are rewarded with social or economic privileges. Rawls (1971 : 15, 62; see also 94, 101-5, 151), for example, argues that economic inequality can be the instrument of a radical social ethic. For him, justice is satisfied if unequal rewards help to increase the production of wealth, provided that such additional increments are distributed to the disadvantaged: '... there is no injustice in the greater benefits earned by a few provided that the situation of persons not so fortunate is thereby improved ... Injustice is simply inequalities that are not to the benefit of all.'

These economic, sociological and ethical attempts to legitimize inequality are sometimes underlined by resort to psychological argument. Notwithstanding that the case for equality seems to be self-evident, there appears some doubt whether people really want it. John Wilson (1966 : 165, 162) has concluded that people are psychologically ill-equipped for equality:

We positively prefer to treat the other person as an enemy, or as a superior; or as an inferior: at any rate, not as an equal. Equality-relationships are very hard to sustain and demand a high degree of psychological maturity. It is not to be wondered at if we often fail to sustain them: but usually we do not even try ... our behaviour in political and social contexts in fact suggests that we are usually more concerned with equity than with equality. We want our rights, or what we conceive to be our rights: we do not want partnership ...'[4]

Thus professional associations and labour unions strive to maintain salary and wage differentials, and incomes policies are regarded as unacceptable if they unduly threaten existing patterns of income distribution (Hindess 1971 : 40).[5] Vaizey finds evidence of inegalitarian pressures at work in 'the phenomenon of working-class deference' and in 'racialism, the dislike of immigrants'. With reference to education, Pedley (1963 : 11) concluded that the British of the 1960s wanted a school system geared to creating the opportunity to become unequal and there is little evidence of a change of mood in this respect in the mid-1970s. Advocacy of equal chances to become unequal has become a rallying cry for the Conservative Party under Mrs Thatcher presumably on the assumption that there are votes to be won from the exploitation of inegalitarian sentiments.

Meritocracy and equality of educational opportunity

Nevertheless, as the 'equal chances to become unequal' rhetoric recognizes, advocacy of inequality has also to masquerade as a species of equality. In modern societies, acceptance of a functionalist insistence upon the necessity of equality tends to require that the conception of inequality known as equality of opportunity should be written into institutional arrangements, especially for education. If economic and social efficiency is the objective, then it appears that the most able must be identified early and educated to the hilt of their potential, quite irrespective of their social origins. If the efficient operation of the social system requires the maintenance of inequalities of wealth, status and power, then these privileges should be rewards for qualities and skills which are relevant to social efficiency. If they ever did, accidents of birth, family and social-class origin seem no longer to supply societies with appropriate talent. Indeed, Shanks (1961: Ch.6) has argued that Britain is a stagnant society largely because of its continued attachment to the class system as an allocator of social roles, especially through a divisive educational system. To foreigners this tends to be the whole truth about the British *malaise*. Elsewhere intelligence, talent, diligence and appropriate professional training seem the only criteria for the allocation of privileges which are functional for greater efficiency. Hence, equality of opportunity, requiring removal of hindrances to the development of individual talent, has to be engineered through the educational system. In line with the conception of equality of opportunity, the substitution of intelligence for birth or wealth as an educationally relevant discriminator, and the scholarship system involving the selection and subsidy of working-class children, seemed a progressive educational reform in the early years of this century (Halsey, 1972a : 6). It was the manifest injustice which resulted from neglect of demonstrable capacity to benefit from further schooling which provided the initial impetus to claims for equality of educational opportunity which, over the years, have seemed irresistible. These injustices are graphically chronicled by Roberts (1973 : 144-5), writing of his own schooling in a Salford slum in the second decade of this century:

> ... we left in droves at the very first hour the law would allow and sought any job at all in factory, mill and shop. But, strangely, I myself wanted to go on learning, and with a passion that puzzled me; an essay prize or two, won in a competition against the town's schools, had perhaps pricked ambition. 'Isn't there some examination you could take?' asked my mother. I inquired of the headmaster. 'There were', he said vaguely, 'technical college bursaries, but he didn't put pupils in: one needed things like algebra and geometry to pass — quite difficult stuff.'
>
> 'Some homework, then', I suggested. He shook his head: he didn't give homework. Still, my name would go up. I could sit, of course. The old man raised no objections, merely instructing me to 'get through'. I sat an incomprehensible paper and failed. When the results were announced weeks after, without having a hope of success, I felt sick with disappointment.

Roberts eventually became a graduate and university teacher. His account focuses three facts about the schooling available to the industrial working class (especially the lower working class) at that time. Elementary education consisted of some half-dozen years of schooling which was an end in itself; secondly, the only available secondary or further education was private and financed from student fees; thirdly, the elementary school curriculum (what Tawney, 1973 : 8, called 'educational shoddy') was not an adequate preparation for access to even those few private institutions which existed in a large industrial centre like the Manchester-Salford conurbation. The iniquities described by Roberts may seem peculiarly British (or, at least, European), an unsurprising reminder of educational obscurantism in a notoriously class-ridden society. But recent 'revision' of American educational history has unearthed a similar picture of education provided there for the lower classes (Katz 1971, 1973).

Roberts's comments on English education at this time also underline how the problem of equality of opportunity tends to be posed in terms of the *clever* lower-class child: equality of opportunity is closely connected with the idea of social *mobility*. From the vast social substratum of the disadvantaged, a few are chosen for secondary education (and even fewer for higher education) with its consequent social and economic reward: entry to the middle class, an enhanced social status and higher standard of living. Simply stated, equality of educational opportunity implies that no one should be prevented through social or economic impediment from getting the best possible schooling from which he can benefit. Irrelevant matters to do with social class, economic status, nationality, sex, ethnic origin, religious affiliation, race or geographical location should have no bearing upon access to schooling. On the other hand, demonstrable differences in intelligence, achievement, talent, interests or tastes may justify differential educational provision. Everything hinges on this distinction between differences which are educationally significant and those which are educationally irrelevant.[6]

Until the 1950s it was assumed that the century-long movement towards equality of opportunity in education had been substantially successful (Halsey 1972a: Ch.1). The total exclusion of working-class children from secondary and higher education described by Roberts seemed finally to be a thing of the past. Over half a century there seemed to have been a good deal of social mobility, evidenced by the growing number of children with working-class origins in the professions and other white-collar occupations.[7] However, from the mid-1950s, an accumulation of sociological data from different national sources indicated only such limited success in securing equal access to post-primary educational institutions that our educational arrangements came to be judged a failure against this criterion of equality of opportunity. No doubt all strata of the working class were represented in academic secondary schools and universities in numbers which indicated a dramatic increase over half a century, but they were still grossly under-represented in proportion to their numbers within the total population. Evidently, real obstacles still lay in the way of under-privileged children's access to the fruits of the educational system.

However, perhaps failure was endemic in the concept of equality of educational opportunity itself. It is evident that equality of opportunity is a conceptually ambiguous notion and it has recently been attacked from both ends of the political spectrum: from the left because its application leaves the social *status quo* completely undisturbed; from the right because it implies unacceptable social change. The first of these criticisms is perhaps the more familiar. From the radical viewpoint, equality of opportunity is essentially a conservative notion, taking the universe as it finds it, intimating nothing of social or human ends; it is essentially an instrumental concept, mechanistic and ethically neutral. As a recipe for social engineering it merely makes for mobility within the *status quo*. Hobsbawn (1975 : 137) suggests that 'it is a sort of entrepreneurial Businessman's or bourgeois concept which is something quite different from, and indeed incompatible with, egalitarianism'. From this point of view it almost seems that the word equality is an accidental occurrence in the phrase (or, perhaps, cynically included to exploit its emotive overtones), where everything really hangs on the word 'opportunity' which, in turn, seems logically inconsistent with the notion of equality. When the emphasis is upon opportunity, the implication is that outcomes will be unequal. He who is offered and seizes an opportunity receives a bonus, something which the others haven't got (Lucas 1975 : 46):

> Equality of opportunity implies comparison. My opportunities are being compared with yours ... equality of opportunity tends to be applicable only in the context of a competition where a number of people are competing for the same goal in accordance with rules which can be assessed as being equal or unequal.

On this view, life (and schooling) is a race in which there have to be

winners and losers. At best we can only devise a fair system of
handicapping and, although theoretically a perfect handicap would
lead to everyone's breaking the tape at the same instant, this is the
last thing we really expect from a good race. In any event, dead
heats are a rarity in the real world and those involving an entire
field of competitors are probably unknown. And when we cash this
sporting metaphor in terms of the requirements of any society, the
notion of a dead heat would be socially and economically dysfunctional. Handicapping may do justice to individuals but, as we have
seen, keeping the social universe moving requires an emphasis
upon differences in individual achievement and role performance.
This, in turn, requires differential rewards or prizes to call forth
effort and the display of necessary talent. This concept of equality
of educational opportunity was particularly evident in the British
Black Papers (see Cox and Dyson 1969a, b, 1970).

It has appeared, then, that the attempt to reconcile moral
assumptions about human equality with functionalist economic,
sociological and psychological arguments for inequality, was
destined to issue in those educational arrangements which have
come to be known as meritocratic. Social justice in education
seemed most likely when apparently irrelevant considerations of
wealth, class, sex, race, or religion ceased to influence the allocation
of educational resources. If élites are sociologically inevitable then
those recruited from the highly intelligent and diligent products of
the educational system seem preferable to those derived from birth
or wealth. This does seem to have the merit of substituting relevant
distinctions between people — those associated with intelligence,
talent, skill, knowledge and energy — for irrelevant differences
when distributing economic and social privileges. As John Wilson
(1966 : 58) puts it: 'We can say that equality is "increased" or a
state of "absolute equality" is approached as we progressively
remove accidental features, and concentrate more and more on
natural features that all men might reasonably be expected to have,
at least in some degree.' Nevertheless, meritocracy has come to have
pejorative overtones, an outcome no doubt intended by Young
when coining the term, with its echoes of aristocracy. For if, in one
sense, meritocracy does require upsetting the *status quo* (we would
have a *new* aristocracy) it does assume the continued existence of
privilege, of social, economic and educational inequalities, and of

hierarchies based on wealth, status and power. The social pyramid is altered only in terms of the class origins of the upper strata, to the extent that a minority of working-class children become upwardly mobile. The meritocratic conception of equality of opportunity intimates nothing of a classless society; its aim is not classlessness, but one of giving everyone a better chance of being re-classified socially. That is, the meritocratic principle of social mobility merely legitimizes inequality, making its continued existence acceptable as a kind of safety-valve (Bourdieu 1973 : 71):

> ... the controlled mobility of a limited category of individuals, carefully selected and modified by and for individual ascent, is not incompatible with permanent structures and ... it is even capable of contributing to social stability in the only way conceivable in societies based upon democratic ideals and there-by may help to perpetuate the structure of class relations.[8]

It might be expected that such a class-reinforcing educational system would evoke hostility from the ideological left, whilst receiving approval from conservatives. Some political Conservatives do, indeed, see a considerable electoral asset in the slogan, 'Equal opportunity to become equal'. But other defenders of tradition see little of value in meritocratic education. They employ a version of the functionalist argument for inequality to call in question the sociological and psychological consequences of increasing social mobility. Utley (1975 : 4) argues that 'in any tolerable society continuity is essential. It is to be achieved only when people grow up in stable roles.' Hoggart (1968 : 241-52; see also Jackson and Marsden 1962 : 219) has also pointed to the schizophrenia which he believed inevitably afflicted the scholarship boy. And Bantock (1975a : 130) concludes that 'a society based upon meritocracy implies a too great mobility and this in turn a lack of continuity of meanings'. In this criticism of meritocracy, Bantock is summarizing Eliot, and it is he and his followers who have been particularly concerned to stress the inseparability of the family from formal educational institutions. For them, meritocracy is suspect precisely because of its threat to the existing class structure, not because it destroys class, but because it entails recruitment to the 'superior' classes of persons lacking their traditional values. Bantock (1963 : 181) argues against '... too rapid assimilation of the culturally

impoverished who have high IQs into sections of the community
which carry a good deal of social and economic prestige; the rise of
the merely clever in these terms to positions of social influence is a
culturally doubtful manifestation'. On this view, intelligence and
the capacity for hard work are no substitute for the qualities of
character (including disinterested commitment to public service)
which allegedly result from breeding and upbringing of a particular
kind. From this point of view, family background is judged
especially relevant to education. Bantock refers to the 'propitious
environment' provided by family and other extra-school institutions. Moreover, if the family is, thus, a crucial support for formal
education, then 'the pursuit of equality of opportunity to an
extreme point leads to demonstrably unacceptable intrusion into
the institution of the family' (Howe 1975 : 51).

The importance of the family for education also leads Coleman
to dismiss equality of educational opportunity as 'a false ideal' for
reasons to do with the economics of education. He believes that in
removing incentives to families to invest in their children's education, the aggregate of resources in a society available for education
is reduced and, hence, the maximization of educational opportunity is threatened.[9] This is to take the view that it is politically
irrelevant where educational resources come from: what are all-
important are the outcomes from the educational system. The
conception of equality of educational opportunity focuses upon
inputs to the educational system. But if it is outcomes which ought
to be equalized, perhaps the last thing we need to contend for is
equality of inputs on behalf of individuals or groups (Coleman
1973). Indeed, it seems reasonable to suppose that just as maximization of the physical health of a community evidently requires
diversion of medical resources largely to those who are sick, so it
appears sensible to assume that maximization of educational
outcomes may require public expenditure largely on behalf of those
who appear educationally disadvantaged. On this view we should
stop worrying about continued private expenditure of educational
resources by those families which seem well able enough to look
after themselves, if this makes increased public resources available
for the schooling of those who cannot. Instead of insisting upon
equality at the point of input, why not focus upon equalizing
outcomes or benefits, accepting that this might require unequal

inputs, whether from public or private sources? This is to invoke the logic of Shaw's parable of the captain and the cabin boy (1946 : 46; Tawney 1974 : 50), what Rawls (1971 : 100-1) calls 'the principle of redress':

> ... undeserved inequalities call for redress; and since inequalities of birth and natural endowment are undeserved, these inequalities are somehow to be compensated for. Thus the principle holds that in order to treat all persons equally, to provide genuine equality of opportunity, society must give more attention to those with fewer native assets and to those born into the less favourable social positions. The idea is to redress the bias of contingencies in the direction of equality. In pursuit of this principle greater resources might be spent on the education of the less rather than the more intelligent, at least over a certain time of life, say the earlier years of school.

Positive discrimination is necessary in favour of the disadvantaged: the desirable widening of opportunity which is necessary to diminish economic and social inequality has to be sought in ways which probably call for unequal provision within the educational system itself.

Equality of results

However, in attempting to escape the ambiguities and inequities which attach to the notion of equality of opportunity by turning instead to outcomes or results, we merely seem destined to replace one set of conceptual confusions for another.[10] For although a focus upon equality of outcomes seems to locate the argument within a different and less ambiguous set of value assumptions (substituting egalitarianism for meritocracy), the notion of equal results or benefits is very difficult to concretize educationally or socially.

Equality of outcomes implies that in some sense people should *become* equal as a result of their schooling. But it is far from clear what it would mean to advocate equal outcomes as the result of an educational experience. There are obvious difficulties in giving content to the notion of equal learning outcomes within educational systems. What would count as equal learning for the school population within a given society? Would everyone matriculate, or get a bachelor's degree or, perhaps, a doctorate — and with equal grades? In cultural terms, would we aim at bringing everyone to the same level of knowledge and skill? The apparent absurdity of these questions suggests that some process of levelling down would be essential to the achievement of equal outcomes. On the other hand, it is possible to consider equality of result with reference to those outcomes which are extrinsic to the educational experience itself. One can take an essentially instrumental view of education, being primarily concerned with what follows from differences in educational provision in terms of occupation, wealth, prestige and power. Historically, a good deal of the discussion of educational equality relates to outcomes which lie outside the educational process itself. That is, the debate about equality has focused largely upon the instrumental values of schooling: its impact upon social mobility, its effect upon earning power, access to professional life, to political power and so on. From this extrinsic point of view, equality is assessed in terms of socio-economic outcomes. In this context, the questions about equality become: should schooling be used to engineer a classless society; to secure equal incomes or job satisfaction between individuals? The extrinsic reference is central to Christopher Jencks's discussion in *Equality* (1972) which, as the title of its first chapter indicates, was intended to shift the focus of the educational debate 'From equal opportunity to equal results'. However, in viewing schooling instrumentally in relation to these socio-economic inequalities, advocacy of equality of outcomes tends to lead to dilution of the concepts of both equality and education. And even where schooling is valued for its intrinsic educational ends, dilution of the concept of education seems inevitable where there is commitment to equality of educational results. This is particularly evident in some recent American analyses of the problem.

For example, Green (1971) concludes that the achievement of educational opportunity is 'a dismal prospect', partly because equality of outcome is inconceivable except at a very modest level of academic achievement. Beyond the elementary level, and probably not even that far, keeping educational achievement equal between individuals would entail levelling down to an extent that any educational reform directed towards such an outcome would be politically unacceptable. Equality of academic achievement could only be secured by depressing the rate of learning of some children (mostly middle-class children) to that of the backward child. Even if the achievement of the backward child did not become the norm (the school convoy proceeding at the pace of its slowest ship), considerable levelling down would be logically entailed in securing a common average level of achievement. Green concludes that this would be politically unacceptable to the American middle class, but it is doubtful if it would be any more acceptable elsewhere. Parkin (1973: Ch.5), for example, cites Polish middle-class resistance to improving worker education.

In face of the political and pedagogical difficulties in raising the learning capacity of some students without either depressing the standards of others or accelerating their progress even further, Green (1971 : 35) concluded that the intractibility of the problem is astonishing: '...the attainment of equal educational opportunity will be a persistent issue in most developed societies for the next decade; [but] there is no politically acceptable escape from the issue; and ... there is currently no politically acceptable solution to the problem'.[11]

Dilution of a different kind is implicit in the assumption that since achievement of equal outcomes between individuals seems pedagogically out of the question, equality should be sought not for individuals, but only between groups. Conceptions of equality have usually been individualistic, the focus being upon persons who, in some sense, were assumed to have a right to equality simply in virtue of their human nature (Green 1971 : 35); see also Halsey 1972a : 8). But given the apparent intractability of the problem of securing equal outcomes between individuals, American discussion of the problem of equality has tended to conclude that the most important personal datum is that which classifies an individual as a member of a class, an ethnic or religious group. Thus, Green (1971 : 18) argues: 'It can be set down as a kind of definition that any society will have attained a condition of equal educational opportunity when firstly the range of the distribution of benefits and secondly their distribution within that range is approximately the same for each relevant social group within the student population.' This 'does not mean that everyone must reach the same level of achievement. It means only that the *range* of achievement and the distribution *within* that range should be about the same for each social group.' It is clear that the equality of outcome envisaged here is that representation of the different social groups — classified in terms of class, racial or ethnic origin, sex, etc. — at the various educational levels should be in proportion to the size of the group within the general population. Thus, the principle of equality of results would be satisfied not if every working-class child (or Black, or Italian immigrant) had a quality college education, but rather when working-class children were present in institutions of higher education in numbers proportionate to the size of the working class within the total population, and given the proportion of college students from other social groups: implicitly not every middle- or upper-class child should be in college either. Similarly, not every woman has the right to higher education but only a number of women relative to the ratio of women to men in the population and to the proportion of males in college.

This dilution of equality of educational outcomes to refer to groups rather than individuals has not been universally acceptable. Critics have noted that in the United States, inequalities amongst Whites are larger than inequalities between Blacks and Whites. As one critic (Duncan 1973) puts it: 'It seems quite shocking that white workers earn fifty per cent more than black workers. But we are even more disturbed by the fact that the best paid fifth of all white workers earns six hundred per cent more than the worst paid fifth.' The conclusion has to be that since both individual and group inequalities are unacceptable, we are really faced with decisions about the priority involved in removing two injustices, and cannot take refuge behind the assumption that the principle of equality is satisfied when inequalities between groups are diminished. Attacking group inequalities first may be politically expedient where persisting social inequality seems a greater threat to social order than do the inequalities suffered by marginal individuals and families within any social group. But the decision to opt for eliminating the more visible, potentially explosive inequalities between groups seems acceptable only in the language of priorities. Green's and Coleman's conclusion that the principle of equality is satisfied when the range of achievement between groups is equalized does not find wide support.[12] From a humanistic point of view it is not clear why vast inequalities between individuals within social groups should be more acceptable than similar inequalities between human beings across social groups. Indeed, what Glazer (1976) calls 'policies of statistical parity for ethnic groups in employment, housing and education' have clearly discriminated against particular individuals by attaching 'benefits and penalties to individuals simply on the basis of their race, colour and national origin'. Glazer admirably underlines the paradox that positive discrimination aimed at reducing inequalities between groups violates the principle of the Civil Rights Act of 1964 which disallowed discrimination in housing, employment and education on grounds of 'race, colour, religion or national origin'.

Education and equality of moral worth

If the notion of equality of educational outcomes is diluted by attempts to limit its application only to a modest level within the educational system or to equality between groups, a third type of dilution is implicit in attempts to circumvent the problems inherent in the notion of equal outcomes by changing the definition of what constitutes an education. Perhaps equality of outcome is possible if we diminish the educational importance of academic achievement in intellectual and cognitive terms, and instead we elevate the claims of character development and affective education. John Wilson (1966 : 61-3) notes a tendency for egalitarians to want to reward 'moral choice' and human qualities like conscientiousness, kindness, persistence. He believes that the emphasis upon moral rather than intellectual qualities is an attempt to get at the characteristics which are the real core of the self: 'a man "really is" his moral qualities: other attributes such as intelligence and still more his wealth and position in society are not really "him"'. This is why egalitarians tend to 'frame the rules of the game so that only these things count. If — and it is a big "if" — all men share these abilities to an equal degree such a game would offer some hope of an absolute principle of equality'.[13] Wilson himself rejects this hypothesis that there is any serious sense in which some things can be done equally well by everyone. However, he is clear that the assumption of some equal gifts — like diligence, industriousness, determination, courage, honesty, kindness — is crucial to the notion of equality. Without this assumption the concept is morally lame for, no matter how favourable to equality are the rules of the game, 'if I have not the power (in the form of personal resources), then strictly speaking I do not have the opportunity or the chance'. Thus the egalitarian,

> ... in so far as he is compelled to allow competition at all, will want the rules to favour capacities which we all possess. In practice, this comes down to setting up the kind of game *which can be won in as many different ways as possible*, and in which the criteria of desert are not too closely attached to any one particular set of talents ... [Wilson gives examples of other criteria than wealth which might be introduced for winning the hand of a beautiful woman — being handsome, clever, witty, attentive] ... Thus although in one sense the egalitarian cannot, whatever system he arranges, give any more people a chance to *win* (since there is a limited number of winners) he can give more people *hope*. (Wilson 1966 : 185)

There has undoubtedly been a recent trend towards emphasis upon other human capacities than the intellectual and other skills and achievements than the cognitive. Critics of comprehensive schooling are probably correct in noting a tendency for egalitarian-inspired reforms of this kind to diminish the importance of intellectual objectives in the curriculum in favour of development of those traits which, it is assumed, are more equally distributed within the population than is measured intelligence. Of course, it is an unproven assumption that kindness, endeavour, emotional warmth, disinterestedness and so on, *are* distributed any differently from intellectual capacity. But that objection loses some of its force in face of the argument that intelligence is not universally func-tional for social efficiency and that other human qualities contri-bute to social well-being. Thus, the argument for modifying our concept of what it means to be educated, by shifting the balance in favour of other than intellectual capacities, is not simply a moral one. It is, in part, a functionalist argument that we would be better, more efficient societies for cultivating other kinds of human qualities. Critics of meritocracy often have in mind that rule by the merely clever is frightening (witness all the bright, clever young men involved in Watergate). Evidently, IQ and industry are not everything. It is arguable that leaders need other important characteristics. Especially in the United States there is a long standing mistrust of intellectuals in public affairs. Richard Hofstadter (1963 : Part V) has observed a tendency for American public figures to be admired for their goodness rather than their intellectual acumen, and Iain Macleod, a former British cabinet minister, was once dismissed by a colleague, Lord Salisbury, as 'too clever by half'. Perhaps the point is that we need to distinguish different kinds of excellence required in different leadership roles. Nuclear physicists probably need a high IQ. Those who function in more person-oriented roles, in social services, for example, may need other dispositions and qualities.

It has seemed an additional attraction of the view that the pursuit of equality should be sought by emphasizing 'character' at the expense of intelligence, that thereby we shall escape from the illusion that human worth (and, hence, capacity to benefit from schooling) is measurable. We may be deluded in believing that intelligence is measurable but we generate continuous and acrimonious debate by thinking that it is. But, as Wilson reminds us, it seems self-evident that we are all equal as moral beings and we rarely attempt to rate the population in hierarchies of moral or emotional merit. However, what seems to have the merit of being an egalitarian strategy for eliminating privileged schooling by opening doors to qualities which everyone possesses, can become a double-edged weapon. As Tumin (1967 : 104) argues, the attempt to take the sting out of low status ranking or economic reward by suggesting that only moral conduct is worthy of admiration, is really a device which 'enables privileged groups to maintain their favourable positions'. Lower ranks are enabled 'to feel a greater equality with their superiors' without their being any disturbance of the socio-economic and political *status quo*. Moreover, as Parkin (1973 : 99) notes with reference to Poland, there is a tendency for the middle-class to seek to maintain a privileged position by the reintroduction of criteria of selection which are not amenable to empirical test:

>...where privilege goes hand-in-hand with power it may be possible for the most advantaged members of the dominant class to defend their position — for example, by changing the criteria of recruitment in a way beneficial to themselves and their offspring. One way of doing this is, for example, by making the assessment of 'character' an important part of the selection

process. Because the kinds of personal attributes that go to make up character are not generally open to objective measurement the assessment of such attributes can be made by the occupants of privileged positions.

It is by no means clear that non-meritocratic focus upon moral and emotional rather than intellectual qualities will favour egalitarian objectives. As we have already observed, in stressing the 'propitious environment' afforded by family circumstances, conservative educationists are sensitive to the value of other educational qualities than mere intelligence. Bryan Wilson (1975 : 17) makes a plea for privileged educational treatment on grounds other than the possession of demonstrably high intellectual capacity by appealing to the contribution to the social good which is often made by 'the educated man of less intelligence'. Yet his appeal to the educational importance of 'other social virtues' (civic concern, social responsibility, and civic standards) is on different grounds from that of the egalitarian. The latter stresses the *equal* importance of these other virtues in order to identify sameness or equivalence through which equal educational treatment can be justified. On the other hand, the anti-meritocratic conservative is stressing *unequal* distribution of non-intellectual qualities in order to defend privileged educational provision (largely on grounds of social class) for individuals who would not satisfy the intellectual criteria largely employed in selection for different types of secondary schooling. Bryan Wilson has in mind, for example, the 'cultural style' which he believes characterizes some kinds of family life and compensates for limited intelligence: '... a cultural inheritance of good talk, informed opinions and the accumulation of cultural appurtenances — of which books and musical instruments are perhaps the most conspicuous — which are regarded as essential sources for the enrichment of the individual's private life'.

Equality: an educationally irrelevant concept?

If equality is conceptually ambiguous, practically elusive, seemingly unwanted, sociologically and economically dysfunctional, perhaps the problems which confront us in the theory and practice of education are best approached with different conceptual tools. And especially, to focus upon the cultural rather than the material outcomes of education is to raise additional doubts about the educational relevance of equality. For it is arguable that attempts to define educational outcomes in terms of equality are abortive because equality is essentially an economic notion, inappropriately applied to considerations of the distribution of knowledge and skill and the acquisition of a personal culture. Discussing equality in the context of his examination of the relationship between ethics and education, Peters (1966) implies that equality *is* an economic concept, relevant only to the problem of distributing scarce resources amongst competing claimants. That is, it only makes sense to discuss equality when the distribution of some scarce resource — whether material or social — is at issue. Except in the context of pollution, we don't normally think it relevant to talk about equal access to fresh air or sunshine. If you enjoy walking in the rain — which proverbially falls on the just and the unjust — you just do it; you don't have to assert your right to do it equally with the economically and socially privileged or the politically powerful. On the other hand, food, clothing, money, housing are in relatively short supply as are (by definition) rank, privilege and status. Problems of access to these economic and social 'goods' are the stuff of which discussions of equality are made. But it is not clear that 'culture', which we 'distribute' through the educational system, is quite like food, housing, clothing and other economically scarce goods. Perhaps it is more like fresh air, sunshine and rain, freely available and not subject to economic constraint.

It is not clear that education does fall unambiguously into the category of things in relatively short supply, i.e., economic commodities. Indeed, it has been the conventional wisdom that differentiated educational provision between individuals or groups does not derive from limitation of supply in relation to demand, but from other, non-economic factors. The autodidact is by no means an unfamiliar figure in the history of education. If you have a mind to get at it, knowledge is publicly available, and with the advent of free libraries there is little impediment to a person's reading Shakespeare, Plato, Einstein, and becoming an expert on any one of these, or simply delighting in them as enrichment of his own personal experience. No doubt the whole of human knowledge is not freely available in every small town library, but one would have to conclude that some remarkably well-educated people have emerged from environments little endowed with the paraphernalia of libraries, schools and so on. In effect, in advanced industrial societies, the willing learner is usually faced with more freely available resources for learning than he is likely to exhaust in a lifetime. A diminishing appetite for skill and knowledge is evident long before one has exhausted the possibilities. This sort of assumption was behind the nineteenth-century confidence in the liberating power of literacy: simply teach a person to read and you make available to him the whole of human knowledge, radical political propaganda no less than the received wisdom of the group. In any school classroom, the fact that individual pupils achieve unequal results in, say, a mathematics lesson, does not follow from mathematics being in short supply so that, with a limited amount of mathematical knowledge and skill available for distribution, more of it for one student means less of it for another. From the standpoint of the 'supply' of mathematics, nothing stands in the way of every pupil's becoming a skilful mathematician. The notion of a fixed supply of human knowledge leading to unequal learning outcomes is absurd. If there is unequal learning in a classroom, the limiting factors are largely from the side of demand, not from a scarcity in the supply of knowledge.[14] Thus, in the past, one of the working assumptions of educational systems has been that inherited intelligence puts an absolute ceiling on many people's capacity for learning.

This last is a crucial point. For, on the surface, it seems that denial of education to a majority of people — or its limitation beyond the elementary level — has usually been justified in terms of their apparent inability to benefit from more education, not because education was in short supply, thus needing to be rationed to those who could use it or afford to buy it. Certainly in Britain, the inter-war rationale of differentiated secondary education was in terms of psychological, not economic, theory. The clearest formulation of this psychological justification for dissimilar provision of secondary education was in the Norwood Report (1943) which identified three different types of intelligence requiring nurture through a tripartite system of secondary schools. It was not argued that the community could not afford to send every child to grammar school and university, but rather that it would be a disservice to a majority of children to do so because of their incapacity or disinclination to profit from 'academic' schooling. No doubt, without this encouragement from contemporary psychological theory, and if everyone had aspired to attend university, arguments from economic scarcity would have been adduced to justify differentiated secondary schooling. Then, as now, it was probably assumed that in advanced industrial societies, occupations requiring a high degree of knowledge and academic training were merely the tip of an iceberg whose submerged bulk was the mass of skilled and unskilled manual occupations necessary to support economic affluence. There is a perennial fear that if too many people are too well schooled in non-practical subjects there will be a shortage of people prepared to occupy themselves in manual and, especially, menial jobs: hence the view of the school as an agency of social selection. This sociological argument sustains the economic one: even if resources for schooling were not scarce and in limited supply, it would still be necessary to maintain inequality of educational provision to avoid flooding the labour market with over-educated workers. But even in the relatively affluent 1950s, when arguments were advanced that additional economic resources should be made available for higher education precisely because the economy needed better educated personnel, any significant expansion of higher education was opposed in some quarters on the grounds that 'more means worse'; that is, it is not the shortage of resources but the incapacity of most people to profit from it which is the rationale for differential, unequal, educational provision. The conviction dies hard that equality and quality are irreconcilable educational objectives. In the period since the Second World War, the statutory period of schooling throughout Western Europe has been advanced by two years to give effect to a mandatory leaving age of sixteen. Yet this 'reform' has found vocal opponents, not least in potential students, many of whom already appear to find what schooling they have an intolerable burden. Here again, it appears that personal ability, interest or talent are the relevant factors, not a shortage of economic resources: in economic terminology, the supply of education seems far in excess of demand. Students seem to have as much education as they want, or are capable of, so why go on about equality as if the constraints were essentially economic?[15]

Jencks appears to be attributing widespread dissatisfaction with schooling to a natural disinclination amongst most people to acquire the civilized arts and intellectual accomplishments. This stands in sharp contrast to the conclusions of mainstream educational theory — especially progressive theory — that resistance to schooling is environmentally induced and, thus, that coming to value education is mainly a matter of motivation. On this view man is essentially a learning animal and if educational institutions frustrate learning, the fault is in them, not in the learner. The remedy is not to assume a widespread aversion to life of the mind, but to reform schools so that they work with the natural learning grain of the mind. [16] After two centuries of popular schooling this remains an act of faith. For, empirically, all the evidence seems to favour Jencks.

Socialism or education?

However, it is far from clear that Jencks is prepared to follow the logic of his conclusion that the sum of human happiness varies inversely with the equalization of educational provision. He does not propose a dismantling of systems of popular education or reduction of the aggregate of economic resources applied to schooling. But in view of his assumption that there is little appetite within the population for the 'goods' traditionally associated with education — its intellectual and aesthetic outcomes, for example — schools become trivialized to the status of child-minding institutions. Whilst prepared to acknowledge that schools are worthy of public support, even of increased financial support, he recommends improving them for much the same reason that we improve public highways and transportation systems, public health services and so on; that is, simply because all of these improvements make travelling, being in school or in hospital more comfortable and congenial. His belief is that schools need to be improved on the simple humanitarian ground that children and their teachers have to spend a good deal of their time there. Wherever they are, particularly if they are obliged to be there, people have a right to expect the amenities of any institution to be as good as possible. So, even if we abandon the mistaken and unreasonable expectation that schools will transform society, we ought to go on pumping public funds into them simply to increase their amenity value.

This is essentially the argument which Jencks deploys in dismissing the case for equal educational provision. Education, he argues, is unlike wealth, and the demand for it is not a function of economic imperatives. Accepting the Benthamite principle that 'society should be organized so as to provide the greatest good of the greatest number', and linking this with the economic principle of diminishing returns, he argues that the sum of human happiness is likely to be increased by a more equal distribution of wealth. From applying the two principles he concludes (1972 : 9)

> ... people with low incomes value extra income more than people with high incomes. It follows that if we want to maximize the satisfaction of the population, the best way to divide any given amount of money is to make everyone's income the same. Income disparities (except those based on variations in 'need') will always reduce overall satisfaction, because individuals with low incomes will lose more than individuals with high incomes will gain.

Although Jencks believes that this argument for equal distribution as the way to maximize a population's satisfaction applies to most goods, it does not apply to the distribution of education. Quite the contrary: total satisfaction and happiness is diminished by equalizing educational provision. Education's 'goods' — 'ideas and the life of the mind' — are valued increasingly the more one already has of them. And whilst there may be people with little education who value things of the mind (though Jencks does not concede this), it is a disservice to most people to offer them more of something to which they evidently attach little value (Jencks 1973 : 11):

> If schooling and knowledge are thought of strictly as ends in themselves, it is impossible to make a case for distributing them equally. We can see no reason to suppose, for example, that people with relatively little schooling value additional schooling more than people who have already had a lot of schooling. Experience suggests that the reverse is the case. In so far as schooling is an end in itself, then, Benthamite principles imply that those who want a lot should get a lot, and those who want very little should get a little. The same is true of knowledge and

cognitive skills. People who know a lot generally value additional knowledge and skills more than those who know very little. This means that in so far as knowledge or skill is valued for its own sake, an unequal distribution is likely to give more satisfaction to more people than an unequal distribution.

The trouble with this conclusion is that unless schools make some positive difference in whatever respect, there is no point in children and their teachers being there at all. They tend to be there only because, however mistakenly, there is a common assumption that something of value accrues, if not to the individual child, at least to the community. Jencks's discussion of the remaining value of schools (once their instrumental value is discredited) is extremely weak and inconclusive. There is the hint that they serve us simply as custodial institutions: in a complex industrial society with a good deal of specialization of function and geographical dispersion of domestic from other economic and political associations, schools have the economic value of enabling parents to go out to work without worrying unduly what their children are up to, and without other workers (especially the police) being distracted from their own jobs by hordes of children on the streets. But, at the very point of thus trivializing schools, Jencks draws back from this conclusion, though without offering anything positive about the business of schooling which would justify this vast, near universal expenditure of time, energy and money.

This lack of a coherent educational theory is especially puzzling in view of Jencks's prescription of a political solution to the economic and social ills of the United States (1973 : 265):

> As long as egalitarians assume that public policy cannot contribute to economic equality directly but must proceed by ingenious manipulations of marginal institutions like schools, progress will remain glacial. If we want to move beyond this tradition, we will have to establish political control over the economic institutions that shape our society. This is what other countries usually call socialism.

Unfortunately, Jencks was as circumspect in elaborating his conception of socialism as he was in defining education, maintaining that 'the purpose of *Inequality* was not to argue the case for socialism, which is complex and problematic'. However, in a subsequent clarification of his position he attempted to resolve the double ambiguity in the final sentence quoted above — which other countries does he have in mind, and are they agreed on what socialism is? He instanced Czechoslovakia, New Zealand, Sweden, Yugoslavia, Poland as examples of countries which 'almost all have either communist governments or strong parliamentary socialist parties that have held power for appreciable periods of time since 1945' (1973 : 163-4). In fact, neither communist nor democratic socialist ideologies trivialize education in quite the way Jencks does. To the contrary, it is difficult to recall any socialist programme which has not had the reform of the educational system at its core. In social democracies like Sweden and the United Kingdom, the replacement of segregated secondary schooling by comprehensive schools has seemed essential to diminishing social inequality, and in the Soviet Union and Eastern Europe education is evidently of major importance for social engineering. It is part of Marxist doctrine that schools are a key instrument of bourgeois hegemony and that its replacement by working-class hegemony requires radical reform of the educational structure.[17]

Perhaps multinational research conducted on the model provided by Jencks would demonstrate that socialists have been deluded in thinking that educational reform is a necessary condition of radical social reform or revolution. But perhaps not: for in socialist ideology, education is more than merely instrumental to socio-economic objectives which might, demonstrably, be secured in other ways. Arguably, a theory of education is intrinsic to socialism. For socialism is not just about economic equality: it refers to a total cultural configuration, a different kind of society in terms of objects to be valued and cultural artefacts and activities which are taken to be worthwhile. It requires a particular conception of political organization and the distribution of political power, implying a need for political education. The central role attributed to work in human life as the opportunity to participate in the creation and recreation of a civilization implies also the importance of vocational and aesthetic education. Familiarly, socialists speak of 'new men', 'new societies', 'new humanitarian culture' (Westergaard 1975 : 252). These notions, however vague, intimate an emphasis upon what people value, what they know, the skills they have at their command, their perceptions of interpersonal relationships, and their aesthetic sensibility, rather than merely upon what economic resources they command and the consumption goods at their disposal. Hence, even supposing that economic equality had been engineered — by compulsory incomes policies, progressive, redistributive taxation, the provision of free welfare services — educational institutions would still be of utmost importance in socialist societies for transmission of knowledge, values and skills necessary to achievement of the good life, once economic and other inequities had been removed. Yet Jencks does appear to believe that socialism would be achieved solely by resort to economic regulators affecting things like taxation and income control.

The criticism that Jencks is operating with a trivial conception of education does not require rejection of his thesis that schools have been required to shoulder responsibility for social and economic changes which it is not in their power to deliver. A political initiative towards socialism is probably the only instrument likely to achieve economic equality, even the less than 'all-embracing' or 'absolute' equality which Jencks has in mind. But, as we have argued, a theory of education is integral to socialism not merely as a mechanism of social engineering. However mistakenly from Jencks's point of view, it is part of the socialist *credo* that the sum of human happiness can be increased through wider dissemination of those cultural 'goods' which he takes to be of interest only to the few. Whatever their economic circumstances, people have a life to live in which they expect to derive satisfactions from work, recreation, political participation and from as many as possible of life's daily encounters with the environment. Their cultural resources inform their perceptions of daily experience. No doubt one's economic resources (particularly a necessary minimum of these) are not irrelevant to the quality of one's personal culture, but nor is cultural satisfaction simply a function of the price of 'goods' in the marketplace.[18] The conventional wisdom is that it is also related to the quality of one's education. Even if Jencks is correct in believing that 'ideas and the life of the mind' are not widely valued, it is apparent that the average man does depend upon the cognitive assets which he acquired in school. Against Jencks's trivializing of school and the knowledge and skill acquired inside its walls, there stands the common man's experience that however little schools may have contributed towards his income or social status, he did obviously leave school with some cognitive assets, even if only in relation to the three Rs. He is literate and the sense he is able to make of a newspaper, as well as his capacity to communicate with all kinds of public and private institutions, depend upon skills acquired in school. He is numerate and, however simply, his mathematical perceptions were trained in school. And in ways which are less capable of assessment and measurement he has a personal culture — deriving at least in part from the history, literature, science and geography he studied at school — in terms of which he makes sense of the newspapers and books he reads, the television programmes he watches, the conversations in which he participates, as well as its being the conceptual structure upon which recurrent educational experiences are constructed. Quite simply, as critics of Jencks have shown (Moynihan and Mosteller 1972 : 21ff.), most of us are capable of doing things relevant to vocational, domestic and political life, as well as in the pursuit of 'leisured' personal interests and cultural experiences, which we would be unable to do without exposure to forms of knowledge and skill from the school curriculum.

We have already questioned how far 'distribution' of the cultural 'goods' associated with schooling are subject to economic constraints and suggested that there is knowledge and skill freely available which many students do not seem to want. But before concluding that most people have no interest in being educated, it is important to consider assumptions that there are alternative cultural values which might, more appropriately, be focused by schools concerned to win the commitment and engage the interest of the likely 'drop out'. Current educational debate, for example, questions the relevance of the 'high culture' which is assumed to be the pre-occupation of schools, and it canvasses the respective merits of different class sub-cultures. This, in turn, raises questions about the desirability and possibility of a common culture as the basis of cultural equality. But with reference to these cultural correlates of schooling, the debate engendered by Jencks resolves little: it merely poses other social, political and cultural questions which are the subject of the remainder of this book.

2

Education and
social class

Some conceptions of social class

Although social stratification has always been the basis of formal
educational provision, until relatively recently social class did not
figure as an analytical category in the literature of education.
Schools were always socially functional and, historically, education
was conceived in terms of social categories requiring initiation of
the young into political-economic roles as guardians, courtiers,
governors, gentlemen.[1] In the mid-nineteenth century, Matthew
Arnold commended a tripartite system of secondary schooling in
which the various curricula were derived from a hierarchical view of
occupation and social roles in industrial societies. But it does seem
to be the case that only with the emergence of the sociology of
education as a contributory discipline to educational theory has the
concept of social class been used in examination of the deficiencies,
and in proposals for the reform of publicly financed educational
systems. No doubt since the inception of popular education, success
and failure in school has borne some relationship to social class
background, but theory of education, with its essentially individ-

ualistic orientation, tended to neglect this as a variable before the 1950s. The traditional textbooks formerly prescribed for the study of principles of education rarely mentioned social class. In those texts,[2] the assumptions were *humanistic* in the sense that an individually oriented educational theory defined the objectives of education in universal terms ('the educated man'), and learning problems were conceived either as originating in genetic differences between individuals (a matter of inherited IQ) or of personal attributes of the learner, like laziness or Churchillian idiosyncracy.

However, social class has become a central concept not only in the intellectual equipment of sociologists of education, but also in popular discussion of educational theory, where generalizations about the class correlates of education are usually little better than clichés. This tendency for theories about education and social class to degenerate into slogan-mongering probably derives from the considerable ambiguity which attaches to notions of social class in mainstream sociology itself, ambiguity which occasionally prompts the conclusion that 'it no longer has a meaning or place in social analysis' (Silver 1973 : xxx). It is therefore somewhat surprising that the conceptual ambiguities of the word 'class', which are the concern of a good deal of mainstream sociology, are rarely examined in educational literature.

In the sociology of education, the interest in social class lies mainly in evidence of social class as a determinant of educability or, more exactly, as a correlate of success in school. In this context, reference is to class as an economic category, since distribution of students amongst different types of secondary school or 'track', and access to higher education, is correlated with parental income or occupational level using one of the various indices of economic and occupational stratification.[3] Evidence from a variety of national sources shows lower-class children to be under-represented in academically oriented secondary schools and in higher education, whilst middle- and upper-class children are disproportionately successful in gaining access to the limited number of places available in these same institutions, given the assumption that intelligence and talent is randomly distributed throughout the entire population. These data have been taken as evidence of the existence of social injustice in advanced industrial communities calling for reforms (whether of the educational system or in relation to relevant contextual institutions) designed to diminish inequality in the distribution of educational resources amongst the various social classes.

However, for the educationist this demonstration of the correlation between economic stratification and success in school poses a number of problems. Clearly, it is not simply the income or occupational differential which unambiguously inhibits or encourages success in learning. An economically dependent conception of stratification does not explain the undoubted success in schools of many lower-class students. Earlier explanations of the inhibiting effects of lower-class origin focused on material manifestations of poverty: income deficiency, malnutrition, chronic disease and physical malformation, inadequate clothing and housing and so on. But significant improvements in social services, which have rid schools of the grosser manifestations of poverty and have effected improvement in general standards of health, seem not to have led to corresponding improvements in the proportion of lower-class children in selective secondary schools and higher education. This fact has led some sociologists to look for cultural and psychological correlates of economic indices of social class in order to explain academic performance in school.

In this respect, the most influential analysis has been that which has focused upon different cultural and disciplinary styles associated with family life in different social classes and, especially, upon linguistic differences between classes, finding explanation of lower-class difficulty with schooling in the inability of working-class speech to support academic discourse.[4] This 'cultural deficit' account of lower-class failure has been challenged, however. The school, some critics argue, is a middle-class institution, and although this is assumed to have a wealth of implication for educational practice, its meaning is rarely concretized in a way which would make it a useful conceptual tool. Before attempting to elucidate this and other class-dependent educational clichés further, it is necessary to note some alternative conceptions of class as a basis for further analysis of the relationship between education and social class.

Social class may be conceived as a single, specific dimension of social stratification or as a multidimensional category. The first of these notions of class, indicating only one dimension of social stratification, is usually attributed to Max Weber, who identified three areas of social stratification: class, status and power. In this tripartite analysis of social stratification, class figures as an economic concept, an index of occupation, income and wealth: 'classes ... are aggregates of individuals and families in similar economic positions' (Meyer and Buckley 1969 : 45). As Runciman (1969 : 30) puts it: 'To the notion of economic class are linked such terms as wealth, income, prices, capital, market'. It is this conception of class which, as we have seen, is basic to much of the analysis of educational chances in class terms. Status refers to the esteem which a person attracts and, hence, his access to social relationships in homogeneous social groupings; it is a concept in which notions of prestige and deference, condescension and exclusiveness are central:

> Status ... refers to the differentiation of prestige and deference among individuals and groups in a society ... Prestige rests upon interpersonal recognition, always involving one individual who claims deference and another who honours the claim ... Status groups treat of each other as social equals, encouraging intermarriage of their children, joining the same clubs and associations, and participating together in such informal activities as visiting, dances, dinners and receptions. (Meyer and Buckley 1969 : 46).

The notion of status carries an ambiguity which is absent from that of class. Class location is capable of a degree of statistical measurement. Especially with reference to income and occupational hierarchy, one's class is defined more or less accurately according to the subtlety of the classificatory categories employed. But status is not measurable in this sense. Inevitably, there is a substantial subjective component in attribution of status: 'the status-structure of their society is in fact determined solely by the *feeling* of its members' (Runciman 1969 : 30). To the extent that status does have an objective dimension it is defined by other people who, informally or by formal procedures like the 'blackball', admit others to their circle or contrive to keep them outside. A strong element of subjectivity is attached to status since status groups or strata are nowhere 'officially' designated as they are for class by the Registrar General, for example. Thus, whilst success in business confers status in some groups, in others this is *infra dig*. Religious devotion, athletic prowess, intellectualism or political flair may each be esteemed or not according to the group making the judgement. Again, an element of subjectivity follows from the fact that it is often individuals rather than reference groups who classify other people. It is not uncommon that in the different circles one frequents (usually a multiplicity of groups, not all having congruent value systems) there is disagreement about the esteem which is attached to a particular human activity, quality or achievement. The obvious example of this would be within families where there is often a mixture of classes — in the economic sense — and differing valuations of 'success', especially between generations.

The third category of stratification, power, refers to political effectiveness as a criterion of stratification. Power is 'the ability to control the behaviour of others ... sociologically it refers especially to the control that certain groups and individuals are able to exercise over the life chances of others' (Meyer and Buckley 1969 : 49). With reference to this political dimension of stratification, a problem arises in assessing the power wielded by a trade union leader as against that of an industrialist, a bishop, or a civil servant. There are several hierarchies of power such that the question 'Where does power lie?' requires an answer both from within and between institutions.

From an educational point of view it is interesting that education does not figure as a category within which one might be stratified, especially since attendance at 'the right school' seems a guarantee of prestige in some societies. In fact, Runciman argues (1969 : 33), education is merely one of those criteria by which one acquires prestige or authority or wealth, but it does not constitute a category separate from class, status or power because 'the polymath does not constitute a high ranking stratum in the way that the rich, or the social aristocracy, or the holders of government do'.

Runciman justifies the tripartite distinction of social hierarchies as follows (1969 : 31): class, status and power

> ... may be distinguished in terms of the kind of aspiration which they represent. To want wealth is not necessarily to want prestige or power; to want prestige is not necessarily to want power or wealth; to want power is not necessarily to want wealth or prestige. It can even be said that the difference between a rich man, a celebrity and a ruler is something like this: A rich man

collects cattle and hoards grain, or the money which stands for them ... A ruler collects men. Grain and cattle or money mean nothing to him except in so far as he needs them to/get hold of men ... A celebrity collects a chorus of voices. All he wants is to hear them repeat his name.

On the other hand, criticism of this triple distinction of social hierarchies derives from the fact that there is often a good deal of correlation between the economic position a person occupies, the power he exercises and the esteem he enjoys. Though there are clearly cases where wealth conveys neither power nor status, and the reverse is often true, it is also evident that power, for example, often has an economic basis as well as being a source of prestige. Indeed, the Marxist notion of social class holds that everything of cultural significance derives from the economic base where men are distinguished as owners of capital or sellers of labour. In spite of wealth, status and power being analytically distinct and sometimes empirically unrelated, they do often mesh, and function as mutually reinforcing.

It is for this reason that an alternative conception sees social class as a single, multi-dimensional complex, a total life-style or cultural configuration. Aron (1969) calls class 'a synthetic product of multiple factors', and the question then becomes one of the kinds of factor which compound the class synthesis. The recognition that class, status and power are usually interdependent and mutually reinforcing may simply lead to a notion of class as a composite of Weber's categories: 'The class system is the totality of relations constituted by expressions of deference, accorded to individuals, roles and institutions in the light of their place in the systems of power, property and occupations'.[5] However, a common assumption would be that class is defined by a richer complex of factors than power, income, wealth and property. Education, artistic taste, religion,[6] speech, manners, dress, geographical location and size of residence, ownership of property and source of income all seem to mesh into that web of factors which define one's social class.

However, a single, multidimensional index of social class is especially liable to subjectivity: 'The consciousness that each has of his station does not always coincide with the consciousness of others' (Aron 1969). This subjective element in social classification

leads some sociologists to conclude that class is an entirely psychological notion having no existence 'in any natural or objective
groups at all' (Jarvie 1972: Ch.4). Aron (1969) delineates this
nominalist conception of class as follows:

> A class is not a real ensemble, but a conglomeration of individ-
> uals. Individuals are differentiated from each other by multiple
> criteria and social status or class is only one among several
> discriminations determined essentially by psychological pheno-
> mena. Each is in the class which is imposed by the idea which
> others have of the position he occupies. Each has a status which is
> defined by the esteem of others. A definition of this kind regards
> the psychology of individuals, with all the contradictions it may
> allow for, as the essence of the phenomenon.

Accepting this notion that 'people do not belong to a social class
system — *we put them into one*', Jarvie concludes that any
allocation of people to 'objectively identifiable social groups is
false', corresponding to no facts about those it classifies. It is,
indeed, a fact that such classification is attempted, but such
attempts derive from people's theories about class and their acting
as if these were true. In that sense the concept of class is disposi-
tional:

> It describes people's disposition to believe and act in certain
> typical ways ... a social class is a *quasi* group of people who *think*
> they have similar interests, and who share common beliefs about
> the system of social class, their own position in the system, and
> similar dispositions as to the behaviour appropriate to their
> position in that system.

Thus, it is not in objective, material, natural facts which class is
immanent. It is rather people's beliefs, theories and myths which
function as self-fulfilling prophecies: 'those theories, because they
are acted on, themselves create and sustain the imagined divisions'.
Jarvie concludes that the notion of social class is a conceptual debris:
'the class system does not exist at all'. It is people's myths about
class which 'so tragically separate them'. For Jarvie, it follows that
the healing of these divisions is an educational enterprise: if class is,
so to speak, only 'in the mind', then the problems of class do not
yield simply to social engineering, but require changes of mind

which follow from more accurate perceptions of the way the social universe actually is. A major task of sociology is the 'refutation of a vast mass of popular myths, followed by attempts to devise educational checks which will impede the uncritical transmission of such erroneous theories, simply by showing how little they correspond to the facts' (Jarvie 1972 : Ch.4).

One of the tasks undertaken in this book is an examination of some current beliefs about social class which are assumed to have significance for educational theory and practice, especially those which sharply dichotomize middle-class and working-class cultures and values. Whether or not class is a nominalist myth as argued by Jarvie, it is clear that any conception of class depending upon 'multiple discriminations' is largely subjective, being only a particular group or individual's synthesis and stratification of complex phenomena.[7] And viewing class as a subjective, multidimensional complex of factors does seem to be essential when attempting to explain some of the so-called determinants of educational phenomena. Confusion of class (in the economic sense) seems to occur when working-class children 'succeed' in those schools which, on one sort of analysis, are a preparation for middle-class occupations.[8] And something more than a mere economic concept of class is at work when we speak of working-class children and their parents having middle-class aspirations. The success of working-class children in selective schools seems to require analysis in terms of the notion of 'status dissent'. Yet what, in class terms, is being dissented from (or assented to) when we speak of families in these terms? Again, the notion of schools as transmitters of middle-class values, or the idea that there is a working-class culture of which schools should take account, requires a definition of class in something other than raw economic terms. The psychological and cultural components of class at work here require complex explanation. Much the same is also true of the notion that society and education might be classless. Except in Marxist terms where this dissolution of class would hinge on a transformation of the ownership of property, the classless society could only have meaning where factors entering into classification were so complex that no stratification would have more than momentary validity. Whether a classless society is possible is debatable, but the assumption that is is has underpinned much advocacy of comprehensive education. However, faith in the comprehensive school as a solvent of social class has not referred simply to the possibility of facilitating upward mobility and securing a more equitable distribution of individuals to social roles irrespective of social-class origin. Earlier advocacy of comprehensive education looked for its impact upon the class system through transmission of a common culture. Here, again, a more complex notion of class than that of being an economic category is at work, when classlessness is believed to depend upon universal internalization of a common culture.

The school as a middle-class institution

It is often asserted that the school is a middle-class institution, but it is rarely made explicit whether this claim is being made descriptively or normatively and, especially, whether criticism is intended. As a descriptive statement, it could be an assertion that schools could not be other than middle-class institutions. As such, the supposition would be that it is in the very nature of schools to be middle-class: they were founded to do things which the middle class values. This would be to assume that education points to a certain quality of life, a life-style which is, roughly, that which happens to be preferred by the middle class; that middle-class values are inevitably at the centre of any experience which can be categorized as 'educational'. It follows, alas, that other social classes will never succeed in school unless they accept the middle-class life-style as a valid objective of their own development.

However tenable this conception of the nature of education, it is probable that those who assert that schools are middle-class institutions are making a very different point, a value judgement in condemnation of schools as they function in modern society, and a denial that schools fulfil their proper obligation when transmitting middle-class norms. The slogan is usually to be inferred as a condemnation of schools for being thus incorrigibly and uncompromisingly middle-class in orientation. Schools, it is implied, ought to be something other than middle-class. Either they ought to be classless, that is their preoccupation should be with things to which the notion of social class is irrelevant; or they should be class-biased institutions in reflecting the dominant class profiles of their distinctive populations. This second alternative requires that there should be a plurality of schools. Some of them, those which serve a middle-class clientele could, no doubt, be predominantly middle-class in character; but others, especially, should focus upon the life-style and culture of the working class. A variant of this second alternative implies that a middle-class oriented school is an option for the effete, if not the decadent: contrary to the view that middle-class values represent the best of which humanity can conceive, middle-class values can be seen as corrupt and corrupting, even for the middle class itself (Labov 1973). If it is true that the working classes are wasting their lives at bingo and the like, corresponding middle-class activities are 'fiddling the income tax', attempting to better the Joneses and so on. Indeed, the notion that the middle class is defined by its attachment to money[9] is to see it as rooted in evil. The pejorative use of 'bourgeois' to characterize middle-class values sums up the conviction that they are no basis upon which to universalize educational provision.

Four distinctive positions can be distinguished with reference to the class orientation of schools.

(1)   Schooling, by origin and by definition, is a middle-class institution: schools could not be other than middle-class in orientation.

(2)   Schools should be class distinctive and class reinforcing: we need a plurality of schools serving different class interests, working-class schools alongside middle-class schools. This argument for separate schools can be widened to refer to ethnic, racial, religious and other cultural differences.

(3)   Schools should be multi-class institutions, comprehensive in the sense of taking account of the varied vocational, economic and cultural needs of different class and cultural orientations, whilst recognizing that such differences should be harmonized within a cultural mosaic where the common experience both sustains and is enriched by the parts.

(4)   Schools should be classless: this alternative is itself subject to varying interpretation (see below). In one of its versions it draws its justification from assumptions about the technological and socio-economic dynamics of advanced industrial society which seem inevitably corrosive of social class (see Ch.5 below).

In the remainder of this chapter it is the first of these assumptions that schools are inevitably middle-class institutions — which will be the subject of discussion.

However inappropriate its values and culture appear from the perspective of other, lower classes, it is sometimes assumed that, in some sense, the middle-class life-style is the only rational option, such that the school is necessarily faced with the task of discovering how to take working-class children as it finds them whilst, at the same time, ensuring that they are brought to an appreciation of middle-class culture. Upward mobility is widely accepted as a legitimate aspiration for the socially under-privileged, not least amongst many of the disadvantaged themselves. There are several reasons why the presumption might be in favour of the middle-class way of life and initiation into middle-class norms be deemed the only social option facing schools:

(i)   middle-class values might be ethically superior;
(ii)   middle-class cultural norms might be intellectually and aesthetically superior;
(iii)   a middle-class life-style affords better life chances with reference to health, longevity, education and so on;
(iv)   it is the required life-style for an advanced technological society.

This last assumption will be examined at length in chapter 5. Briefly, it holds that there is a shift in advanced industrial societies away from manual and towards non-manual, white-collar occupations at either a professional or quasi-professional level. Although as we shall presently see, there is disagreement about the social implications of this 'technological' trend, sequential census returns do appear to confirm that there is a diminishing proportion of the work force employed in those manual occupations traditionally conferring working-class status. This seems to indicate a withering of the working class and corresponding aggrandisement of the middle class. The implication is that, whether they wish it or not, and whether its values and life-style have the merit assumed in points (i) and (ii) above, an increasing number of people is destined to make a living in middle-class occupations and, on economic criteria of class, to become middle-class by definition. There are two educational correlates of this technologically engendered socio-economic shift. Potentially middle-class in terms of economic criteria, an increasing number of people need to be socialized into the values and cultural style of the middle class. Secondly, it is assumed that knowledge, and not manual skill, is the major occupational resource in advanced industrial societies, such that the traditional concept of the school as an agency for the transmission of knowledge and symbolic skills becomes more relevant than ever. If this socio-technological analysis of post-industrial society is valid, then it does seem that there is strong support for the view that schools ought to minister to the middle-class way of life.

Our third assumption — that the middle class enjoys better life chances — has similar educational correlates. Evidence on the respective life chances of the middle class and the working class shows the expectations of the former to be much higher than the latter. Statistically, members of the middle class live longer, have lower infant mortality rates, are less susceptible to disease associated with malnutrition and inadequate housing, enjoy longer schooling and better access to education (Tumin 1967 : Ch.7; Littlejohn 1972 : 118-20; Aiach and Willmot 1975). Educationally, the question is one of how far superior life chances are related not only to favourable economic circumstances, but also to having knowledge, whether 'general knowledge' acquired from prolonged schooling or particular knowledge of appropriate social, economic and political institutions. It has become a commonplace that the middle class is the main beneficiary of social reforms intended primarily for amelioration of poverty. Presumably the poor often lack the appropriate knowledge and skill to make the best of resources intended to improve its own life chances, whilst the middle class has the cognitive resources to exploit public welfare institutions to the full. If such knowledge and skill, the fruits of its prolonged and often privileged schooling, is a factor in improving life chances, then anyone valuing the educational, health, fiscal, social and other advantages enjoyed by the middle class would do well to seek 'a middle-class education'.

So far, in instrumental terms, there seems everything to be said for the view that schools cannot be other than middle-class in orientation. It is when we encounter claims for the ethical and cultural superiority of middle-class values that the case for a middle-class orientation of schools becomes dubious. Examination of these claims will be taken up in discussion of the assertion that schools are middle-class because they transmit middle-class values. But first, we examine the claim that schools are middle-class institutions because they are managed by the middle class; that is, they happen to transmit middle-class values not necessarily because these are superior, such that education entails their transmission, but rather because the middle class controls the process of transmission.

Middle-class management of the educational system

Schools could be categorized as middle-class institutions because they are managed by the middle class. In this, of course, they would not be essentially different from most institutions which are the apparatus of the modern State and which, ostensibly, serve the whole community. Members of the middle class manage most religious, cultural and recreational institutions, including bingo halls, socialist political parties and, increasingly, trade unions (Hindess 1971). Even in communist states, the bureaucracy is drawn from an élite whose life-style is privileged in relation to the categories of class, status and power. All this simply reflects nothing more nor less than the fact that in highly specialized economies, those who acquire professional skill as administrators become, by definition, members of the middle class: that is, they find themselves in occupational roles which, in terms of status, power and economic reward are on all fours with occupations peopled by the middle class.

Given this assumption that schools are run by the middle class, two possibilities follow: either, the schools are run to serve only the interests of the middle class, or it is conceivable that schools might be managed disinterestedly, without prejudice relating to the class origins of their clientele, even with a view towards amelioration of the condition of underprivileged groups in society.

The first of these alternatives conceives schools as hegemonic, part of the apparatus of the State designed to maintain the authority of the ruling class.[10] As hegemonic, schools function to service the exploitive imperatives of the capitalist consumer society. Their function is primarily economic in existing to promote the values of consumerism. Illich's proposal to de-school society was derived in part from his criticism of the school's efficiency in performing this function. Schools are also hegemonic in confirming a majority of working-class children in subsidiary roles as manual workers. Littlejohn observes that the appearance of a selective bias in access to selective secondary and higher education 'is liable to convey the impression of a middle-class conspiracy against working-class children' (1972 : 124). But the stability of the *status quo* also depends upon keeping the ruling class open to recruitment from below. Hence, in fostering upward mobility, schools are also efficiently fulfilling their hegemonic function. As agencies of social selection (preoccupied with testing, examination, qualifications, the award of diplomas and certificates) schools are thus renewing and refreshing the ruling class without eroding its authority in any way. Hence, even concern with clever working-class boys and girls is self-interested and not evidence of an altruistic or humanistic concern that the individual should make the best of himself. 'Contest mobility', the 'career open to talent', 'equality of educational opportunity' are, thus, simply prudential notions, resorts to expedience, lacking any ethical justification. The appeal to ethical concepts like equality or social justice are, on this view, a rationalization or veneer intended to cover the essentially conservative and hegemonic function of social mobility as engineered through the schools. This view of schools as instruments of middle-class hegemony was underlined by Anthony Crosland (quoted in Raynor 1969 : 39) when minister of education for England and Wales:

> Our schools have been essentially middle-class institutions and our educational system geared to educating the middle classes, plus a few from below who looked like desirable recruits to the middle class. The remainder were given cheaper teachers and inferior buildings and were segregated in separate schools.

Crosland was a prominent advocate of comprehensive education: it has been long and widely assumed that the comprehensivization of secondary schools would be counter-hegemonic.[11] As social solvents they would erode middle-class hegemony, and in Crosland's view, pave the way for a classless society. However, this moral case for comprehensive education has tended to give way to functionalist justification. From this standpoint it can be argued that the recent comprehensivization of secondary education throughout Western Europe is simply a device to make selection more efficient. Avoidance of social and economic wastage has been a prominent item in the more recent rationale of comprehensive schooling, and earlier arguments for common schooling as a 'social solvent' have given way to debate about the relative efficiency of comprehensive as against segregated secondary schooling in securing greater examination success.

An alternative account of middle-class management of schools requires that the middle class functions disinterestedly in running the schools on behalf of children *as* children no matter what their social origin. The earlier case for comprehensive schooling, predicated upon the moral imperative towards a classless society, required this conception of the middle class as capable of disinterested social service. Even critics of the middle class often subscribe to this conception of the middle class as one which serves. Raymond Williams (1961b : 63), for example, refers to this tradition of disinterested middle-class social service: historically, harsh middle-class ideals were tempered 'by a major ideal of public service, in which the effort towards civilization is actively promoted by a genuine altruism and the making of positive institutions'. This commitment to disinterestedness has been particularly evident in those members of the middle class who have been educationists by profession. We have already noted that educational theory has been explicitly individualistic and humanitarian. Each student is assumed to be an individual bringing his own unique complex of intellectual, emotional and cultural capital to school; its task is to bring this unique potential to fruition. This is probably the account of their task which most teachers would give and, undoubtedly, it is an honest version of the teacher's role. Moreover, whatever the dispositions of individual teachers, the ideology of teacher training institutions is unfailingly individualistic and humanitarian in emphasis. Social-class differences function in this ideology only in facilitating or hindering the development of 'the educated man' whose characterization is usually absolutely neutral as to class, nationality, race, colour or creed: education is a quest for improvement in terms of behaviour, thought and feeling which are thought to have nothing to do with social class.

Those who regard schools as hegemonic, concerned with the integrity of the *status quo*, find this liberal, democratic, individualistic account of schooling naive. On turning to the real world of the classroom, this conventional wisdom dissolves into something quite different. Critics of middle-class domination of school would argue that despite their 'better selves' as evidenced in their election platforms, their conference resolutions, the policy statements of their professional associations and their answers to examination questions in educational theory, when it comes to actually managing the educational process, middle-class politicians, bureaucrats and teachers are quite incapable of acting disinterestedly in treating children as children without perceiving them as members of a particular social class. For example, with obvious exceptions, school buildings and resources in inner city schools are old, depressing if not in decay, and in striking contrast to the newer schools in middle-class suburbs designed to facilitate the implementation of progressive educational ideas. The defence of this state of affairs may lie in the rationale of the economics of urban renewal and planning, the provision of new schools being economically related to slum clearance and rehousing. But it does seem a fact that most publicly financed social institutions do ultimately redound more to the benefit of the middle class than to any other.

However, it is in relation to those professionals who encounter children daily in schools that the argument persists that schools are managed by the middle class in its own interests and against the aspirations of the lower classes. The long-standing debate about intelligence testing centres on the question of the possibility of devising tests which are culture-free. Whatever the logical possibilities here, the fact is that educational psychologists rate highly in each of the hierarchies of class, status and power. Inevitably, with the best of intentions to do otherwise, they devise instruments of assessment which miss the point of working-class perceptions of the universe. When it comes to the actual teachers in schools, middle-class themselves, they inevitably transmit middle-class values and reward those who learn to share this particular perception of reality. The notion that there are middle-class values obviously requires examination in any discussion of the accusation that schools are middle-class institutions and the ambiguities in this notion will be discussed presently. What must be examined at this point, however, is the assumption that teachers *are* middle-class themselves; or, since on conventional classifications of occupations they seem unquestionably so, in what respect which has pedagogical relevance can they be dismissed as middle-class.

As a matter of fact, in most educational systems the teaching profession has not been homogeneous as to social background, schooling, professional training, nor in receipt of a unitary salary scale or as objects of social esteem. Indeed, the various social strata have usually tended to recruit their children's teachers from amongst their own ranks.[12] In Britain, upper-middle-class commitment to exclusive public schools derives partly from their being staffed by products of these schools themselves and the ancient universities. Purchase of a 'better' education for one's children is not seen simply in terms of educational efficiency, where efficiency is measured in terms of factors like the size of classes, examination results and the training of teachers (typically, public school teachers were not trained) or the availability of educational technology; rather, the 'best' education is measured by the access it affords to a privileged life-style — a social network, exclusive cultural activities — facilitated by the fact that teachers themselves are in the network. Similarly, that social stratum comprising the lower-middle and skilled working classes has drawn its teachers from its own ranks. In publicly provided systems of education a distinction has to be drawn between the elementary and the high school teacher, the former having (until quite recently) little more than a complete secondary schooling in a teacher's college or normal school, the latter having a university education, often without professional training. The present trend towards an all-graduate profession, and the blurring of the distinction between the elementary and secondary traditions with the development of comprehensive schooling, has not altogether obliterated the distinction between the two traditions. There is little empirical evidence on the class origins of teachers in relation to kinds of schools in which they teach, but it is a familiar fact that many teachers in publicly maintained educational systems having working-class backgrounds. From both sides of the Atlantic there is evidence that at least one-half of teacher trainees come from working-class families. (Corwin 1965 : 162-3; Taylor 1969 : 185-8; Floud and Scott 1965). This fact should caution circumspection we allege that schools fail because middle-class teachers are unable to understand the language of working-class children. The social values and cultural dispositions of those who have made this journey from working to middle class are complex, ambivalent and their pedagogical expression too subtle to be dismissed in a cliché about transmitting middle-class values.

For one thing, it is plausible that teachers with working-class backgrounds only fail to understand working-class speech, manners, values and attitudes in the sense of failing to understand why anyone should want to hold on to a life-style which they take to be manifestly inferior. If some teachers are derogatory of working-class life it is because they think they understand it only too well and reject what they consider to be the intolerable hindrances it puts in the way of favourable life-chances. That is, middle-class values and life-style are preferred from personal experience of both, and it is probable that some of those who seem most unsympathetic to working-class culture are, like the officer who has risen from the ranks or the convert to Catholicism, 'more catholic than the Pope'. This phenomenon was observed by Klein (1965 : 418-19), writing of people in her survey who condemned working-class spending habits:

> Many of these middle-class people were distinguishable from manual workers not by family origin but only by present occupation. They were reacting against a life they had left behind ... teachers who had come from working-class families had a distinct tendency to opine that the wrong kind of boy was being allowed into grammar school nowadays: this in spite of the fact that they themselves had been 'the wrong kind of boy' in earlier days.

This attitude in teachers of working-class origin may be deplorable, but their conversion is not to be found in teaching them facts about working-class culture which they do not know, so much as in whatever is involved in the creation of sympathy for what they do not value or, possibly, what they fear.[13] Yet the assumption that teachers *are* middle-class does lead some critics of the school to assume that a solution to the problem of school failure is to be found in teachers learning a 'new' language because it is believed that working-class English is utterly foreign to them.[14]

Part of the problem of dismissing schools as class biased by reference to the class composition of the teaching profession is that it depends on an altogether too crude conception of social stratification: it assumes value homogeneity within classes, for example. Yet not only does there seem to be a good deal of overlap at the margins of the different social strata, but there are also hierarchies within classes themselves. Thus, the teacher of working-class origin who despises working-class culture is not necessarily doing this from the perspective of newly won middle-class culture. As Roberts shows in *The Classic Slum* (1973), there always has been disdain for the lower, unskilled working-class from the skilled working-class. The insistence of craft unions on maintaining wage differentials is obviously a species of class distinction, with implications also for social prestige and access to political power. Yet the working-class teacher has probably originated in the upper-working class and status dissent (rejection of lower-class norms) was a likely factor in his aspiration towards upward mobility. Hence the hypothesis: *if* teachers with working-class origins typically resent lower-class students and despise their cultural values, the explanation may lie in phenomena related to working-class stratification itself, not in middle-class values.

The notion of value heterogeneity within classes has further ramifications with reference to the assumption that schools transmit middle-class values. It is a familiar enough notion that each social class has its upper, middle and lower strata which blur at the edges, but it is less often explicit that the dichotomy of 'us' and 'them' may be as divisive within classes as between classes (Lockwood 1975 : 242): 'they' can refer to other middle-class people who earn their livings in different ways. Conflicts of interest are as likely to divide the middle class as they are the working class, and the fact that different middle-class groups acquire their incomes from different sources both reflects and reinforces the different value orientations of their members. In the American context, Cook and Cook (1960 : 94-5) distinguished 'two tops' in society subscribing, on the one hand, to the tough-minded values which are an 'interactive composite of wealth, power and competition', on the other hand, to the tender-minded values of creativity, service to others and 'the never-ending search for meanings'. Familiarly, the tough-minded middle class in commercial and industrial management are apt to be suspicious and even derisory towards 'liberals' and 'lefties' commonly found amongst the artistic and academic middle class and, to some extent, those engaged in broadcasting and journalism. With reference to status stratification, differing middle-class groups apparently display little in common when attributing status to life-styles which they value. Both their status symbols and their membership of cultural and recreational groups differ significantly. No doubt they also have different perceptions of what constitutes

power, and their divergent political ideologies commit their alleg-
iance to differing political parties and pressure groups. Indeed, to
the extent that the 'us'-'them' distinction has an essentially
political connotation, the bureaucratic 'they' in Washington or
Whitehall seems often as alien and threatening to the middle class
as to any other. Moreover, on a strictly economic view of class,
although they may occupy similar strata with reference to income
levels, the different sources of their incomes should have consequences for their political interests. Those deriving income from the
private sector of the economy — whether as salaries or profits —
seem threatened by the growing middle-class group of tax-
supported occupations in the public sector. Whilst the interests of
the former would appear to be furthered by the election of
conservative, retrenching, free enterprise parties, those of the latter
depend upon government by left of centre parties committed to
increasing public expenditure. For, to the extent that income
derives differently from the profitability of private industry or from
public finance, there is a latent conflict of interest between middle-
class groups, especially in times of economic recession. Moreover,
those in fee-earning professions — especially in what Gretton (1917
: 101-2) called 'the parasitic middle class' — constitute yet a third
category with interests potentially different from the other two.
Indeed, middle-class salary earners are apt to feel as exploited by
the escalating fees charged by legal, medical and real estate
professionals as does any social group. Obviously, as critics of a
naively Marxist conception of class (as defined by one's relationship
to ownership of the means of production) have argued, the
professional middle class is impossible to classify: witness the
spectre of university teachers wondering in public whether or not
they are working-class (see below, pp.130-1).

Williams (1916 : 317) suggests one explanation of this ambiguity
in our classificatory social categories. The attempt to include both
middle- and working-class in a single class system rests upon a
category mistake, since 'middle' has primarily a social significance,
whilst the reference of 'working' is economic. Thus, middle-class
and working-class 'are not true alternatives. The alternatives to
"middle" are "lower" and "upper"; the alternative to "working" is "independent" or "propertied".' It has been suggested
that the complex of psychological, cultural, economic and political

factors which is at work in defining value orientations and group self-images is best analysed and classified by reference to the notion of 'occupational community' rather than to the blunt instrument of social class. With reference to the notion of working-class solidarity, there exists a growing body of research throwing doubt on the assumption that there exists a homogeneous working class displaying class solidarity and a distinctive class consciousness (Bulmer 1975). Divergent value orientations are clearly identifiable within the working class and this has led to the assumption that the politically and socially relevant focus for research in industrial sociology ought to be the occupational community. This requires a redefinition of occupational community so that 'the concept is not restricted to quaint, vestigial local work based communities', but relates to the 'extent to which people see themselves as members of what they regard as an occupation', a perception having significance in terms of 'relationships, culture and identity'. Salaman (1975 : 227) concludes:

> ... although it has frequently and cogently been argued that the traditional and orthodox distinction between middle and working classes is still empirically meaningful (that is that there remain substantial differences in work and market situation, in patterns of association and relationship, consciousness and values etc.) it is also clear that there are important occupationally based differences within these two classes, both with respect to the 'objective' aspects of the location of occupations within the division of labour and with respect to ideologies (or, viewed differently, occupational or class consciousness).

There seems no reason why the conception of occupational communities as the explanation of distinctive value systems should not be applied to middle-class divergent value orientations as a more fruitful basis than raw social-class analysis for attempting to establish relationships between education and socio-economic groupings. Skidelski (1969 : 19-20) provides some evidence that whilst parents involved in business prefer the traditional public school, progressive boarding schools tend to attract parents in 'creative' occupations (musicians, writers, painters, television producers, entertainers) and the professions, especially academics, psychiatrists and architects. He concludes, tentatively, that 'parents engaged in commerce are more likely to have a utilitarian idea of education, measuring success in terms of examinations and opportunities to "get on". Professional and creative parents are likely to assign a higher value to self-discovery and fulfilment in work'. A similar distinction between educational styles preferred by different groups within the middle class is traced by Bernstein (1971-3 : Vol.3, Ch.6)[15] to an ideological conflict between the 'old' and the 'new' middle class. The conception of education as play 'was first institutionalized within the private sector for a fraction of the middle class — the new middle class'. The new middle class is defined in relation to the division of labour as, for example, 'those who are filling the ever-expanding major and minor professional class concerned with the servicing of persons'. Although Bernstein's own analysis draws largely upon the concept of social class, it does give some support to the view that the notion of occupational community could be a more fruitful point of departure for an understanding of some of the educational corre- lates of socio-economic distinctions.

Nevertheless, it is still claimed that despite evident differences in value orientation within classes, there remain underlying values common to different occupational communities within each class which have educational significance transcending their differences. It remains to explore this notion that there are basic values common to all groups within the middle class which permeate the educa- tional system.

The school and middle-class values

The notion that schools transmit middle-class values relates partly to curriculum content, and partly to the disciplinary ethos of the school which has come to be known as 'the hidden curriculum'. With reference to the manifest content of the curriculum, 'values' refers to cultural values (in the sense of culture which I have categor- ized below as 2n, see Chapter 4) and, particularly, to intellectual and aesthetic norms and standards. On the other hand, the values which inform the disciplinary ethos of schools are ethical and social.

Discussion of values with reference to the manifest cultural content of the curriculum is taken up in subsequent chapters. In the present context, it is simply necessary to note the argument that the culture of the school (even in the diluted form in which it appears in schools deliberately contrived for the less able) derives from a high culture which is a minority taste and preoccupation, characteristic of the life-style of the middle class. It is a curriculum whose relevance is to life-activities like reading *The Times* (whether New York or London), reading magazines like *The Times Literary Supplement* or *The New York Review of Books*, theatre and concert going, visiting art galleries and museums, book collecting, foreign travel and so on. It is also argued that not only are members of the middle class the typical consumers of this culture, they are also its creators: 'the skills and insights, scientific and humanistic, which sustain our civilization have been developed by those who either are middle class or have become so in the process of acquiring such skills' (Bantock 1975a : 153).

A rebuttal of this notion that the middle class creates this culture essentially for its own consumption is that it is an odd claim that history, science, geography, mathematics and technology represent middle-class culture. Writing of the English grammar school, Jackson and Marsden (1962 : 221) underlined the absurdity of this notion:

> It seems to us that what we call our central culture and what the teachers call 'middle-class values' are by no means the same thing ... When the headteacher says 'I see grammar school education very strongly as a matter of communicating middle-class values to a "new" population', he is surely not saying something akin to Matthew Arnold's classic statement, but something contrary in spirit; provincial and partisan.

There is ample evidence that this central (or high) culture has been attractive to generations of working-class people such that it is an essential component of anything worth the name of 'working-class culture'. On the other hand, superficially, there is a case for arguing that those activities we have noted above are minority tastes and that, in the late twentieth century, they are more likely to be engaged in by members of the middle class than by members of the working class. This, for example, is the view of one American critic of the curriculum (Kvaraceus 1965 : 124):

> In differentiating the curriculum, attention must be given to the current structure of the monolithic upper-middle class curriculum that assumes that all high school pupils will become daily

readers of the *New York Times* and will subscribe to the *Saturday Review* and will eventually turn out to be the worthy alumni of some university or college — preferably the Ivy League. Attention must be directed to the development of a meaningful curriculum for the non-mobile or stable lower-class youngster for whom middle-class goals do not represent reasonable or realistic goals. The core of this revised curriculum should centre around the communication skills, leisure time pursuits, husband-wife relationships, child-rearing skills, beginning job competencies, and social-civic responsibilities.

It is interesting that these vocational, domestic, leisure and political competencies should not be considered the appropriate outcomes of a curriculum designed for all children of whatever social class: if they are, why single them out as curricular objectives only for lower-class children unable to accept middle-class goals? More to the point is the assumption that the traditional curriculum has nothing to contribute towards the knowledge and skill required for these fundamental life preoccupations. It will presently be argued that what is dismissed, often pejoratively, as 'high culture' has a reference much more mundane than to the esoteric preoccupation of the coterie of readers of the New York or London *Times* (see Ch.1).

However, it is especially through its 'hidden curriculum' that the school is deemed to have a middle-class orientation in terms of those values which inform its disciplinary ethos. At an apparently trivial level this seems evident in what might be called the 'hats and gloves' syndrome. In some schools, a good deal of time and energy is devoted to manners or etiquette in insisting on what is 'proper' with reference to superficial matters of personal appearance and dress. Secondary schools often appear to spend an inordinate length of time in seeking out those who are wearing jeans, long hair, jewellery, make-up and so on. Often this scrutiny extends to junior members of staff — male staff wearing beards and women wearing slacks, for example. Positively, the syndrome requires the wearing of uniform as well as insistence on things like cleanliness and short hair. This emphasis upon 'correct' dress and appearance is probably much more common in British schools than elsewhere. With recent permissiveness this almost military conception of personal appearance as an index of personal worth seemed to be eroding. Nevertheless, it persists, and there is evidence in the mid-1970s that some school administrations are tightening up 'standards' in these areas, anticipating support from a backlash against the excesses of permissiveness and the desire for 'discipline' in the face of community violence and urban terrorism. For example, in mid-1976 an English secondary school headmaster addressed parents thus:

> Experience has shown beyond reasonable doubt that if a young person is concerned with his or her appearance then that person will also be concerned with punctuality, attendance, behaviour, responsibility and achievement ... experience has also shown that if pupils are allowed to be slovenly in appearance then this slovenliness will be reflected in all that they do.

Of interest here is not the assumption that a correlation between concern for appearance and achievement has been established 'beyond reasonable doubt', but that these claims are in the context of a letter asking parental cooperation about the provision and wearing of school uniform. 'Slovenly appearance' consists in not wearing 'correct school dress', that is, the regulation uniform. Indeed this attempted justification of 'correct' school dress is essentially military in origin. Army discipline in emphasizing correct dress, smartness of appearance, short hair, etc., assumes that respect for authority and prompt response to orders is inconsistent with appearance which is 'sloppy' and behaviour which is idiosyncratic. Much the same sort of rationale obviously unerpins the view that personal discipline in respect of dress, cleanliness and appearance is a necessary basis for the discipline required in academic learning.

The 'hats and gloves' syndrome prompts two comments with reference to the schools' values and social class. The hidden curriculum, as it refers to matters of etiquette, is probably as much a consequence of generational as of class differences: younger teachers often find the constraints of school etiquette and manners as odious as do students. Secondly, so far as etiquette reflects class values, it is a lower-middle-class characteristic to emphasize the 'proper' or genteel in terms of surface manners and appearances. The distinction between 'U' and 'non-U' of a generation ago was drawn in a way which isolated the 'non-U' lower-middle class; upper-class speech and behaviour demonstrably had much in common with lower-class culture in this respect. Perhaps the trouble with teachers is often that they are not middle class enough. The disciplinary norms which schools urge upon children represent the philistine values of the lower-middle class and rebellion in schools against what is perceived as repressive discipline is a reaction against the values of the new, suburban lower-middle class. More seriously, with reference to the cultural objectives of education, it is not always clear that the teacher's own personal culture is adequate as a resource for the initiation of students into those humanitarian values, the 'Western' culture, which liberal educational ideology takes to be the cultural data of education. This criticism is implicit in a recent English survey of the values of students in a large northern college of education. Some 70 per cent came from homes with all the material paraphernalia of suburban middle-class life but very few parents confessed to an interest in the arts, religion or politics. Of the students themselves it was apparent that 'classical music, the theatre, art and literature were things which usually did not touch their lives ... Many did not even regularly read newspapers' (Lomax 1971): few had any interest in religion, politics or social problems. Although Bantock (1969) believes lower-middle-class cultural norms to be so pervasive that our culture in the twentieth century belongs to the lower-middle-class man, Hoggart takes these manifestations of lower-middle-class culture in the school as 'the accents of marginality', possibly a transitional phenomenon: 'It is now already a little misleading to speak of the middle class way of life in this connection. What has come about bears only about as much resemblance to the traditional upper middle class way of life as it does to the traditional working class' (quoted by Klein 1965).

If not this preoccupation with superficial manifestations of gentility, what are the central values of the historic heroic middle class? In the relevant literature, listed values vary but include: ambition, future-orientation or capacity for deferred gratification; commitment to leadership and participation; politeness, punctuality, respect for authority and property; belief in education, health and cleanliness; physical non-aggression, impersonality and privacy, escapism, a tradition of gentlemanly service exemplified in the valuation of honour, dignity, integrity, kindness, considerateness, philanthropy, courtesy, chivalry, charity and disinterestedness (Bell 1962; Cole and Cox 1968; Cohen 1955; Kvaraceus 1965).

Apart from the occasional blot, this list is such that a roll-call of those who subscribe to it would constitute the communion of saints; as indeed, their implied absence in the working class would make it a criminal sub-culture. In fact, in Western culture, these have usually been regarded simply as human values, not distinguishing characteristics of any class, but virtues by reference to which persons are deemed human. As Gross argues (1962 : 121-2), these values are insufficiently discriminatory, too conceptually imprecise, to be useful tools of sociological analysis and description. If people are to be classified by reference to the values to which they subscribe, it is necessary to go beyond these abstract, first-order human values to the second-order norms through which they find concrete expression in the lives of individuals or groups. Kohlberg (1971 : 71-2) makes this point with reference to the presumption that politeness is a distinctively middle-class value:

> Politeness ... may reflect a universal concern over propriety of behaviour, but middle-class definitions of politeness are different from ghetto definitions of politeness. Our moral objection to spitting in another child's face is not that it is 'impolite' but that it is a violation of the other's dignity, of respect for the other as a human being. An advocate of 'Black Power' and 'Black Values' may legitimately object to a teacher's indoctrinating children with middle-class lily-white conceptions of politeness, but he cannot object to teaching respect for the fundamental rights of other human beings. His only basis for being heard in his claim for 'Black Values' is the basis of regard for the equal rights and dignity of blacks as human beings.

Education and the value of future-orientation

Educationally, the crucial middle-class value is taken to be orientation to the future, a preference for future over present gratification. Yet this value (assuming that it is appropriate to speak of future-orientation as a value in this way) is especially difficult to employ as an index of social class. And since the absence of this value orientation is taken to be a crucial impediment to working-class success in schools, it is worth focusing on this as a test of the notion that the school's values are middle-class.

It is odd that a social group which invented the Friendly Society, the Co-operative Movement, Penny Banks and Trade Unions should be said to lack future-orientation. Educational history is also replete with working-class initiatives in pursuit of its own education, involving considerable personal sacrifice. Blinkered dedication to immediate gratification is hardly typical of generations of workers 'voluntarily often sacrificing scant leisure' to attend adult classes for purposes quite unconnected with immediate personal gain (Hodgen 1925; Simon 1960; Silver 1975). Bulmer (1975 : 197) cites a number of commentators who, as early as the 1850s, 'were welcoming the existence of a ''new'' working class — respectable, temperate, members of Co-ops and Penny Banks'. The working class has often been as careful in taking thought for the morrow as any stratum in the socio-economic hierarchy. It has also paid careful attention to utopian reformers preaching 'a new view of society' and has been receptive to the claims of other-worldly religious sects with their promises of future recompense for present suffering. It does not diminish the importance of this capacity for deferred gratification that it was pursued collectively and solidistically rather than individually; nor that the sums involved were small — a few pennies per week — from the perspective of the economically affluent; nor that abstention was often accepted negatively or defensively — an insurance against the rainy day — rather than in positive expectation of future gratification. The moral energy of this patient, future-orientation was remarked by a continental observer of the English working class towards the end of the nineteenth century (Baernreither 1889 : 7):

> ... the danger is that reform can never ripen, since those who are most closely interested in the reform — in other words, those who hope that it will better their position — either cannot or will not wait. ... The self-denial and self-sacrifice of the earlier generation of working men purchased the progress of their successors of today, and even now the English workman quietly endures all the uncertainties and hardships of the present, in the hope that, by slowly but steadily pushing onwards, he may bequeath to his children a good, and possibly to his grandchildren, a still better future.

Implicitly, Baernreither here focuses the crucial role of present economic comfort or deprivation in shaping one's perception of the future, and this raises doubts about whether future-orientation or deferred gratification can properly be categorized as values at all. It is odd that anyone should be said to value the future as such, especially for its own sake. What is usually being claimed when we speak of future-orientation is that certain things are valued which can only happen in the future. Valuing education for one's children is usually in expectation that it will fit them for particular social and economic roles. It is *their* future life-style which is in question.

It is important to recognize, then, that valuing always has an economic dimension in that it involves making choices with reference to the marginal utilities of desirable but competing objectives, and the diminishing returns to a particular form of behaviour. As with material economic goods, the pursuit of options in cultural or moral terms is subject to conflict: otherwise the notion of choice is otiose. But choice is rarely simply a matter of distinguishing desirable from undesirable consequences of action. Valuing partakes of economic criteria precisely because it has to be done with respect to desirable alternatives which cannot both be satisfied at once or in equal measure: hence the need for calculations in terms of marginal utilities and diminishing returns. Indeed, the notion of deferred gratification is quite meaningless except in the context of present satisfactions or obligations. We save for next year's holiday either because we cannot be on holiday now or because we have just come back, surfeited, from holiday, not because we simply prefer being on holiday next year instead of now. It is not clear why one would wish to postpone a desired holiday, being in a position to take it today, if one were not either under an obligation to work to make a holiday possible, or just back from holiday and welcoming the change to normal everyday preoccupations. That is, one could be postponing one's holiday until next year in order to have something to look forward to, simply because the marginal utility of a recent experience is low and one wishes to maximize satisfaction next year. Deferring gratification is in this case no sacrifice and is, indeed, a form of present gratification.

But, the objection might be, in deferring gratification, there is sometimes an element of sacrifice as when middle-class parents forgo things they could use or enjoy now, in order to provide for their children's future, especially their education. This notion of sacrifice (carrying an implication of moral superiority) recurs in explanation of middle-class behaviour in relation to education: for example, 'the middle-class child is ... prepared early to sacrifice the present for the future'. Corwin (1965) continues, in explanation of the discrepancy between middle-class and working-class values:

> Since thrift and planning can occur only in a relatively secure environment where the future is foreseeable, lower class children do not learn those habits as virtues. They are not enthusiastic about the prospect that years of economic sacrifice in school might bring them greater reward in the future.

Despite locating these discrepant attitudes to the future in an economic context, the overtones of moral superiority implied in the reference to sacrifice and virtue are clear. Yet, what is strikingly unreal about this conclusion is that the notion of sacrifice should be introduced at all. It has far too potent evocations to stand simply for the act of giving up some luxury that one might otherwise have had. Especially in the North-American context from which Corwin writes, it would seem puzzling to the lower-class child to know what exactly it is that the middle-class child is sacrificing in the present and, by contrast, what luxuries of consumption he himself currently enjoys at the expense of his own future. For it is one thing to deny the present in order to cater for the future when a comfortable standard of life is available, but quite something else to invest in the future when basic needs are not even being met. You can look to the future when you have enough satisfactions today, even when these are not luxuries; when these is no economic elbowroom whatever, getting through this week is the dominant preoccupation: 'when one's belly is empty, one's only problem is an empty belly' (Orwell 1970 : 127). Yet some expression of regret that the working class lacks future-orientation, preferring immediate gratification, seems predicated on the assumption that working-class life is a perpetual Roman orgy of eating, drinking and merry-making. In fact, present gratification for the working class has usually meant simply being adequately clothed, fed and (more rarely) housed. If valuation implies choice, it is inappropriate to speak of working-class values in a present-future dimension, for not to choose the present expenditure of its economic resources would be to prefer hunger, cold, malnutrition and the giving up of such modest recreational consolations as would make the difference between life and mere existence. The poor live so close to subsistence, to life's brutal imperatives, that they *must* choose the present. Even to speak of choosing the present is inappropriate when you cannot help but opt for present gratification in order to remain fit and healthy. For the working class throughout most of its history choosing immediate as against deferred gratification has been a matter of Hobson's Choice. In much the same way, there is an obvious sense in which the middle class does not choose or value the future above the present: its members rarely defer gratification of basic biological needs and modest recreations. At most, future-orientation is a matter of degree in relation to economic circumstances.

It is clear that the middle class has no monopoly of those human values which the educational literature on social class usually takes to be self-evidently middle class. The pursuit of moral superiority would not be a good reason for adopting a middle-class life-style. But in rejecting this notion that moral superiority attaches to the middle class, one has to avoid throwing the ethical baby out with the social-class bathwater. For it may be that some of those attributes which are inappropriately assumed to be distinguishing marks of the middle class are of importance in the pursuit of education. For example, the ability to defer gratification is taken to be educationally functional, so far as an education is conceived primarily as a preparation for life, not as an experience having immediately relevant interest or satisfaction. The assumption then must be that children capable of future-orientation have a capacity for boredom such that they are able to tolerate presently unsatisfying, even meaningless rituals often associated with learning, seeing through them to the dividends which will subsequently accrue — selection for academic secondary schools, university scholarships, graduation and a licence to practise one of the professions or, at least, entry into a secure, status-conferring white-collar occupation. It tends to be part of the conventional wisdom, however, that this filtering or screening process for privileged social roles has little to do with education.

But aside from this debatable assumption that matters concerned with earning a living have not very much to do with life (hence, cannot be part of education for living — see Ch. 5) there does arise the question of how far a willingness to defer present gratification is necessary to being educated, where education is defined without reference to extrinsic aims, as initiation into worthwhile or culturally significant experiences, or full development as a human being, or whatever improving process is implicit in one's preferred statement of educational aim. The progressive educational tradition from Rousseau through Dewey has emphasized that education is not a preparation for life but a presently satisfying experience. The future is unpredictable (as Rousseau put it, the 'Great Reaper Death' may carry the child off before his and our aspirations for him are realized — so much for deferred gratification) and often enough asking the child to defer gratification is really in pursuit of our own present gratifications (what we want him to become). Hence the insistence of the progressives that the child is not 'an adult writ small', not 'a candidate', 'on the waiting list'. I have suggested elsewhere (Entwistle 1970 : Ch.5) that this tendency to dichotomize present and future is mistaken educationally: we obviously take care of the future by taking care of today. Nevertheless, there is a sense in which any educational experience must transcend the present and immediate. For if, as Dewey put it, experience is not to be merely 'written in water', it has to be stored against future contingencies. And this necessary storage of experience requires that it be caught up in a symbol system of one kind or another — linguistic, mathematical, artistic. And, familiarly, it is the learning of symbol systems in school which often generates boredom and, by definition, distances the learner from his present, immediate, concrete experience. R.S. Peters has written of education requiring that one gets 'on the inside' of worthwhile activities. And there is an obvious sense in which a novice is 'on the outside' of any activities needing to be learned. If there were no mystery, no difficulty, no unforeseen impediments to acquiring knowledge or skill, it would hardly be appropriate to speak of learning at all. Similarly, the gratifications of worthwhile experiences only reveal themselves with mastery. And mastery, as Whitehead insisted (1955 : Ch.2) depends upon a stage of precision in any learning experience, requiring drill, repetition and attention to the 'grammar' of a 'discipline'. This is not to say that the precision of learning cannot be a source of immediate gratification, but even the most creative of academic tasks (one suspects artistic creativity too) has its periods of discipline, routine, repetition, frustration, 'seeing through a glass darkly' and *longueurs* which are only gratifying in the perspective of the total task or performance and, hence, by definition, not immediately satisfying or less satisfying than possible alternative activities. Thus, capacity for deferred gratification is essential to success in schooling, even when this is conceived as an intrinsically educational process.

It is in this sense that a learning experience which is educative requires a capacity to transcend the imperatives of this time and this place, and involves some recognition that satisfaction in life often comes from 'casting one's bread upon the water', worthwhile knowledge, skill and interests inevitably generating a bonus of unforeseen gratification. Whether from temperament, economic deprivation or stupidity, some children cannot escape the prison of their immediate appetites, and one may have to conclude that such are incapable of being educated. And if there are sub-cultures whose time-orientation is inescapably towards the present, and if those with an ability to transcend the constraints of time and place are to be found substantially within the middle class, then the school, even as the source of properly educational experiences, may be a middle-class institution. It is, indeed, ironical (if reference to the school as a middle-class institution is intended critically) that working-class children seem to prosper educationally when they are integrated into schools with middle-class children (see Coleman 1969). But before accepting the conclusion that there is a completely different cultural perspective in the working class, unfriendly to the educational experience, one needs to examine working-class life and culture more closely than is often the case when it is defined simply by exclusion with reference to those 'superior' values and cultural activities which are said to be middle class. This examination is undertaken in Chapter 4. But first it is necessary to examine the alternative view that, whilst schools as they now exist may well enough meet the needs of the middle class, the working class needs working-class education in its own schools, managed by the working class with the aim of transmitting working-class culture.

3

Education and
the working class

The working class and the community school

It is necessary to draw a number of conceptual distinctions before
considering different prescriptions for education on behalf of the
working class. First, a distinction must be drawn between *working-
class education* and *education of the working class*. *Working-class
education* implies that there is a type of education appropriate to
the working class, different from that which is relevant to other
classes. This view derives from the assumption that the working
class has its own culture and values: being working-class is to
require distinctive skills, techniques and forms of knowledge which
define a peculiar educational content, a particular kind of curriculum.

On the other hand, *education of the working class* refers simply
to the class origins of the clientele of various educational institutions. Thus, a working-class school would cater exclusively for
children with a working-class background, but this fact alone would
not commit it to a curriculum of a particular kind, since its
educational objectives would not differ from those of a middle (or

any other) class school. Or, in a large school serving a socially heterogeneous neighbourhood, it would be clear that some children came from working-class homes. This might present a school with certain problems and challenges. But the class background of the clientele of any school would be considered irrelevant to consideration of educational aims and objectives and, on the whole, to the definition of content and method. This is to assume that education is one and indivisible: its aims are universal. The philosopher of education typically talks of *the* concept of education or *the* aims or objectives of schooling, in a sociological vacuum and without reference to limiting categories like class, nationality, race or religion. He recognizes that education has a social dimension in accepting that man is a social animal and that some of the skills and forms of knowledge he has to acquire are functional for his life in relationship to other people and within institutions. However, formal definitions of education tend to be humanitarian and individualistic, making assumptions about rationality and a capacity for moral and aesthetic sensibility on behalf of persons *qua* human beings.

The above distinction is related to one of a slightly different kind. Anyone concerned with working-class betterment as an objective of movements for social and educational reform, in terms of notions like 'the good life' or 'the good society', is faced with two different possible outcomes of an educational system. Education may be conceived as *classless* or as *class specific, class confirming* even *class divisive.*

The notion that education should be classless derives from an estimation of the desirability and the possibility of achieving a classless society. In turn, there are two versions of the classless society; the social democratic or non-Marxist socialist and the Marxist. The first of these is committed to a conception of a classless society where class divisions dissolve upon recognition of some more fundamental notion of the nature of persons as human beings and unique individuals.[1] Raymond Williams is an exponent of this position.[2] Toward the end of *The Long Revolution* (1961b : 317, 321) he casts doubt on the value of the notion of social class: 'Anyone who is used to either professional or amateur attempts at social classification will know how intricate it has all become. The question we need to ask, however — and it is only very rarely asked

— is what all this classification is for, what actual purpose in society it serves.' Then, of his perception of his own location in the social system: 'I have never felt my own mobility in terms of "a rise in the social scale", and certainly I have never felt that I wanted to go on climbing resentful of old barriers in my way: *where else is there to go, but into my own life.*' (my italics) This implies that to be educated is to be developing self-consciousness, not class consciousness.

An alternative notion of the classless society envisages the development of social homogeneity by a process of assimilation of other classes by one social class. The view is sometimes canvassed that the classless society is being formed by a process of bourgeois-ification; that is, in a capitalist society, it is the middle class which assimilates the lower classes to itself. As we have already noted, the frequent criticism of schools as middle-class institutions relates, in part, to this notion of bourgeoisification. Middle-class oriented schools are discriminatory only for those who have no desire to be caught up in middle-class ways of life, for whom bourgeoisification is irrelevant or uncongenial. For Marxists, the process is in the other direction: social homogeneity is a consequence of the dictatorship of the proletariat. Classlessness is realized by a process of proletarianization.

In principle these two variants of the process leading to classlessness — the social democratic and the Marxist — should have quite different implications for schooling. In practice, their adherents have tended to make very similar proposals for school reform. This perhaps indicates an inconsistency in the position of traditional Marxist educationists which may explain the rise of a revisionist, neo-Marxist movement in education.

An alternative to both of these classless extremes as objectives of the educational system is the notion of schooling as essentially class specific and class confirming. From this point of view, the most important thing about a person is his role as member of a social class, such that his primary need is to develop attitudes, perceptions, values, skills, techniques and tastes which are functional for membership of that class. The ideal is a stratified society with strong class consciousness which it is the function of schools to develop. There may be economic amelioration and widespread affluence, but the integrity of different social classes is preserved and, perhaps, class consciousness is intensified. In terms of the distinction drawn above between working-class education and education of the working class, it is the former which, on this view, would be the concern of appropriate educational institutions.

Nevertheless, it is not clear what this class confirming conception of working-class education would consist of. From a strictly economic view of class, working-class education could only be an education appropriate to a life spent in manual labour. Whether, alongside the vocational and pre-vocational training which might be entailed by this, there is also an implication of the need for the school curriculum to focus a particular life-style — working-class culture — is also a relevant consideration, including the question of the degree of exclusiveness which characterizes working-class culture, as distinct from other sub-cultures, or from the mainstream or central culture (see Ch.4). It is also important to consider whether this economically defined working-class education should be post-school education, that is, adult 'vocational' education, concurrent with entry into gainful, full-time employment, thus allowing for a period of schooling in which working-class children remain available for selection into the whole range of economic roles within society.

Broadly there are two views of working-class life in terms of its attractiveness as a preferred way of life. One is that working-class life is to be avoided: no one having the choice would continue to live within the working class. This is a conception of the working class as different *and* inferior: reference to it as a *lower* class seems to have moral and cultural as well as mere economic overtones. Presumably it is also the reason why in some cultures people are loath to classify themselves as working class, despite earning a living from manual work.

An alternative perception is that working-class life has its own rewards and satisfactions with qualitative cultural significance: it is different but equal, and is sometimes regarded as preferable to other life-styles. There are people who are proud of being working class. From this point of view it is possible that the persistence of the English class system (which evokes either derision or dismay in foreigners) is as much a function of the working class wanting to maintain its identity as it is of other classes denying workers power, esteem or economic equality.

However, it is probably the first of these judgements which represents the conventional wisdom. Working-class life and status seem something to be avoided wherever possible. The movement towards comprehensive schooling, especially where its justification derives partly from the importance of deferring (but not ultimately abandoning) selection, is predicated upon this assumption that no one, from choice, would wish to be committed to manual labour and a working-class life-style: hence, no one ought to be consigned to that sort of fate by other people's decision. For example, attacking those who wish to preserve a system of segregated secondary schools, Rubinstein and Stoneman (1970 : 23) argue: 'They ignore the fact that, at the age of eleven or even earlier, many of our children have their future as manual workers determined with very little chance to move into other occupations.' But it is not clear why this would be objectionable if no opprobrium were attached to manual labour or if it were a preferred way of spending one's working life for some people. The implication is that opportunity for upward mobility is the right of every child. For *upward* mobility: movement towards the different kind of occupation and life-style which are associated with non-manual labour is almost always conceived as preferable, rarely as something which is different but equal. It is interesting and paradoxical that this conception of manual labour and working-class status as something from which to escape is implied in the political Left's historical opposition to specialized vocational schools for children.[3]

There are a number of reasons for this perception of working-class life as something to be avoided. The first is economic in origin. 'The working class' and 'the poor' have often been interchangeable terms, though in modern society such identification of the working class with the poor may be far from the truth: both the affluent worker and the penurious middle class are familiar enough. But, historically, the working class has usually appeared in a constant struggle to attain and defend a barely adequate standard of life in face of the disciplines, privations and exploitation of capitalism. Working-class betterment through the labour movement has been the theme of a century and a half of social history culminating in the Welfare State. It is a commonplace of sociological theory that life chances in the working class compare badly with those of other classes. And, it is argued, this essentially precarious existence of the working class persists notwithstanding superficial affluence: it is the possibility of unemployment of the weekly wage earner which leads some to reject outright the notion of the affluent worker (Parker 1971 : 88). Although through nearly three decades of full employment this has seemed of little relevance, the growing threat of massive unemployment in the mid-1970s is a reminder of the tenuous grip of the manual worker upon the standard of life. By contrast, it has been the comparative security of white-collar (and, especially, professional) work which has made it a preferred occupational choice. Economic theory has always insisted upon the need to account for a non-monetary component in assessing the rewards accruing to different categories of work. Amongst these non-monetary factors favouring white-collar occupations (as well as relative security of tenure in work) have been the greater physical amenity of the workplace, often greater variety in work tasks, status as 'staff' and a degree of autonomy in managing the job and organizing the working day. Thus, whatever comparability there may be in economic reward, it is in the categories of status and power than manual workers seem at a disadvantage. The rationale for this discrepancy between the status of manual and non-manual occupations is not obvious since some forms of manual work are obviously more demanding of intelligence, knowledge, skill and aesthetic sensibility than are some clerical and quasi-professional white-collar jobs. Conventionally, the distaste for manual labour is thought to derive from Aristotle's dismissal of it as 'servile' because it is paid. But few professional workers would today escape this taint of servility. Perhaps the only relevant distinction which justifies the esteem attaching to non-manual occupations is the 'leisured' element which is implicit in their performance by comparison with working discipline in the factory and workshop where most manual work is conducted (see Ch.6).

It has to be conceded that these perceptions of the inferiority of working-class occupations in terms of economics, social esteem and power are middle-class perceptions, even if they are often shared by both status-dissenting and deferential sections of the working class. Indeed, it could be argued that one aspect of the middle-class orientation of schools is their often derisory dismissal of working-class occupations. This stands in sharp contrast with the view that working-class life has merit and is even to be preferred. Certainly there are members of the working class who take a disdainful view of other sub-cultures and their occupants.

Historically, the notion of working-class education as class confirming and class specific (especially in confining working-class children to manual occupations) has been associated with political and educational conservatives. In both Europe and North America, elementary education was taken to be appropriate education for the working class, terminal in early adolescence and unrelated to the system of secondary education. Then, with differing national emphasis and on a different time scale, secondary education was thought suitable for some appropriately gifted working-class children. Eventually, it was considered the right of all children. Although in Britain provision of secondary education for all initially took the form of differentiated (for example, tripartite) secondary schooling, since the 1950s comprehensive schooling was increasingly advocated by the political Left as the only acceptable democratic option. In the past decade, however, mainly on behalf of so-called disadvantaged groups — ethnic minorities (especially Blacks), children in Educational Priority Areas — this assumption that children are best served by central provision of comprehensive schools has been called into question by political radicals. These have taken the view that the local community is probably the best provider of both an appropriate curriculum and school management. A variety of reasons are apparent for this retreat into localism.

(1) There is an assumption that the apparently progressive movement from elementary schooling to universal comprehensive education has really been along a blind alley so far as the working class is concerned: it has been a confidence trick perpetrated by the middle class (Katz 1973; see also Hodgen 1925):

Public schools have always represented conservative social forces expressing and reflecting the aspirations, the fears and the interests of the more affluent members of communities ... In large measure the founding of public systems of education represented the attempts of 'better people' to do something to the rest ... Although official educational rhetoric has proclaimed the schools agencies of upward mobility for the children of the poor, in fact they have more often protected the status of the well-to-do ... For those who control the system there has been no point in making fundamental structural alterations.

Others have concluded that although the movement towards nationally financed and uniform school systems was well intentioned and moderately successful, this tradition has now exhausted its capacity, both culturally and economically, to sustain further necessary development on behalf of the disadvantaged (Midwinter 1975).

(2) A related assumption is that it was a mistake to extend the period of compulsory schooling into middle adolescence. Illich and Reimer have implied that children could be freed from compulsion to attend school as early as eight years of age. Midwinter (1975) thinks it is a mistake to have extended compulsory schooling beyond fourteen. It appears that other critics of conventional schooling would prefer no statutory leaving age, the decision about withdrawal from school being left to the individual student. However, this criticism of extended compulsory schooling tends to be associated with advocacy of some form of recurrent education, people having the right to opt back into the publicly maintained educational system at intervals when they feel a need for continued education. With reference to limited (or absence of) compulsory schooling, de-schooling can be seen as a version of the community school option: both Illich and Reimer deplored the impoverishment of the community as an educational resource and their respective educational webs and networks put the local community and its resources back at the centre.

(3) The quest for decentralization and community management of schools is partly a protest at the increasing bureaucratization of publicly maintained school systems. Bureaucratization is taken to inhibit flexibility in schooling, particularly in accommodating individual teaching and learning styles and meeting the educational needs of differing sub-cultures.

(4) Community school advocacy assumes that any local community is adequately endowed with pedagogical (including curriculum) and management resources.[4] All sub-cultures are assumed to be adequate or valid ways of life and there tends to be what Harrington (1973 : 265) called the 'idealization of the dispossessed'. Oddly, there is also sometimes an assumption that anything

outside the local community is a 'remote middle-class world' (Halsey 1972a : 144).

(5) The community school is student centred in the sense that the learner is himself considered capable of defining the learning stiuation; he is the best judge of what counts as educational knowledge.

(6) It is believed important to keep educated persons within each local community. Although a degree of occupational mobility is necessary to provide communities with professional workers from within the community itself, social and geographical mobility is dysfunctional for the community school. Some of the disadvantaged need to become doctors, lawyers and various kinds of social worker, but they should return to the local community upon graduation to live within it and serve its people. [5]

It is not suggested that those committed to a community-oriented educational system would subscribe to all of these assumptions. Some of those sympathetic to decentralization and community control also recognize that these may be incompatible with the achievement of other valued objectives, including racial integration. And because different individuals and groups emphasize different objectives for community schools, it would be misleading to suggest that there is a coherent, community school movement. The most that can be claimed in terms of ideological homogeneity is that advocacy of community-orientation comes from radicals of the Left, including neo-Marxists who reject traditional Marxist commitment to comprehensive education and the transmission by schools of a universal or mainstream culture.

Although nineteenth- and early twentieth-century conservative advocacy of elementary schooling as appropriate for the working class seems ideologically poles apart from current radical rejection of comprehensive, centrally provided schooling in favour of local community provision, it is not clear that the practical implications of the two positions for the working class differ at all. Historically, the conservative assumes a position which is not substantially different from Robert Lowe's classical conclusion that working-class culture is essentially modest, if not mean, from which it is only possible to look up: the lower classes 'must be educated that they may appreciate and defer to a higher cultivation when they meet it; and the higher classes might be educated in a very different manner, in order that they may exhibit to the lower classes that higher education to which, if it were shown to them they would bow down and defer' (Simon 1960 : Vol.I, 356). The modern radical ostensibly takes the opposite view. It is working-class culture which is vital, intellectually and aesthetically energetic, emotionally warm, direct, concrete, getting to the heart of the matter. By contrast, the so-called higher cultivation is bourgeois, that is corrupt, effete and circumlocutory in its verbal expression.[6] But despite this ideological polarity when evaluating working-class culture, both the educational conservative and the new radical advocate of the community school are at the same end of the spectrum distinguishing class-confirming education from education conceived as classless and universalistic. This claim that the conservative and neo-radical positions are not essentially different in their practical consequences will now be examined.

Modern educational conservatism and working-class education

G.H. Bantock is an example of the modern conservative tradition in education. Best known for his defence of segregated secondary schooling on behalf of a minority of abler children, against the trend towards comprehensive education, he has recently posed as a radical exponent of a new kind of curriculum appropriate to the education of 'the folk'. This would be 'affective-artistic rather than cognitive-intellectual', concerned not with the transmission of a literary culture and cognitive skills, but based upon what Bantock takes to be a genuinely folk culture, a culture saturated with kinetic skills, especially found in movement and dance.

No doubt Bantock would reject categorization as a latter day conservative in the tradition which saw elementary education as peculiarly fitting for the working class. He explicitly criticizes the elementary tradition as a mistaken and abortive attempt to provide popular education in the form of a watered down version of the high culture (1975b : 213, 216, 220)[7]. But despite his conviction that his own popular curriculum would provide a superior emotional education which is at present lacking in schools,[8] the cognitive poverty of his proposed curriculum would probably sell the working-class child even shorter than elementary education allegedly did.

It is also true that Bantock does not see his proposal in class terms. Instead of reference to the working class he prefers the archaic notion of 'the folk' who, presumably, are not identical with the working class. But two things render the class implications of his proposals inescapable. First, he is sure that education cannot be conceived simply as a function of schooling. What he calls 'the propitious environment' for schooling (1975a) has reference particularly to family life and the conditions it is able to provide for different kinds of educational experience. Thus, his movement oriented, 'affective-artistic' curriculum is most likely to evoke a sympathetic response in those whose daily life is saturated with movement, presumably in manual occupations. It is difficult to conceive who these would be except members of the industrial working class. On the other hand, the literary oriented curriculum will fructify in the lives of those children whose homes provide 'the social conditions of quietness and privacy which books demand for their proper assimilation' (Bantock 1975a). These social conditions are likely to occur in conditions of generously spacious housing which, of economic necessity, are the homes of the professional middle class. It is interesting that in no more than an aside, Bantock (1975a) acknowledges that the dullards from the middle class will go to private schools; one wonders who else but the children of the working class this leaves as objects of his popular curriculum in tax maintained schools.

However, Bantock's most disingenuous disclaimer about the social implications of his proposed 'differentiated curriculum of cultural transmission' is that 'it does not constitute a political device to justify simply an élitist discrimination' (1976 : 85). No doubt he is sincere in believing his motivation to be strictly pedagogical, that is, 'to meet the reality that every teacher in the land encounters — the differences in achievement and potential achievement by which he is faced'. Clearly, he believes himself outside the tradition of those who see popular education as a device for political control through 'the gentling of the masses'; he protests that he is not proposing 'an education for helots'. Nevertheless, the political implications of this blueprint for popular education are evident and far reaching. To stress emotional education whilst diminishing the cognitive component of schooling inevitably implies that the cognitively weak will be controlled by others. Emphasizing emotional at the expense of intellectual nurture can only be a prescription for bringing the emotionally sensitive under the control of the intellectually competent. Implicitly, the appetites of the former must be in control, for without cognitive resources to *think about* social, political, economic and cultural concerns, they must be made to *feel* right about them; in the absence of a capacity for rationality and without cognitive resources to understand and make decisions about life's enterprises in the political and economic domains outside their narrow domestic territories, they have to learn to rest content with the decisions of others, trusting experts and leaders, being affectionately disposed towards them, and avoiding any gross emotional response which would simply be a letting off of steam in relation to the hazards and injustices of life. The emotional safety valve is to be in movement and dance.

If this account looks like a caricature of what Bantock intends for the affective-artistically but not cognitive-intellectually educated folk, it can only be a result of the lack of any clear conception of the skills which ordinary people need in relation to the political culture and the economic system, and for involvement in the major enterprises of national life and international affairs. The educational value of the proposed curriculum derives from Bantock's assumption (1975b : 223) that 'body awareness is projected into a variety of kinetic disciplines which combine practicality with imagination, affective expression and discipline and which exploit characteristic twentieth-century cultural forms'. But what, concretely, are these characteristic twentieth-century cultural forms; do they include the political culture, the economic system and technology and, if so, how is knowledge and understanding appropriate to these mediated through kinetic disciplines of mime and dance, or 'through emphasis upon the physical life, outward bound projects, the opportunities which form part of the new physical education'? It is interesting that Bantock elsewhere claims that the arts have too small a role in the education of abler children (1963 : 153). This is in the context of his advocacy of literature on the grounds that literary education has a contribution to make to 'thinking about political and social matters'.[9] But whilst it is not difficult to conceive how literature might contribute towards the development of political consciousness, one has to be much less sanguine that the non-literary artistic modes of mime and dance carry the same potential for awakening socio-political insight and criticism.

It is evident that here Bantock is operating with a very narrow conception of culture as recreations and pastimes (what is categorized in Ch.4 as C4n). No doubt these must be essential components of any modernized curriculum because they do, indeed, assume characteristic twentieth-century forms. Criticism of the disproportionate share they have in Bantock's curriculum (about 60 per cent), or doubt that they can assist in developing critical awareness in those areas of life which are political and economic, is not to be read as indicating that recreations and pastimes are of no importance. It is simply that to ignore political and economic institutions is to rule out dimensions of the culture which are genuinely popular in origin. It is argued below that the distinctively working-class culture is to be found in the institutions of the labour movement, and working-class solidarity has to be understood in relation to these. But in common with other writers who make a great deal of working-class gregariousness, Bantock confuses solidarity with sociability and, thus, trivializes working-class culture as 'social warmth and a stress on the immediacies of social contact', implying an inability to transcend the limitations of time and place.[10] It has already been argued that this myth of working-class need for immediate gratification (whether spiritual or material) will not stand up to the facts of social history.

Nor will the assumption that 'the folk' can be relegated simply to the role of cultural consumer. But this assumption of passivity is required by Bantock's conclusion that they will be 'spectators of course, not participants' in those media which transmit the modern forms of culture. This takes the media and their values very much for granted, including the political question of who controls them. It also leaves unquestioned the spurious drivel which an educated minority creates for the spectator of these characteristic twentieth-century cultural forms: it is well-educated graduates who write television advertising jingles and copy for the tabloid press. To be sure, Bantock does write of the need to cultivate 'critical awareness where print is involved' and for inducing 'some awareness of the possibilities of the media which form the leisure-time activities of the bulk of the population' (1975b : 223). But it is not evident how an education rooted in the arts of mime and dance is adequate to developing a critical awareness of media like newspapers and television. Any critical activity with regard to the former requires a capacity to understand the subtleties of print which Bantock takes to be beyond the capacity of the folk. And although television depends more upon sensitivity to oral and visual communication, its content shares with that of the print media an interest in matters which do not lie simply in the fields of entertainment, the arts and recreations. Both types of medium attach considerable importance to news and current affairs. In neglecting this 'serious', politically implicated content of the media, Bantock is guilty of the McLuhanite fallacy that the medium is the message (see below, p.106). Hence, 'a critical awareness' of the media, including 'some awareness of their possibilities', requires above all some familiarity with those areas which is as much their concern as are the arts — political, economic and social affairs, science and technology. Knowledge related to all of these non-artistic concerns is important if the possibilities of the media are to be realized. Anyone interested in the reform of the media ought to know what might be involved politically, economically and technologically, in the search for alternatives through which their possibilities for personal enrichment might be enhanced, either for recreation or serious engagement with public affairs.

In fact, if a radical proposal for curriculum does not explicitly concern itself with either the political culture or the economic system (whether by inclusion of politics or economics as subjects in their own right or through some other organizing principle), such neglect is either thoughtless or it is deliberate on the assumption that these things don't really matter. Bantock sharply dichotomizes culture (examples he gives are 'pop song or Bartok, comics or classics') from problems of hunger and poverty and what he calls 'the exigencies of *weltpolitik*' (1963 : 202). But aside from the fact that anyone concerned for the cultural potential of modern media cannot ignore their political implications (as Williams, 1962, has clearly shown), to speak of working-class culture — or the culture of the folk — without acknowledging that this culture has derived from concern with the conquest of hunger and poverty is to trivialize working-class culture. It is from out of this concern with material poverty and its cultural correlates that working people have contributed uniquely to the political culture throughout the period of industrialism. A curriculum attempting to do justice to the culture of the folk ought, especially, to pay attention to the history of the common people in terms of their contribution to the development of political and economic institutions. But Bantock expressly excludes the study of history from his popular curriculum, [11] presumably because history is an example of the cognitive-intellectual academic style. One can only assume that the emotive potential of a study of working-class history is ignored because the sight of the historical working class lifting itself from poverty by its own bootstraps might persuade working-class children that their future social role need not be that of a passive spectator. There is no possibility of political education — or informed citizenship — in a curriculum whose cognitive focus is derived only from the theoretical aspects of movement and dance. And neglect of the art of citizenship is not corrected by provision of teaching with reference to those aspects of citizenship which relate to family life. Most children eventually marry and become responsible for the upbringing of other human beings, and there is everything to be said for assisting them to fill these marital and parental roles with intelligence, moral sensibility and taste. But family life does not exhaust the possibilities of citizenship and, indeed, its quality probably owes a good deal (both spiritually and materially) to the part which one plays in other social institutions.

Thus far one has been critical of Bantock's proposals for a popular curriculum only in finding implications in his work which he himself disclaims. But to argue that his proposals are class-biased and politically implicated is not to dismiss them as practically unrealistic. For the essence of the conservative position, especially in the Black Papers to which Bantock has been a contributor, is that mass stupidity is a fact of life for which we must legislate in our educational and cultural arrangements. Bantock has had repeated resort to a metaphor taken from Blake: 'The fool sees not the same tree that the wise man sees' (1952, 1976). It is beyond the scope of this chapter to examine, by reference to Blake's other comments on the nature of wisdom and folly, whether Blake himself saw this dichotomy in relation to the natural talents and inclinations of all human beings such that they could all be categorized as either wise or foolish. But whatever is implied by Blake, Bantock's use of the metaphor in order to dichotomize the entire school population implies a minority which is wise and the majority which is foolish. In a recent essay on popular education he is quite explicit in seeing children as either stupid or able, a conclusion which does not promise very much for a culture of the folk. Any possibility of Bantock's prescriptions being taken seriously as educationally valuable is diminished by his recurrent need to characterize the folk, pejoratively, in this idiom.

However, there is also a common patronizing judgement, often shared by status-dissenting members of the working class itself, that the lower classes *are* essentially stupid. There is also academic sociological data on this point. For example, Josephine Klein (1965 : 87-96) concluded that in the three working-class communities she observed in Paddington, Liverpool and Ashton, responses to life were characterized by cognitive poverty:

> Even the most sympathetic writers on working-class ways of life remark on what appears to be a stubborn determination not to develop — and not to allow others to develop — attitudes or behaviour which would make for a more interior life ... Cognitive poverty describes habits of thinking rigidly, concretely, without speculation, without pleasure, over a narrow range of interests ... There is unvarying ridicule of minor deviance. There is interest in personal detail as contrasted with an interest in wider and more abstract issues, concern with which is felt to be incomprehensible as well as slightly ridiculous and unfitting for members of the group. There is a preference for the familiar, as contrasted with a view that considers the novel as more interesting and challenging.

Gans (1967 : 26-7) wrote in not dissimilar terms of the working-class community he observed in the United States: 'People find it extremely difficult to accept the validity of values and interests which conflict with theirs; they have trouble relating to strangers and making a decision in a group — or for the group.[12] Perhaps these social scientists are only saying, euphemistically, what Bantock makes no bones about — that the working class *is* stupid.

With the reservation that all class-bound culture has elements which are dysfunctional from the viewpoint of universal human values, our own argument will presently be that some lower-class sub-cultures have to be judged inadequate in terms of any morally acceptable conception of the good life. But this conclusion is essentially different from Bantock's in finding no natural or otherwise inevitable division of mankind into the wise and the foolish: indeed, it is not clear that stupidity does aptly characterize members of so-called cultures of poverty. Not wanting to know may, indeed, be a wise reaction to what seems the unalterable weight of poverty and its cultural correlates. Again, it is one thing to find cognitive poverty amongst particular social groups as some sociologists do, but quite something else to legislate, educationally, to reinforce such deprivation by provision of a cognitively emasculated curriculum.

In this disdain for the educational capacity of a majority of people, Bantock's conservatism stands in contrast to the viewpoint of North American educational conservatives. For example, whilst insisting that schools should function to sustain the traditional academic values against the inroads of progressivism, Bestor also believes in the need for transmitting the intellectual culture throughout all sections of the population. He has been no less rigorous than Bantock in attacking Deweyism and his attack upon the life adjustment curriculum is on all fours with Bantock's earlier rejection of Dewey's instrumentalism. Oddly, though, Bantock's contempt for Dewey comes together with his contempt for the stupid when he accepts the Deweyan curriculum for those who happen to share Dewey's 'mental limitations': 'to them it is undoubtedly true that he has brought considerable benefits' (1963 : 47). But Bestor (1952 : 86-7) will have none of this. To the contrary, he believes that it is nothing but a disservice to offer to a majority of future citizens a life adjustment curriculum based upon the assumption of their having chronically disabling mental limitations. To him, the political implications of a cognitively impoverished curriculum for a majority of students are clear:

American public schools have the responsibility of raising up a nation of men and women highly literate, accurately informed, and rigorously trained in the process of rational and critical thought. If the schools fail in this, then we may expect to see the collapse or defeat of democratic self-government through the sheer inability of its electorate to grapple intelligently with the complex problems in science, economics, politics and international relations that constantly come up for public decision.

Bestor immediately makes it clear that the public school's task of providing intellectual training is for 'every part of our citizenry', on the assumption that 'needs which require satisfaction by intellectual means are common to all men'. He is in no doubt that any curriculum has quietist implications which diminishes the cognitive and intellectual component for any student on the assumption that life adjustment skills are his basic educational need: 'The "mudstill" theory of society has come back with a vengeance, and likewise the good old argument that schooling for the ordinary man must teach him to know his place, to keep it, and to be content with it.' Bestor is persuaded that such a gentling process cannot be dignified, after the fashion in Bantock, by the name 'education'. If it were the case — which he denies — that a proportion of the school population was lacking intellectual competence, the only appropriate response to such a conclusion would be that such persons are ineducable and ought not to be in school (1952 : 86-7): '... if professional educators believe that most men have no need for intellectual training, then they should honestly say so and work for the abolition of compulsory school laws. It is sheer dishonesty to advocate schooling for all and then to turn about and argue that men have no need for the very thing which the school is designed to furnish'. It is interesting that Bestor (1955) believes his advocacy of the universal human need for intellectual training should have drawn from American critics the protest that his educational theory is élitist and aristocratic: to the English conservative, Bestor's views look like advocacy of a curriculum based on a common culture which they denounce as utterly unrealistic.

The élitist conception that the health of society depends upon some few who are intellectually trained for the rational life and cultural creativity, relies upon the truth contained in the parable of the leaven in the lump. Bestor's rejection of this sort of élitism[13] derives instead from the more realistic implication of the metaphor of the rotten apple in the barrel. It is the notion of an intellectually incompetent and ineducable segment of the population which is the threat to civilized values and political democracy: 'By its very nature a school cannot be neutral on the question of respect for intellectual effort, any more than a church can be neutral on the question of virtue. If it does not foster respect for the things it was established to promote, then it inevitably fosters the opposite. A non-intellectual school is an anti-intellectual force in society.'

To do him justice, Bantock is not so much anti-intellectual with reference to the folk, as ambivalent or undecided about its need for literacy, rationality and cognitive resources. Notwithstanding his dismissal of the folk's capacity for cognitive-intellectual discourse, he does occasionally lapse into the language of rationality when prescribing for their educational needs: '... in the *analysis* of newspapers we can try to show the *falsity* of the advertisements (with their links with the domestic life) so that the children become used to *asking qualitative questions* in relation to the concrete things they all see and use' (1963 : 216). And again (1963 : 218), 'the purchase of goods for the household can be considered in relation to advertisements on the one hand and the *rational* [my italics] advice given by *Which* and *Shoppers Guide* on the other'. But what cognitive resources (scientific, economic, political, psychological, for example) are necessary to assess the falsity of advertisements? What sort of knowledge is required to take the sort of individual or collective action to do anything about those whose lying contaminates the public media? Or is searching out the falsity advertisements just another game, in line with Bantock's conclusion that the folk will realize itself 'through play rather than work' (1963 : 208)? And where does this analytical, rational probing of questions of truth and falsity stop? Why does it need to stop when domestically related problems have been illuminated?

The truth is that notions of emotional, rational or cognitive development as components of 'a unified sensibility' (to use Bantock's own phrase) can only be conceived comparatively, in terms of more or less, better or worse, never absolutely as over and done with. Though notions of educational ceilings (i.e. absolute limits on anyone's development) may be useful in certain contexts, the likelihood is that these are usually a good deal higher for most people than élitist educational theorists are apt to suppose. For their own good reasons (if only to survive in an unpromising social environment) individuals may build their own cognitive ceilings very low, opting for an anti-intellectual, cognitively impoverished stance on life. But no one has the right to be architect of anyone else's low-ceilinged educational hovel, and the existence of late developers who break through the educational roof is all the justification necessary for the view that for anyone, educationally, only the sky is the limit. For once the possibility of rationality and critical awareness is allowed in relation to any of life's enterprises, there can be no guarantee that the germ of rationality in any life can be sterilized once it has begun to fructify. In assuming that it can, some modern radicals are at one with a conservative like Bantock. Albeit for different reasons, they take the view that working-class education defines a peculiar cognitive and intellectual style. Though this distinctive culture is presumed a valid and adequate way of life, I shall now argue that its practical implications are not dissimilar from those of Bantock's conservatism.

The modern radical and working-class education

The English conservative's derisory views of the majority are not shared by those I have categorized as radical advocates of one or other version of the community school. Quite the contrary: with reference to the educational resources of working-class communities, the community school position assumes the adequacy or validity of working-class culture as the datum of an educational experience. Though she is not explicitly an advocate of the community school, Keddie's dismissal of cultural deprivation as a myth and her claims for the adequacy of all cultures do constitute a theoretical justification for community-oriented schooling. An examination of her notion of cultural adequacy helps to focus the limitations of this position.

In the editor's introduction to her collection of essays, *Tinker, Tailor ...* (1963), Keddie argues that it is not clear of what culture lower-class families can be deprived 'since no group can be deprived of its own culture'. This passage has puzzled a good many of its readers, not only because it startlingly questions the conventional wisdom, but also because it does have a certain logical cogency. Culture is not like property or wealth of which one might be deprived by the bailiff, a burglar or the collapse of the stock market. A person's culture is much more like his education, his knowledge and his skill which he possesses existentially. Except by techniques of brainwashing, it is clearly impossible to deprive a person of what he has learned, of the mental or emotional dispositions which he has acquired: as easy to deprive a man of his height without amputating his limbs, as to deprive him of his culture, his knowledge and skill, his education. These attributes define what one is as a person: a man's culture *is* what he is. Hence, it is part of the meaning of culture, when used in this personal sense, that one cannot be deprived of it. But this logical truth is a trivial truth in terms of its social and educational implications. For it is ludicrous to imagine that the statement 'that child is culturally deprived' means 'I have deprived him of his culture'. What is probably intended is something like 'that child's culture is an inadequate basis for the good life and he ought, in his own interest, to be put in a position where his culture can be enriched'.

The impeccable logic (in the sense just examined) of Keddie's 'no group can be deprived of its own culture' in no way entails her further conclusion that 'so-called minority group cultures may be seen as ... adequate in their own right', or that any culture is 'a way of life that has its own validity'. The qualification 'in their own right' is puzzling. It is odd that the word 'adequate' is assumed sufficient without one of the prepositions 'to' or 'for' which always, if tacitly, accompanies normal usage. Without a prepositional phrase to give it context, the word 'adequate' is vacuous. Nothing is simply adequate. Adequacy must have reference to some standard of performance or some criterion of value by which a person or thing may be judged adequate. It is difficult to see what the denial of the possibility of cultural deprivation and insistence upon all cultures being adequate and valid ways of life could imply except something like 'the culture is adequate for maintaining the standard of life of a group as it presently exists'. But this would be an oddly functionalist position for an exponent of the 'new' sociology of education to take. Having 'its own validity' also suggests that no further questions should be asked with reference to the quality of life of a group: the group is self-sufficient and ought to be left to carry on undisturbed. Neither individuals, nor the group in community, need look critically at the given way of life with a view to its improvement. Presumably, so far as the culture may exhibit manifestations of injustice, exploitation, alienation, these are phenomena about which no one need be concerned — most of all, people from outside the group itself.

Nevertheless, it is the conception of cultural deprivation as a way of life falling short of the possible (even, and especially, when perceived from within that way of life itself) which has been the mainspring of movements for working-class betterment through social reform or revolution. Paternalistic and patronizing they may now be judged but, hitherto, political radicals have subscribed to the notion of cultural deprivation, sometimes tacitly, often explicitly. It is difficult to see how any advocacy of radical social change could be legitimized except by reference to the fact of cultural deprivation or the inadequacy of a particular way of life when assessed against some conception of the good life or the good society. Without such a normative reference there would be no justification for any attempt to upset the social *status quo*. Indeed, one of the founding fathers of Marxism gave an account of the conditions of working-class life in England over a century ago which could only be described as 'culturally deprived'. Engels probably became a socialist when walking the streets of Manchester in the early 1840s, and throughout his account of *The Condition of the Working Class in England in 1844* he emphasized the utter demoralization of the workers and their families: the worker was 'deprived of his humanity', having become 'a soulless factor of production', a mere machine. In other metaphors he was described as 'a vegetable', 'a chattel' and as degraded 'to the level of animals' (Engels 1958 : 11). The detailed descriptions of brutalizing factory discipline, insanitary housing in streets which were open sewers (one recent biographer of Engels, Marcus 1974, concludes that he painted a picture of 'millions of English men, women and children ... virtually living in shit'), loss of domestic skills (the ability to cook, for example) and the affections of family life, leisure largely spent in drunkenness — these are too familiar to relate in detail. Sufficient to record a comment by Engels (1958 : 229) on the condition of child labour which itself became an objective of half a century of agitation for reform:

> Mr Horne, an official of the Children's Employment Commission stated that in Willenhall the workers lack all moral sense, and he gives ample evidence to support this assertion. In general he found that children had no affection for their parents and recognized no obligation towards them. These children were so brutish and so stupid that they did not realize what they were saying. It was by no means unusual for them to assert that they were well treated and perfectly happy, although in fact they worked for twelve to fourteen hours, were dressed in rags, were not given enough to eat and were beaten so hard that they felt the effect for several days afterwards. They simply had no

experience of any other way of life than to slave away from morn til night until they were given permission to stop. They had never before been asked whether they were tired and did not know the meaning of the question.

The conventional, 'enlightened' response to this kind of evidence has been approval of a succession of legislative acts restricting the inroads of the working life into childhood and extending opportunities for education. But it now appears that this enlightened, reforming response can be faulted. The fact that the exploited have no 'experience of any other world' gives no warrant for anyone's acting on their behalf, since they do not see themselves as exploited and claim to enjoy an adequate and valid way of life.

The relevance of Engels's account of working-class life for current discussion of cultural deprivation and its educational implications is not vitiated by the historical distance which separates his England from the modern world. Evidence of the cultural deprivation of any group in any place at any time must falsify the assumption that no group can be culturally deprived. In any event, modern parallels with the conditions described by Engels are not unknown: his account of working-class life a century ago recalls Oscar Lewis's descriptions of the 'culture of poverty' in the present day. In addition to being a condition of chronic economic poverty, the culture of poverty is characterized by the cognitive poverty of its 'members', instilling a fatalism with reference to any possibility of ever achieving a different way of life. Children acquire this fatalism early and, when adult, they do not seek access to power through membership of political parties or labour unions, nor do they make use of even those welfare agencies which exist for amelioration of poverty. Lewis believes that 'most primitive peoples have achieved a higher level of socio-cultural organization than our modern urban slum dwellers'. This assumption is interesting since those who deny cultural deprivation, and assert the adequacy and validity of any way of life, appear to arrive at this conclusion by reference to anthropological evidence of rich and complex culture in primitive societies.[14] It is true, as Lewis observes, that no group of people, however unfortunately circumstanced, fails to develop strategies sufficient to maintain life itself. But though Lewis acknowledges that the culture of poverty has its compensations and adaptive mechanisms, he believes it has little to commend it in terms of historic notions of the good life within Western society:

> ... on the whole it seems to me that it is a thin, relatively super-
> ficial culture. There is a great deal of pathos, suffering and
> emptiness among those who live in the culture of poverty. It does
> not provide much support or satisfaction and its encouragement
> of mistrust tends to magnify helplessness and isolation. Indeed,
> the poverty of culture is one of the crucial aspects of the culture
> of poverty.

This was also Engels's conclusion (1958 : 241):

> Even if I had not given so many examples as I have done to illus-
> trate the condition of the working classes in England, it would
> still be self-evident that the proletariat can hardly feel happy at
> the present situation. It will surely be granted that the state of
> affairs I have described is not one in which either an individual or
> a social class can think, feel and live in a civilized manner.

This statement is at the beginning of his chapter on 'Working-Class
Movements'. For Engels there was no explanation of these
movements apart from the facts of cultural deprivation. The
two are dialectically related as he had hinted in his introduction
(1958 : 12): 'The Industrial Revolution ... turned the workers
completely into mere machines and deprived them of the last
remnants of independent activity. Yet it was this change that
forced the workers to think for themselves and to demand a fuller
life in human society.' For Engels the fact of cultural deprivation
and the notion of 'a fuller life', a nobler conception of man, were
the antithetical components of the dialectic from which revolutionary action — the synthesis — could be forged. Clearly, deprivation
is built into the notions of exploitation and alienation. Only the
conclusion that the working classes were culturally deprived can
make sense of Marxism, and justify the disturbance of existing ways
of life which is implicit in even modest social democratic proposals
for reform. Nothing of reform or betterment is indicated if a
culture can be judged adequate and a valid way of life.

To argue the reality of cultural deprivation in this way, however,
focuses one of the many ambiguities in the notion of culture.
Characterization of the condition of the poor as cultural deprivation
could evoke the response that what Engels and others[15] describe

is essentially economic, not cultural, deprivation. However for a Marxist this separation of economic base from cultural superstructure would make no sense. Any such separation would require a very restricted conception of culture. For one thing, it should be remembered that at the time of Engels's observations, the English working class was almost totally disenfranchized and, hence, chronically deprived with reference to the political culture. And as we have already seen, Engels was also convinced that economic deprivation was a cause of deprivation with respect to other cultural institutions — especially family life and the use of leisure — prompting his conclusion that in the economic conditions he observed no one could feel and live in a 'civilized manner'. In any event, it is apparent that Keddie's conception of cultural adequacy can only be sustained in terms of the anthropological sense of the word as a total way of life. Although Keddie says as little in elaboration of 'culture' as she does with reference to 'adequacy' or 'validity', her characterization of so-called deprived children as 'experienced participants in *a way of life* that has its own validity' suggests the anthropological culture concept. But for an educationist the essential limitation of the anthropological concept of culture lies precisely in its failure to discriminate normatively amongst items in this cultural aggregate. Culture conceived as the total way of life, unexamined, unrefined, unselective, cannot be an adequate conceptual tool for anyone concerned with intellectual, aesthetic or moral development as I have argued elsewhere (Entwistle 1970a : 131-9, and Ch.4 below).

Just as it is difficult to see any justification for advocacy of social reform or revolution apart from conditions of cultural deprivation, it is also difficult to imagine how the notion of cultural inadequacy or deprivation can be separated from the concept of education itself. No one concluding that his own personal culture was adequate would ever submit himself formally to an educational experience. The further pursuit of education implies a recognition of one's own inadequacy with reference to some aspect of the culture. Given that a person believed his skill or knowledge to be adequate it is difficult to see why he would take steps to further his own education. And this is true for anyone, irrespective of social class.

Perhaps this is exactly the point which those who reject the notion of cultural deprivation wish to make. Their concern seems to stem, in part, from application of the notion exclusively to the working class; one has the impression that their polemic is in the spirit of *épater le bourgeois*, evoked by the impertinence of the middle-class kettle calling the working-class pot black. To the extent that new sociologists want to separate the concept 'a valid way of life' (and definition of an appropriate curriculum) from middle-class norms and values, one has little quarrel with their intention. Indeed, in this we are in step with Engels who found the middle class, in its own fashion, no less deprived and demoralized than the working class; also with Arnold who thought it philistine. [16] It is interesting that Arnold could not conceive of culture in relation to social class. Each of his class labels — barbarian (upper), philistine (middle) and populace (working) — carries pejorative overtones as if to say, when it comes to culture, a plague on all your classes. And if deprivation is inseparable from the notion of needing to be educated, an implication of escapism is also written into the concept. Escape from the limiting conditions of one's environment must, by definition, be a consequence of liberal education: liberation from the constraints which any class environment (middle, upper or disadvantaged) imposes upon the individual.

Yet, when curriculum proposals for community-oriented schools serving the lower-working class are examined, these seem certain to reinforce its cultural deprivation. Midwinter, one of the more vigorous polemicists on behalf of the community school, writes as follows (1972b : 2): 'We aim at dignifying the child with the feeling that education and knowledge are about him and his place, that he is in effect an historical character in a geographical setting.' This is a sentiment with which it is difficult not to sympathize: the notion of cultivating self-knowledge by helping the learner to locate himself in a geographical and historical context would be widely accepted as an educational aim. Thus, a child living in Liverpool (where Midwinter has been professionally involved in an Educational Priority Area) would discover precisely what it means to be a Liverpudlian, by contrast with what it means to be a Mancunian, a Montrealer, a San Franciscan, an inhabitant of Tokyo, Lagos, Alice Springs and so on. One's own geographical context gathers significance by comparison and contrast with other localities, whether very similar or vastly different from one's own.

Similarly, the uniqueness of being a Liverpudlian *now* can only be properly understood by reference to life in Liverpool in 1940, in 1915, in 1830 and to the non-existence of Liverpool as a major port before the late eighteenth century. This sense in which self-knowledge is deepened by reference to *other* people, institutions and environments both now and in other times — by escape from the limited horizons imposed by this place at this time — would be too obvious to labour were it not for the fact that Midwinter apparently has something quite different in mind with his notions of historical character and geographical setting. For him, the historical and geographical are not contexts which serve to liberate the imagination, but blinkers which shut out the universe beyond the narrow confines of the locality at the present time. In Midwinter's terms, we are historical characters only because we are alive now: the historical reference is not to a motion film of the human story, but to a still photograph of this single moment in time.

One has to write 'apparently' with reference to Midwinter's view of the relevance of history for the education of these children (1972a : 101, 103), for he offers very little in the way of detailed curriculum content. It clearly serves his polemical purpose only to be negatively critical. But all his references to history in the curriculum are derisory and it is unclear whether he is questioning the relevance of all history teaching or only what he takes to be irrelevant history. Thus, Drake, Shaftesbury, Wilberforce and Rhodes are dismissed as 'the dubious heroes of our island heritage' and 'the teaching of Richard the Lionheart is wasteful and dishonest'. This is repeatedly dismissed as an 'artificial heritage' but we are left in the dark about whether history ever bequeathes us a 'real' heritage.[17] One is left wondering if there are no 'legitimate' lionhearts in English history; or whether there is a history of 'the common people' which might throw light on life in an Educational Priority Area.[18] Much the same ambiguity characterizes Midwinter's references to poetry. He makes much of the school's attachment to 'Cargoes', but it is not clear if the critical references to it are meant to dismiss it as irrelevant poetry (a comment on the ludicrous spectre of children in the 1970s apostrophizing 'big steamers' as inappropriately symbolizing an economically stagnant Britain, in a world where its remaining international commerce is destined to be airborne rather than seaborne from

Liverpool) or are intended to suggest that all poetry is irrelevant. Other references to poetry are no more sympathetic and suggest that it is considered utterly dispensable to an audio-visual culture, since it is incongruous to expose children and their teachers to Wordsworth by day and to 'Coronation Street' at night (Midwinter 1972b : 13). It seems that even those who teach it have no room for poetry in their lives out of school and, since most adults spend their time watching television rather than reading poetry, the implication is that the latter is a curricular irrelevance (Midwinter 1972a : 101).

But it is in terms of his denial of a role for geography in the curriculum that Midwinter's focus upon the local community becomes neurotic (1972b : 13): 'Teachers talk of widening horizons, when by zooming off via telly, coach or book to New Zealand, the Holy Land or the countryside they are frequently *exchanging* horizons and running the risk of producing social schizophrenics.' One obvious retort to this is that, dedicated to a life in front of the television as Midwinter's citizen obviously is, he will be zoomed off whether he likes it or not, nightly, to New Zealand or the Holy Land. At the time of writing he is zoomed off nightly to Montreal where the 1976 Olympics threaten to grind to a halt because of the boycott by African nations. And it is difficult to see how anyone could begin to understand the African boycott without a knowledge of New Zealand and the human geography of Africa and New Zealand. One can only assume that the Olympics are also assumed to lie beyond the horizons of the lower-class child. But in the modern world, the notion of a social environment which is bounded, for anyone, by the immediate physical environment is woefully inadequate as a curriculum focus. In July 1976, nothing could have been physically more remote from Liverpool or Montreal than New Zealand (obviously as much a curricular *bête noire* for Midwinter as is 'Cargoes' or Richard the Lionheart); but nothing could have been politically or culturally more significant for anyone with either an interest in sport or in political affairs.

Yet Midwinter's implication that any knowledge which transcends the immediate imperatives of time and place is irrelevant for children in Educational Priority Areas must cast doubt upon the radical, social and educational aims which he claims and which are also cogently expressed in the document *Educational Priority* which (amongst other things) examines and commends his work: '... the curriculum should be aimed primarily at the critical and construct- ive adaptation of children to the actual environment in which they live'.[19] One's disquiet at the conservative implications of social adaptation to life in an industrial slum may be relieved, provided that 'critical and constructive adaptation' implies also that the environment itself has to be radically changed. Since the writers in question do refer to the likelihood of these children having to live out their lives in Educational Priority Areas, however, such a radical outcome cannot be assumed. Arguably, the only radical attitude towards ghettos or slums is that their replacement is an urgent human priority, but the fatalism assumed by Midwinter and his colleagues seems to take it for granted that this is not a likely eventuality over the next half-century at least.

Reservation about the limited historical, geographical and cu- tural reference of the EPA curriculum also relates to its doubtful value in promoting an understanding of the nature and scope of the social problems of these inner-city environments. For there is a suggestion that the extra-local environment which has, necessarily, to be experienced vicariously is of little relevance to local concerns. Amazingly, this broader environment is simply dismissed as a middle-class world: the EPA child should come to realize 'that education is about himself and his community just as much as about a more remote middle-class world' (Halsey 1972a : 144). The obsession not to be found genuflecting to middle-class values becomes absurd when everything outside a local community is represented in those terms. For one thing, are there not other local communities no less afflicted with social problems, an awareness of which might be a help to understanding one's own? And how far are problems shared by the disadvantaged the world over, rooted in institutions and circumstances which are national or global in origin? Indeed, the 'remote middle-class world' is the likely source of a good many local problems, and to deny the relevance of knowledge of this wider environment is to frustrate the possibility of radical social change. For example, the authors of *Educational Priority* (Halsey 1972a : 118) write of the need to equip children 'to meet the grim reality of the social environment in which they live and to reform it in all its aspects, physical, organic, technical, cultural and moral'. It is not made clear, concretely, what these five aspects denote. But two common problems of Educational Priority Areas (the world over) are immigrants and unemployment, themselves not unrelated. Yet 'compassionate, tolerant and critical' (Halsey 1972a : 195) examination of these two problems must surely relate to knowledge of the broader national and global environments in which they have their origins. Compassionate understanding of immigrants can only derive from knowledge of the economic, political, religious or cultural tensions which were the impetus to migration from their often distant homelands. Tolerance of their idiosyncracies must grow out of an understanding of completely different cultures. Similarly, problems of unemployment are neither generated in nor soluble by the local community. Unemployment results from technological, financial and political decisions which other people make, often in multinational economic institutions in foreign parts. Historically, generations of unemployed have often only found employment through a willingness to abandon the local community for other economically more propitious environments. It is this fact of the extra-local context of most of the social ills that afflict local communities which has led other radicals to conclude that the shift to a macro-focus is essential because of the importance of 'large-scale market forces and of the national, even international, socio-political context of events' (Westergaard 1975 : 252-3). Simon notes how Chartist lecturers appreciated the importance for political education of an earlier generation of the disadvantaged of what is now often dismissed as an irrelevant 'high culture': one of them reported that 'unless there were some stirring local and political topics, I lectured on Milton, and repeated portions of *Paradise Lost*, or on Shakespeare, and repeated portions of *Hamlet* ... or I recited the history of England, and set the portraits of great Englishmen before young Chartists, who listened with interest'. Simon goes on to observe that although 'immediate political issues necessarily predominated in Chartist literature, the journals also contain much cultural and scientific material which provided matter for reflection and discussion'. Chartist newspapers devoted a great deal of space 'to educative articles on economic, cultural and scientific subjects' (Simon 1960 : Vol.I, 249-50). Apparently Engels took the view that many English working men knew more than the German bourgeoisie (Simon 1960 : Vol.I, 256). Although Chartism may have 'failed' politically there is no gainsaying its educational contribution to the working-class movement, and it is odd that earlier strategies for social amelioration should appear to have no lessons to teach modern educational radicals or those on behalf of whom they display concern. It may be impossible to transform communities without the commitment, knowledge and skill of their own inhabitants, but it is deluding them to imply that major resources for change lie within these communities themselves. The sort of radical social change envisioned in the rhetoric of *Educational Priorities* requires both the concerted efforts of the wider national and international communities and, if the EPA resident is himself to play his part, knowledge of the broader cultural, political and economic context from which social transformation must derive.[20]

But there is a second kind of delusion implicit in *Educational Priority*. Its focus is upon pre-school and primary school, and it is an odd kind of child-centred educational theory which expects six- and ten-year-olds to grapple with the social legacies of two centuries of industrialism. For example (Halsey 1972a : 143).

> Not only could it be argued that a community based or an environmentally oriented curriculum was, on moral and social grounds, the most suitable, it could also be pressed that children should not be presented with extra-environmental (in this broader sense) material. Here the child-centredness of the progressive educationist and the social precepts of the community educator meet.

But it is one of our educational myths, which doesn't stand the test of a day's experience in the classroom, that young children (and, especially less able young children) are incapable of generating interest in anything but what they can see happening at the parish pump, on the main street or in the supermarket. Anyone who has seen even a moderately competent primary teacher at work knows that children do not threaten to fall asleep at the mere mention of remote historical characters, geographically distant places and cultures, fictional and poetic works or scientific theories.[21] What is relevant from any of these areas of knowledge for learners of any age or social circumstance is always a matter for debate. It is, however, a fact of experience that if interest and enjoyment (cf. Midwinter's plea for 'jam today') as well as social relevance is in question, then vicarious experience of the broader environment given by time and space, the arts and sciences, is welcomed by young children.

None of this criticism of the parochialism of the proposed EPA curriculum should be taken to imply that many of the suggested teaching strategies could not be profitably employed in the service of a culturally richer curriculum. Attempts to forge links between home and school, adult educational initiatives, the involvement of local colleges of education in community education, projects and extra-curricular activities, the approach to language skills through socially relevant materials — all these are quite consistent with the development of curricula conceived, intentionally, to transcend the limits of the local community by locating it and its problems in the wider context of history and of the national and international communities. But without this wider reference, there is nothing in the specific examples of the proposed curriculum to persuade one that the possibilities acknowledged by its authors of a parochial, soporific, second-class outcome will be avoided. Reservation has already been expressed at the aim of social adjustment without the wider reference which these 'community educators' regard as irrelevant, if not misleading. Midwinter writes (1972b : 7), without qualification, of education as 'a social activity geared to adjusting children to their society', a conception obviously supportive of the existing social hegemony. His occasional playful thrust at the middle class is really a ploy intended to obscure the conservatism of a curriculum predicated upon the need for children to adjust to a hierarchically structured society, its privileges and injustices remaining intact. Nothing else could be expected from a curriculum with a mainly local and present time focus whose advocate is expressly hostile to transmission of knowledge from those subject areas which transcend time and place. But the distant past and the geographically remote are apt to thrust themselves upon us quite unawares, as have Israel, New Zealand and South Africa in recent Olympic Games, and as history and geography do daily on television, radio and film. Midwinter makes a great deal of the unreality of classroom life (Wordsworth, New Zealand, Drake) by comparison with real life on television ('Coronation Street'). But watchers of 'soap operas' also watch the news and current affairs programmes, as well as fictional presentations which require some knowledge of history if they are to be understood.[22] If one really wished to make curricular reference to what impinges upon a working-class child's attention in real life, especially 'real life' as it is mediated by the audio-visual media, this would as often refer to the geographically and historically remote as to the recent past and the geographically proximate. Evidently, Midwinter's radical popular curriculum is as cognitively barren and politically and socially enslaving as is Bantock's.

Working-class education and the politics of non-literacy

The fusing of modern conservative and radical positions on working-class education is particularly evident in questioning the importance of literacy. Midwinter concludes (1972a : 25) that in Educational Priority Areas, if not elsewhere, the important issues are social and not basically literacy or numeracy. Bantock's position has already been intimated in our earlier discussion of his prescription of an artistic-affective curriculum deriving from the disciplines of movement and dance. For him, the characteristically twentieth-century cultural forms which will be appropriate vehicles for renewal of an oral and kinetic culture of the folk are the electronic media, not the printed word. He is clear about the benefits of a print culture only for those whose social environment is propitious for an education rooted in a literary culture — essentially, the professional middle class.

The modern radical's view that literacy is dangerous for lower-class children derives from the assumption that a ruling class sees in literacy a means towards controlling the masses as compliant, passive, 'good' citizens and consumers. This point is put vociferously in Postman's essay 'The politics of reading' (1973 : 89):

... an important function of the teaching of reading is to make students accessible to political and historical myth. It is entirely possible that the main reason middle-class Whites are so concerned to get lower-class Blacks to read is that Blacks will remain relatively inaccessible to standard-brand beliefs unless and until they are minimally literate. It just may be too dangerous, politically, for any substantial minority of our population *not* to believe that our flags are sacred, our history is noble, our government is representative, our laws are just and our institutions are viable. A reading public is a responsible public, by which is meant that it believes most or all of these superstitions, and which is probably why we still have literacy tests for voting.[23]

Here Postman stands the conventional wisdom about literacy on its head, for it has been long and widely assumed that it is the ability to read which liberates persons from the likelihood of political tyranny (Allen 1972 : 440):

> The suppression of the individual which for so long characterized the governance of nations rested on the ignorance of the many and the learning of the few. With the invention of movable type there was created a source of widespread learning that held hope for the eventual abolishment of ignorance and for removal of the barriers to the participation of the common man in the determination of his destiny.[24]

Goody and Watt take reading and writing to have been crucial for the development of democracy in Ancient Greece (1962 : 3, 332).

However, some support for the view that the ruling class has tended to see literacy as an instrument of its own social hegemony derives from its eventual, if reluctant, acceptance that an industrial working class had to be literate. Initial hostility to universal literacy soon gave way to acceptance of the three Rs as the foundation of elementary schooling without the need for a prolonged and bitter campaign for literacy. Quite early in the debate about the desirability of popular education, the upper class accepted the notion that a degree of literacy would be expedient since there could be 'safe reading' as a mode of control of the masses (McBride 1972 : 379; Hurt 1972 : 14-15). The conventional historical view is that literacy became acceptable in order to enable the new factory worker to read regulations posted on the factory walls, including the signs and directions aimed at preventing industrial accidents (Strong 1972 : 67-8). Whilst this insistence upon literacy has seemed in the best interests of both employers and workers, radicals are apt to emphasize the benefits which accrue to capital from the existence of a literate work force. Postman argues (1973 : 88) that whilst an ability to read may be an insurance against industrial accidents it also implies the regulation of one's behaviour by others:

> It is probably true that in a highly complex society, one cannot be

governed unless he can read forms, regulations, notices, catalogues, road signs, and the like. Thus, some minimal reading skill is necessary if you are to be a 'good citizen', but 'good citizen' here means one who can follow the instructions of those who govern him. If you cannot read, you cannot be an obedient citizen.

That is, instruction in the three Rs constitutes an education for obedience. This hegemonic function of print is underlined by Levi-Strauss (Charbonnier 1973 : 18):

> When we consider the first uses to which writing was put, it would seem quite clear that it was connected first and foremost with power: it was used for inventories, catalogues, censuses, laws and instructions; in all instances, whether the aim was to keep a check on material possessions or on human beings, it is evidence of the power exercized by some men over other men and over worldly possessions.

Nevertheless, if the discovery of print puts power into the hands of the literate then, from the viewpoint of the oppressed, the logic of this fact is that liberation from the tyranny of print can only derive from literacy itself. Goody (1973 : 45-6) shows how the non-literate in the Third World are vulnerable to several kinds of exploitation and that development, modernization and independence are 'all about' the fact that the illiterate 'are at the mercy of a hostile world, geared to the man who can read and write'. To the extent that the existing social hegemony is vested in print, its replacement (as distinct from its mere destruction) would seem to require mastery of the skills of literacy. Moreover, the traditional radical view of literacy has been that however paternalistic may have been the motivation of those who allowed the case for literacy, the nature of reading is such that the consequences of a literate population are potentially explosive with reference to the social order. Teaching a man to read may make him a pliant consumer and a rote conformist to factory regulations, but it also makes accessible to him the whole of the literature of his mother tongue, including its radical component — the works of Godwin, Paine, Owen, Lovett, William Morris, Marx (in translation), radical newspapers like Cobbett's *Register*, the *Republican* and *Black Dwarf* — no less than the plays of Shakespeare or the poetry of

Keats. This liberating potential of literacy was assumed by John Stuart Mill (quoted in McBride 1972 : 297): 'Of the working classes of Western Europe at least it may be pronounced certain that the patriarchal system of government is one to which they will not again be subject. That question has been several times decided. It was decided when they were taught to read and allowed access to newspapers and political tracts.' From this point of view, factory legislation can be seen not as an imposition from above, but as something which working men are inspired to demand as a right. It is on this kind of assumption that the United Nations Declaration of Human Rights includes the right to literacy, and the conventional wisdom tends to be that the right to read is 'as fundamental as the right to life, liberty and the pursuit of happiness' (Allen 1972 : 440; Malmquist 1972). Certainly, the Third World tends to see literacy in these terms.

The democratic assumption is that citizens ought not to be, and need not be, mere literate sheep and that literacy is a basic requirement for political autonomy. Traditional radicals, including traditional Marxists, have taken this view that the implications of literacy are revolutionary, even if only negatively in the sense that the illiterate are not the material out of which revolutions are made. Lenin believed that revolution could not be made by illiterate peasants. Gramsci enjoined working-class organic intellectuals, upon whom the drive towards working-class hegemony would be based, to learn to submit their thought to the discipline of the written word. Only through mastery of print could their thinking gain the precision necessary to engage in debate with intellectuals who were the products of an orthodox higher education and to communicate with their fellow workers (Gramsci 1971 : 29)[25]. Simon takes it to be a fact that by 'creating *thought* among the hitherto unthinking masses' the effect of Sunday schools and other institutions aimed at teaching 'safe reading' was the opposite of that intended by their founders (1960 : Vol.I, 183; see also Silver 1975 : 68-9). And, recently Friere has been a persuasive advocate of literacy as the foundation of a pedagogy for the oppressed.

Even Postman accepts that in the early days of industrialism in Europe and, latterly, in the Third World, literacy may have this revolutionary potential (1973 : 91): '... in recently illiterate cultures

... print is a medium capable of generating intense involvement, radicalism, artistic innovation and institutional upheaval'. It is only in long-established literate cultures that print has lost its dynamic potential to such an extent that books are now rarely the objects of censorship (Disch 1973 : 9). In literate societies of long standing, 'we have accommodated our senses to it. We have routinized and even ritualized our responses to it. We have devoted our institutions, which are now venerable, to its service'. In return, print serves to conserve these outworn institutions: print reinforces the historical sense such that a print technology cannot be the agent of change in traditional societies. There is a 'lack of social amnesia in alphabetic cultures' which means that they are 'inevitably committed to an ever increasing series of cultural lags' (Goody and Watt 1962 : 3, 334-5). As Steiner puts it (1973 : 148): 'In very large measure, most books are about previous books ... writing persistently refers to previous writing.' That is, our contemporary literature is a constant reminder of the great traditions of Western culture in the arts and philosophy, inducing a nostalgia which shackles rather than liberates our creativity. The fact that so much of our cultural capital is stored in print means that in order to revitalize our civilization we have to forget the past by turning to media of communication which are not glutted with this historical cultural deposit. If this is the case it is the electronic media to which we must look 'to unloose disruptive social and political ideas, along with new forms of sensibility and expression' (Postman 1973).

The politics of literacy has, thus, to be understood historically and comparatively. In principle even Postman is prepared to accept the case for literacy and he admirably summarizes its claim to be a source of cultural enrichment and rational thought (1973 : 88): '... the basic purpose of reading instruction is to open the student's mind to the wonders and riches of the written word, to give him access to great fiction and poetry, to permit him to function as an informed citizen, to have him experience the sheer pleasure of reading'. However, whilst Postman believes this acceptable as an educational aim, he finds the claim 'almost totally untrue in practice'. He echoes the judgement of Bernard Shaw half a century ago that the only significant consequence of universal literacy is the mass readership of the tabloid press (1973 : 89):

If one wants to read about America, one may read de Tocqueville or the *Daily News*; if one wants to read literature, one may go to Melville or Jacqueline Susann. In theory, this argument is compelling. In practice, it is pure romantic nonsense. The *New York Daily News* is the most widely read newspaper in America. Most of our students will go to the grave not having read of their own choosing a paragraph of de Tocqueville or Thoreau or John Stuart Mill or, if you exclude the Gettysburg Address, even Abraham Lincoln. As between Jacqueline Susann and Herman Melville — well, the less said, the better. To put it bluntly, among every hundred students who learn to read, my guess is that no more than one will employ the process towards any of the lofty goals which are customarily held before us. The rest will use the process to increase their knowledge of trivia, to maintain themselves at a relatively low level of emotional maturity, and to keep themselves simplistically uninformed about the social and political turmoil around them.

Indeed, Postman takes literate preoccupations to be entirely a function of schooling for both children and their teachers, much as Midwinter takes poetry to be confined to the culture of the school.

Other students of the print culture have pointed to questionable results of literacy which they see as inseparable from the printed word as a medium of communication. It is argued that print is anti-social in reinforcing individualism and privacy (Bantock 1966 : 6-7; see also Goody and Watt 1962 : 3, 338-40):

> ...the book is the instrument of self-consciousness. It points forward to personal, private satisfactions, the creation of individual mythologies in contrast to the oral, communal offerings. The social distance between creator and audience is immensely widened, for the book comes with none of the aural resonances of social life, but as a private possession, portable, respectable, the inhabitant essentially of the study, the room set apart from family living.

The consequence of all this is 'a growing social separateness'. This tendency towards a solitary preoccupation with print, intensifying privacy, individualism and self-consciousness is obviously unpromising for the cultivation of radical political activity depending upon working-class solidarity. Indeed, Goody (1973 : 44-5) suggests that the effect of literacy in the Third World has been in facilitating individual upward mobility (no doubt one of Bantock's 'personal private satisfactions') rather than radical social change on behalf of a majority of citizens.

Perhaps equally unfortunate for the sense of common social purpose which radical political activity requires is the claim that the literary culture is alienating, a source of anomie. Goody and Watt (1962 : 3, 334-5) quote Jefferson's view that 'the printers can never leave us in a state of perfect rest and union'. One consequence of this glut of print is 'the inconsistence of the totality of written expression'. Thus 'as book follows book and newspaper newspaper, the notion of rational agreement and democratic coherence among men has receded further and further away', such that, paradoxically, the very literacy which makes democracy possible also frustrates the consensus upon which it depends.

A further criticism of print technology is of its desensitizing nature in that it anaesthetizes all senses but sight by cutting out all oral symbols and forms of communication. This makes for emotional impoverishment: 'The resonances of the voice speak more directly to the emotions, conjure up a world altogether more alert to the senses than does the word which is read in silence' (Bantock 1966 : 6). Thus, Bantock argues (1966 : 10-11), print makes for a narrowing of experience:

> By 'narrowing of experience' I mean that we stress only certain aspects out of the totality which our senses present to us. The translation of oral symbols into visual abstractions — which is print culture — helps to exclude from sense a whole range of meanings which can only with difficulty be rediscovered in the inner ear; hence our general insensitivity to verse, and the difficulty we have in making poetry in a tone deaf world.

However, as Bantock himself immediately recognizes, there is truth in the common assumption that books open up a range of vicarious experiences which ought to make for a refinement of sensibility. Through books we extend the range of our knowledge of other places, other times, other social classes, other avocations. The print culture, thus,

> extended experience in other ways. What has been lost in sensuous range ... has been made up in the amplification of possible

psychic identity ... The rapid circulation of books — repeatability in this sense — has meant the multiplication of various possibilities. A print culture offers a multiplicity of identities; it tremendously increases the range of possible empathy.

This is, indeed, to imply that print's implications for privacy as against sociability are by no means all in one direction. Goody and Watt (1962 : 3, 55) claim that literacy makes possible a 'world of knowledge transcending political units'. It is this possibility of the enlargement of experience through literacy which underpins the claim that reading is basic to intelligent world citizenship (Smith 1972; Malmquist 1972).

This juxtaposition of two senses of experience and of the pros and cons in relation to print only underlines the several paradoxes which inhere in this particular technology. As we have seen, as well as having apparently contradictory implications for the range of personal experience, the same is true of its political potential which appears, at the same time, both radical and conservative. But this Janus quality which print shares with all human technologies merely reveals the truth that any human artifice exacts a price: its potential malfunctions are the necessary price we pay for its benefits.

A number of points follow from this conclusion. First, it behoves us to look critically at the proposed alternatives to print — the electronic media of communication. Both conservative and radical critics of print take the vital characteristic twentieth-century cultural technologies to be radio, film and television. Eulogized uncritically in deference to Marshall McLuhan, these are taken to be educationally potent in a way which books are not. Yet from the point of view of political control, it is odd that the consquences of the electronic media should be judged liberating and radical by comparison with print. For example, it is taken as a mark against print that the book is silent (Disch 1973):

A book, Socrates argued in the Phaedrus, is always vulnerable to misunderstandings, especially when read by someone who is unprepared for its complexities. Unlike spoken dialogue, which is subject to constant correction, a book is mute; it cannot defend itself against misinterpetation, clarify terminology, or repair deficiencies in logic. Words, like the figures in realistic paintings, 'stand before us as though they were alive'. But if we attempt to question a book about its meaning, the 'words go on telling (us) the same things forever'. Because of these limitations, he warned, teachers who rely on writing will breed pedantic students who appear wise because they know many facts, but who 'for the most part know nothing' of true wisdom.

In passing, it is worth noting that, in another paradox, the book's silence is also its strength. Reading the Socratic dialogue is interesting for the number of occasions when one's own reaction differs from that of Socrates' stooges: when they agree to his prompting, logic often cries out for a negative response. The Socratic dialogue stands conventionally admired as an open-ended teaching method but, as often as not, it is a device for leading students by 'constant correction' to accept the conclusions of the master. On the other hand, precisely because it does not constantly correct the reader, it is a familiar experience that the book may start a train of thought which is genuinely open ended, possibly leading to quite novel conclusions beyond those the author intended. In any event, the oracy of television, film and radio is really akin to the muteness of print. Radio and television talk is essentially one-way and permits only the sort of critical, but unanswered, response which one can make to print. That there is sometimes an appearance of conversation or debate on the electronic media is, for the viewer or listener, quite irrelevant: the questions asked are frequently not the ones which he feels cry out for discussion.

Thus the electronic media have at least the same political significance for authoritarianism, leading, regulation and control as does print. Even more so: for what is claimed as the virtue of an oral culture — its sociability, its emotional warmth — is clearly a danger when transmitted by mass media like radio and television. Bantock, at least, is clear about this (1966 : 17-18): the appeal of 'the characteristic electric media of the non-school environment ... is primarily emotional, the aim to exploit the non-rational element in purchasing'. And what has this exploitive potential commercially must be no less potent for political manipulation. Indeed, it is incredible that print should be seen as an instrument of Fascist manipulation in view of the use made by the Nazi leaders of oratory in the mass rally. (Disch 1973 : 6-7). As Wellek reminds us, 'dictator' derives from *dictare*, to say (1973 : 131; see also Havelock 1973 : 29). Moreover, it is not clear that the electronic media share with print the safeguards of repeatability, the constant checking and reference back which is possible with the individual book and in the library. There is no turning back or jumping forward with speech, no stopping to ponder and reflect. By contrast,

> when reading the individual can control the choice of material, the frequency and speed to suit his thought processes and turn back to make comparisons or refresh his memory in a manner and with an ease that can never be achieved with radio, television and tape recorders ... the printed word on the other hand permits a wider, freer, personal, thoughtful and more creative examination (Boyle 1972 : 433; see also Warner 1972 : 14).

Thoroughgoing McLuhanites, like Postman (1969 : 168), do not of course even admit the desirability of linearity of argument, of this kind of critical approach to the content of the media, arguing that 'the conventional pedestrian academic mode of analytic linear segmentation and explication itself comprises a threat to our survival'. Miller suggests (1971 : 113) that the arguments about linearity and simultaneity apply equally to print and to speech, but with the bias in favour of print. The ease of flicking back and forth over a page or through a text is not matched by the relatively cumbersome mechanics of moving back and forth on tape or record. Arguably, there are devices, much like pagination of print, which allow one to cut back the tape precisely to the point one wishes to repeat. The trouble with this undoubted truth is that what is technically possible is not always economically realistic. We are probably far enough from the time when even every home has the sophisticated gadgetry necessary for video recording and for the counting which is necessary to flip quickly back and forth through the tape. There is also the impediment that public broadcasting authorities and film companies, unlike publishers of print, do not readily make available copyright material. Obviously, besides the technological breakthroughs which would be necessary to make sophisticated recording equipment (including the indexing devices which would parallel pagination and indexing of print) economically plentiful, a good deal of political legislation would be necessary to define universal right of access to broadcast materials.

Easy access to information and entertainment for individual purposes and satisfactions can still most readily be secured through the
agency of the printed word.[26]

It is the persisting legal, technical and economic impediments to
access, repeatability, recording and reversibility with reference to
the electronic media which lead one to conclude that if today one
had to invent the most accessible, economical and technologically
simple device for the communication of information and ideas
one would 'rediscover' the book. As a contributor to a conference
on audio-visual media recently put it (Mace 1971):

> The book is — and will remain for quite some time yet — the
> most readily accessible, easily utilizable, economic and efficient
> means of organizing information and of communicating ideas. It
> requires no support system. I have had this availability proved to
> me a dozen times in the week preceding this conference. Time
> restrictions have prevented me from seeing films, accidents of
> location have prevented my watching TV, voltage differences
> have prevented me from running filmstrips or projecting slides in
> my hotel room. But every customs halt, every lunch-time break,
> every airport wait, has enabled me to read. And the reading that
> I have done has reinforced in me my awareness of the significant
> advantage of a book. Its contents can be a distillation of intan-
> gibles that film, TV and graphics cannot easily present. Consider
> the Hofburg Palace in which this conference is being held. I am
> glad to have seen quality photographs of the building, its archi-
> tectural details and its contents. But these cannot bring to me an
> understanding of the philosophical tenets that underlay Haps-
> burg rule or Hapsburg collapse. The physical battlefields can be
> brilliantly presented by maps, photographs and other audio-
> visual aids. But can the varying states of mind of Austrians,
> Serbs, Poles and other fiercely nationalistic imperial citizens be
> captured as successfully? I think not. It is the book, drawing
> upon letters, diaries, newspaper reports and so on, that most
> richly cultivates the student's mind.

This obvious convenience of print for the various purposes of
acquiring information, ideas or emotional stimulation is obfuscated
by the rhetoric of space age futurism. In yet another context,
denouncing the teaching of reading, Postman writes (1971 : 19-20):

Trying to prepare children for life in the electronic era by pro-
gramming them for reading skills is like trying to get to Mars in a
Chevy Impala. Adding *behavioural objectives* to the curriculum
is like adding power steering to the Chevy: you may have a better
car, but it just won't go far enough. In this case the Chevy
doesn't have the structure to get you where you want to go.[27]

The trouble with this educational metaphor is that most people
have no desire to go to Mars or anywhere else in outer space. What
they want is exactly a more reliable Chevy to take them to places
they do want to go: to work, visiting friends and family and on
spare-time outings to camp, hunt or ski. But the bated-breathless
prophets of incessant change and future shock won't have any of
that. If we have the technology to go to the moon and beyond, that
is where we ought to want to be. Though we may prefer to be
reading books or newspapers, we really ought to be listening to
radio, watching television or, in the age of multimedia, doing all
three at once.

The human purposes of human beings and, especially, their
responsibility for what they do and choose are irrelevant according
to the McLuhanite fallacy that 'the medium is the message'. Whilst
it is evident that any medium of communication derives from its
own technology both peculiar impediments and potential, the
medium is not the message.[28] The miniscule truth in McLuhan's
aphorism is a trivial truth by comparison with the fact that the
media of communication are themselves neutral as to their mess-
ages which derive from the intentions of those who own, manage,
'write', produce and direct the media, whether print or electronic.
The truth about the media is that they can be used to inform and
educate, or lie and mislead, to disseminate radical as well as
conservative ideologies.[29] It is for this reason that the content of
education is no less important than the processes of instruction, and
one has to dissent from the claim 'that the skill of reading and its
later use are more important than any specific content learned in
school' (Harman 1972). Whatever the medium of communication
— whether print or electronic — the person's only defence against
manipulation and misrepresentation is the well-stocked mind: the
educated sensibility which draws upon the culture's store of
established truths. Though this conclusion runs counter to the
conventional educational wisdom that process rather than produce

— a capacity for learning how to learn rather than being learned —
is more important, traditional political radicals[30] have recognized
that to overthrow the existing social hegemony one has to know its
history and master its culture.

By contrast, McLuhanism is the ultimate ideology of dehumani-
zation: the technology generates the message and no one has any
responsibility for what is written or broadcast. But, to the contrary,
the political truth about media of communication is that content is
everything. This is also the educational truth about the media of
communication. Postman (1973 : 88) pretends that without textbooks American children would not be subjected to indoctrination
in political myths which conceal four historical truths: (1) the
achievement of political identity through insurrection against a
legally constituted government; (2) genocide against the indigen-
ous population; (3) slavery as a basis of economic development; (4)
railway building by imported 'coolie' labour. Whether, in fact,
most Americans do come to the end of their schooling in ignorance
of these facts (Postman knows them) is irrelevant to any discussion
of the rival merits and weaknesses of different media of communication. For if they are kept in ignorance of these facts, it is because
of human decisions to present alternative accounts of nation-
building, not because schools use textbooks instead of electronic
devices: if textbooks were suddenly replaced entirely by tapes,
films, TV presentations and the like, the message would remain the
same in default of some decision to tell it differently. After all (with
few exceptions) hundreds of Western movies over several decades
successfully described how the West was won without any implication of genocide or dependence on imported 'coolies'. The film
and television West is as mythical as that of any textbook. Similarly,
when Postman implies the desirability of keeping young Blacks
illiterate to protect them from 'standard-brand beliefs' that our
flags are sacred, our history is noble, our government is representative, our laws are just, and our institutions are viable', he ignores
the fact that any television day in the USA is devoted to demonstrating the viability, justice and sacredness of American institutions
from the family through to the institutions of the economic system
and of law and order. If the message is to be one vast lie about
American (or any other nation's) institutions, it is a good deal easier
to lie electronically than it is in print if only because of the technological imperatives which make television and a good deal of radio

non-repeatable, available neither for checking nor leisured criticism. From the point of view of the politics of education, the content is the message and the messengers are people.

Evidently, abandoning print for the electronic media offers no escape from control by those whose intention is to manipulate other people. No doubt the pervasiveness of film, television and radio provides good grounds for training the young to be discriminating with reference to audio-visual symbols and imagery. But that the need for training in video-oracy is compelling does not make literacy of less importance. The popularity of the recent campaign against adult illiteracy, *On the Move*, is adequate testimony that 'adult illiterates live in a limited world', the social implications of their illiteracy being 'many and varied — in work, leisure and, most important, in their personal relationships'.[31] Those conservatives and so-called radicals who wish to wean the working class from dependence upon print know well enough that it is prolonged and exclusive exposure to the electronic media which really blunts the intelligence and anaesthetizes the emotions.

4

Culture
and education

An educationally relevant concept of culture

There is a familiar distinction between two conceptions of culture, the descriptive, anthropological characterization of culture as a whole way of life and the normative or evaluative conception.[1] However, this simple distinction does not take account of some of the ways in which the word is used by educationists, particularly with reference to the relationship between culture and social stratification. Thus, whilst retaining this fundamental descriptive-normative distinction, it is necessary to mark a number of other distinctions at different levels of generality.

Descriptively, a culture may be conceived as a total way of life or, more narrowly, with reference only to the totality of artefacts which constitute the arts, sciences and philosophy. Further restricted, culture often denotes only the arts. This sense of culture as 'art works' is often further restricted to refer only to the literary arts. Arnold's conception of culture has been criticized for giving undue weight to the book, and Bantock justifies his claim that the curriculum has been concerned with a watered down high culture by reference only to literature (Williams 1961a : 297-8; Bantock 1976 : 89). And a still more restricted definition sees culture in terms of recreations and pastimes: some versions of working-class or popular culture, for example, do focus on such a limited range of activities. As convenient shorthand these four descriptions of culture will be referred to elsewhere as C1, C2, C3, C4 (see the summary table on p.111.)

However, for the purposes of educational theory — and, perhaps, communications theory (that is, development of policy in relation to the media of communication) — mere description of the range of activities and artefacts which make up a culture is of limited value. In the descriptive sense which includes a total way of life (C1), a culture must include strands which are technologically or economically dysfunctional, others which aggravate social injustice, and yet others which offend moral and aesthetic values: anthropologically, the criminal sub-culture is obviously a part of culture, as is the drug culture and alcoholism. As Thompson insists, in criticism of what he calls Eliot's 'sloppy and amateurish' version of the anthropological notion (and Raymond Williams's bland extension of Eliot's characteristic list), any list of the totality of cultural activities and artefacts must include items which characterize the areas of power and conflict: for example (Thompson 1961 : 33), 'strikes, Gallipoli, the bombing of Hiroshima, corrupt trade union elections, the massive distortion of news and Aldermaston marches'. Similarly, the political culture includes 'Watergate' and 'the unacceptable face of capitalism' as well as the Declaration of Independence, the Bill of Rights, the New Deal, Civil Rights legislation and the Welfare State. Hence, each of the descriptive characterizations noted above has a corresponding normative sense of culture, whereby items in the culture may be evaluated as desirable or undesirable, best (and, implicitly, good, better, worse, worst), decadent, corrupt, criminal, altruistic, conducive to mental or physical health, intellectual acuity, moral or aesthetic sensibility. Generally, this normative conception of culture can be characterized as Cn and, with reference to each of the descriptive categories above, as C1n, C2n, C3n, C4n (see the summary table on p.111).

Although the concept of culture in any of its descriptive senses is ultimately inadequate for the educationist, it is not completely irrelevant to his concerns. The total cultural environment (C1) does socialize the student into dispositions which are the raw materials of any educational enterprise. Children bring with them to school

Concepts of culture	
Descriptive	*Normative*
C1 Anthropological — 'whole way of life' — totality of activities and artefacts.	C1n Totality (C1) minus its dysfunctional elements.
C2 The product of intellectual and artistic activity.	C2n The *best* that has been thought and said.
C3 The arts (that is, C2 minus philosophy, science, history).	C3n The best art ('art', music, painting, sculpture, etc.).
C4 Recreation ('leisure' activities).	C4n 'Wholesome' recreation.

interests, prejudices, enthusiasms, strengths and limitations formed, in part, through indiscriminate contact with the total culture. This is also the context within which educational institutions pursue their daily work. The total way of life of the communities within which they are set constitute both opportunities and constraints on their work. But education is not socialization: it is a narrower concept picking out that aspect of socialization which is deliberately conceived towards improvement of the individual or group. [2] It might be objected however that children must be taught the entire totality, 'warts and all', since they inevitably encounter the whole way of life and would be ill-served by a tendency to brush under the carpet the unpleasantnesses of life, like the criminal culture. But if one 'taught' crime in school, it is inconceivable that one's intention would not be to invite the learner to come to some evaluative conclusion about it. To be sure, conceptions of education may differ substantively in terms of what different individuals or groups count as improvement but, formally, to speak of education is to imply betterment. This is to say that whilst the concept of education is procedurally normative (that is, tied to the notion of improvement) its substantive values in a particular context will be relative to the particular society, group or individual, in question. Admission of such relativism does not weaken the notion of a necessarily normative dimension if an experience is to be categorized 'educative'. Even self-education when conceived as learning in relation to an individual's own objectives, whilst utterly and uniquely relative, is also normative. One would not speak of educating oneself if the activities in question were not undertaken with the object of self-improvement, achievement of a higher standard of motor skill, a subtler appreciation of the arts, a deepening of moral sensibility, skill in philosophical argument or deeper understanding of the natural world. Hence, for educational purposes, when proper allowance has been made for the constraints which a total culture may impose upon the work of the school, only certain dimensions of the culture are appropriate.

Normatively the notion of culture (Cn) operates both to limit the range of activities which are culturally valuable, having potential as the soil for personal and social improvement, and to discriminate qualitatively amongst different components of the culture so delimited. Educationists are apt to characterize a culture in terms of a limited range of skills and forms of knowledge variously labelled 'worthwhile activities', 'culturally valuable activities', 'academic disciplines', 'subjects'. That is, however widely the notion of relevance is interpreted, no matter how disciplines or subjects are conceived, and whatever the case for integrated courses of study, some limit is always imposed upon what the curriculum will contain. In even the most 'open' of curricula, the skills of the underworld, the hardest of drugs, and aberrant sexual practices would not be taught. Nowhere is there curricular *carte blanche* with reference to the total culture, and in most societies curricular limits are drawn much more tightly around a core of conventional subjects or disciplines.

However, the educationist's definition of culture must not only be more narrowly descriptive than is entailed by the notion of culture as a total way of life (C1). Even where culture is described by reference to the arts and crafts, the humanities and sciences (C2), or is restricted to the arts (C3) and even to pastimes and recreations (C4), some qualitative judgements seem necessary. There are standards of performance with reference to skill and of truth with reference to knowledge. Some ideas are seminal, others banal. Different works of art appeal to subtler sensibility and even pastimes and recreations differ qualitatively with reference to their moral, intellectual and aesthetic content. In each of the cultural areas C2 to C4, some activities are more fertile for personal growth and development of further interests.

Whatever the totality which confronts the educationist — whether working-class, middle-class, national or Western culture — it will be a cultural curate's egg. Hence, in pursuit of an educationally useful, normative concept of culture, he is confronted with three related tasks.

First, there is the articulation of criteria in terms of which one is justified in speaking of 'the best' culture or, at least, in terms of culturally better or worse. This involves reference to intellectual, aesthetic and moral standards and values. These normative criteria which define 'the best culture' are subject to continuing debate in democratic societies and it is a commonly accepted educational purpose that alternative criteria should receive appropriate consideration. But, historically, a tradition of humanism has developed criteria of interpersonal and social behaviour which rules out exploitation and has found certain forms of human life (whether suffered or chosen) degrading. In turn, these norms have been extended to categories of person not formerly regarded as having claims to recognition as 'fully human' and denied respect as persons — the working class, slaves, subject peoples, women, children. And it is to this humanistic tradition which Engels appealed in seeking to liberate those working-class groups whom he saw deprived of humanity and degraded to resemble machines or animals (1958 : 8). His appeal was to 'MEN, members of the great and universal family of Mankind, who know their interest and that of all the human race to be the same ... members of this family of "one and indivisible" Mankind ... Human Beings in the most emphatical meaning of the word ...' As we have already observed, it is in much the same way that the philosopher of education typically speaks of education in universalistic and humanistic terms. Sociologists of education are apt to presume them naive for ignoring social and economic 'determinants' of educability, or the differentially motivating effects of varied social environments. But philosophers are right in requiring that education, like Engels's MAN, is one and indivisible.

Secondly, there is need to examine particular cultures — regional, ethnic, social class, for example — for the way in which they exemplify, concretely, those concepts and principles which define the subjects, disciplines or forms of knowledge and skill through which the student's cultural horizons are enlarged.

Thirdly, there is the matter of the way in which particular sub-cultures do or do not interpenetrate each other and the cultural mainstream, such that activities and artefacts from different cultures ought to be universalized through transmission in a common curriculum. It is the conventional wisdom that it is only middle-class culture and values which the school attempts to universalize in this way. To the extent that this assumption is valid, curriculum innovation should take account of working-class contributions to the cultural mainstream. With this in mind it is now necessary to examine the notion of working-class culture in relation to other cultures and to the so-called 'high culture'.

The meaning of working-class culture

The argument already advanced that cultural deprivation exists, and that education is predicated upon the notion of cultural inadequacy, does not meet the objection that working-class culture is, at least, normatively the equal of other cultures. It is arguable that demonstration of the existence of cultural deprivation only works with reference to lower-class life in what has been called the culture of poverty. And whilst the 'adequacy of all cultures' thesis seems directed especially at this social stratum, a more aggressive version of the adequacy thesis asserts that working-class culture should define the content of the curriculum for working-class children since working-class culture is 'different but equal' to middle-class culture (Lawton 1975 : 28), even that, in absolute terms, it is superior. This last assumption seems implicit in Labov's comparison (1973) of the language of lower- and middle-class American Blacks. Hence, it is not only conservatives like Bantock and other Black Paper authors who denounce attempts to develop a common curriculum, but also some political and educational radicals from the Left.

However, a conclusion of the previous section was that sub-cultures need to be examined by educationists not so much as exclusive alternatives but, rather, for the relationship they have to the cultural mainstream. This relationship might be sought through examination of the way in which different sub-cultures exemplify, concretely, universal values and principles of social organization. It may also be discovered in the way in which institutions, developed within a particular sub-culture, have become of relevance to other social groups. It seems unhelpful to see sub-cultures as absolutely discontinuous from the mainstream culture. Indeed, the mainstream exists largely as it is fed by tributary cultures which mingle as currents within it. From this assumption, the present chapter also examines some conceptions of working-class culture and their relationship to what is variously categorized as the mainstream, central or dominant culture.

It is not uncommon to encounter the view that the working class does not exist as a cultural phenomenon. This is the case with some American literature which allows the possibility that the working class may be a useful sociological construct for analysis of traditional industrial societies in Europe, but finds that in the United States there is no working-class, although there are economically disadvantaged groups (Parker 1974 : xx).[3] Children from these groups present problems within schools, but these are problems of motivation and of discovering teaching strategies which are appropriate to the task of assimilating disadvantaged students into the mainstream middle-class culture (Kvaraceus 1969 : 95). Elsewhere, the cultural homogeneity of modern societies is argued in the context of attempts to define a common curriculum appropriate to the comprehensive school.

However, as we have seen, these strategies to diminish the importance of social class by stressing cultural homogeneity encounter resistance from both ends of the political spectrum. These alternative and otherwise irreconcilable standpoints hold that working-class culture defines a phenomenon which is completely discontinuous with the cultures of other classes and the cultural mainstream. Familiarly, the working class is believed to perceive the social universe in terms of 'us' and 'them', a 'two nations' conception of class distinctions (Parkin 1973 : 79). The implication is one of irreconcilable class interests and cultural discontinuity. In economic terms *we* are exploited by *them; they* are also perceived as holding all the cards in the power game. Questions of status equality are deemed irrelevant; to those occupying completely different social universes, questions of esteem, deference and equality between classes simply do not arise. The lack of sympathy with other life-styles exemplified in working-class intolerance of working-class deviants to the middle classes is usually taken by others to be a fault, at best an understandably defensive reaction. But within the group itself there is a conception that *this* (our) life-style is preferable because it is better.

If the conception that there is no working class is most commonly encountered in North America, the notion of clearly defined and separate cultural categories also finds its sharpest form in that context. The reference may not be explicitly to the 'working class', but the implication of complete cultural discontinuity in references to Black culture is similar to that which is taken to mark the working class off from other classes elsewhere. Indeed, when they are not unemployed, the Blacks who prompt assumptions of a distinctive Black culture are usually in blue-collar occupations as unskilled or semi-skilled workers. The identity of the Black working class is also reinforced by comparison with the cultural orientation of middle-class Blacks who have 'made it' and, in the absence of significant empirical research in England on working-class speech, the issues facing American Black education have been taken to be instructive for working-class education in that context (Keddie 1973 : Introduction).

At its extreme, the notion of a discontinuous Black culture is predicated upon the existence of a distinctive Black epistemology or *Weltanschauung*. However, concrete examples of this alternative world view are relatively few and rarely prove the point at issue. For example, discussing the desirability of an alternative Black or African psychology, Clark suggests that it should focus not upon the origins of intelligence and its formal properties, but upon the how and why of human behaviour. From this tenable assumption, he then suggests, in explanation of the behaviour of Blacks, that 'Black intelligence manifests itself in a decision to run zigzag down an alley (as opposed to straight) when a policeman pulls his gun on you' and that 'the purpose of this behavioural manifestation is to increase the possibility of personal survival'. But it is odd to claim that this phenomenon is related to a distinctively Black perception of reality. Military training manuals throughout the world's armies probably instruct the infantry recruit to move across ground in much the same zig zag pattern (practical infantry training certainly requires this behaviour) in recognition of the universal principle of ballistics that fired missiles fly (other things being equal) in a straight line, as well as of the commonplace notion that laterally moving targets are more difficult to hit and that it is safer not to appear in the same place twice. Whatever the natural scientific principles involved in this 'military culture', it is odd to claim that it exemplifies an alternative epistemology. Small boys, especially from the lower classes, have always cultivated avoidance strategies from the law, but it is novel to credit them with a different world view. To be sure, the presuppositions of the law and of members of lower-class groups may indicate the existence of alternative value systems — a common enough assumption. And observers of the 'culture of poverty' have remarked the existence of 'lower-class value stretch' or 'normative ambivalence'. Conventional moral values are well enough understood and 'accepted' (e.g. with reference to property and 'stealing', marriage and sex mating patterns, desirable occupations, etc.). Rejection of these is usually not so much a matter of principle as of expedience, from the imperative simply to survive in an unfriendly environment (Parkin 1973 : 92-4; see also Lewis 1970; Roberts 1973). That is, the value stretch involves a bi-value orientation which, in some sense, clearly requires the notion of common moral assumptions.

There is no doubt that this conception of a pluralist society compounded of distinctive sub-cultures with little culture in common is held by some for hegemonic reasons. That is, the notion that working-class or Black culture is distinguished by its own peculiar epistemological and ethical systems, amounting to an alternative world view, is insisted upon from conviction that the existence of this alternative culture is a condition for radical and social change: for the replacement of bourgeois by proletarian hegemony. The contrary view that these sub-cultures are an organic part of a mainstream culture, contributing towards its enrichment and, in turn, deriving nurture from it, is taken to be a guarantee of the peaceful and unchallenged continuation of the existing hege-mony or *status quo* (Parkin 1973 : 80). This is clearly the critical position of some explicitly Marxist writers, but others reveal a good deal of ambiguity on this point. In the hands of some educational and social theorists, recognition of this alternative world view seems necessary, simply as a measure of the task facing anyone who, through education, aims at assimilation of lower-class children into the cultural mainstream. As Basil Bernstein confesses (1971 : Vol.I, 5), for example, his own interest in defining the parameters of a distinctive working-class culture follow from the imperative, 'only connect'. However, it is questionable whether the logic of those who begin by emphasizing distinctiveness to the point of discontinuity does not leave them powerless to connect.

A third alternative to the notions either that the working class no longer exists or that it is different to the point of constituting a different people or nation, is that view that working-class culture stands organically within a pluralist society whose mainstream or dominant culture it both helps to sustain and from which it, in turn, draws sustenance. On this view, the appropriate cultural focus of education is a common culture within which sub-cultures operate and interact. This conception of the relation of sub-cultures to the cultural mainstream will be further elaborated following an examin-ation of the notion of working-class culture in relation to the four conceptions of culture outlined at the beginning of this chapter.

We have already examined something of Midwinter's advocacy of a community relevant curriculum, especially on behalf of children in Educational Priority Areas. This seemed to depend upon a limited conception of the notions of community and environment, and a similar inadequacy characterizes the conception of working-class culture on which his proposals are based. Referring to lower-working-class children in Educational Priority Areas, Midwinter recognizes that these children have a 'rich potential' which is too often unrealized in schools. But when one looks for concrete exemplification of how this potential might be actualized, one is surprised by the triviality of the concept of working-class culture on which it depends. We are offered just two examples of the 'richness in the EPA sub-culture that makes the life of Acadia Avenue seem wan, shallow and namby pamby' by comparison (Midwinter 1972a : 11):

> Teachers will regale one with delicious anecdotes of sharpness or good will or generosity among EPA juniors, like the nine year old girl with an IQ of 70, who could perform prodigious feats of house keeping and who, it was reputed, knew from day to day the exact whereabouts of her city's high ranking officers. The sophisticated traffic-sense of the EPA child is wellnight proverbial, and the aplomb with which infants park and 'mind' the cars of football supporters is, like Private Willis, 'generally admired'.

What can be inferred about working-class culture from these two examples? No doubt the girl, in spite of her IQ of 70, has exceptional gifts. Perhaps she doesn't really have an IQ of 70 and even if she does this would only underline the irrelevance of measured IQ as an index of human capability. Or perhaps all children, suitably motivated, would be capable of similar feats of housekeeping and civic encyclopedism. But whatever the explanation of this child's gifts, the most this example tells us is that intelligence is to be found in any social group; it tells us nothing about working-class culture. This child is not demonstrating a sub-cultural trait so much as social assets which would be valuable in any culture.

The prowess with which infants manage traffic at football matches is another matter, hardly an example of 'sophisticated traffic sense' (which is not to say that working-class children lack sophistication in negotiating urban traffic). It is interesting that Midwinter puts 'mind' in quotation marks. This particular invitation to mind one's car is obviously the modern version of the servile 'Can I 'old 'yer 'orses 'ead sir?', but without the economic value that this service had in the days of horse-drawn traffic. Today, it is nothing more than a protection racket,[4] harmless enough perhaps in infants, but dignifying to neither party to the transaction, and with more sinister potential as a long-term behaviour pattern. As a characteristic example of a rich sub-culture, this really only trivializes it to what could be called 'the artful dodger' conception of working-class culture. There is certainly nothing in these examples, or in Midwinter's other concrete illustrations of what the working class does, which suggests that working-class culture is a total way of life in the anthropological sense of C1.

Like Midwinter, Brian Jackson promises much from his examination of working-class culture, but he delivers something which is only slightly less trivial. In his study *Working-Class Community* (1968), Jackson examined working-class life in the Northern English city of Huddersfield with a view to discovering the way in which the working-class sense of community found expression in a number of distincitvely working-class institutions. These included working men's clubs, brass bands, bowling clubs and a jazz club. The working men's clubs are repeatedly characterized as 'co-operative societies engaged in buying and selling beer'. The brass bands have developed into vehicles for non-music designed only to show off the virtuosity of musicians at brass band contests. Crown green bowling is clearly superior to its middle-class flat green equivalent in the south of England, and the jazz club is an institution for keeping in the neighbourhood disaffected products of the local grammar school. Each of these institutions provides a form of recreation or entertainment with cultural values (culture in my sense of C4), but none of them produces a form of community life which sustains Jackson's claim (1968 : 175) that 'the fact that industrial workers over ten generations made so much out of such squalor and indignity remains one of the little miracles of English social history.' That the English working class lifted itself out of squalor and poverty largely 'by its own bootstraps' is, indeed, a good deal more than the minor miracle which Jackson allows. But this was not achieved through the organization of working men's clubs, bowling greens or brass bands. In this context, it is interesting that the only reference to the working life of the working class is in the description (by Marsden) of the local mill which focuses upon the working day of exploited workers in a situation where no hint of traditional working-class solidarity in defence of its standard of life is at all evident. Typically, according to Marsden (in Jackson 1968), the workers spend their moments of relaxation in sexual innuendo and in observations upon the workers of non-English origin which are mainly racist in tone. The only evidence of working-class solidarity or community is in these discriminatory attitudes of the local, Yorkshire-born mill hands towards their immigrant workmates. In total, the picture of working-class culture which emerges is hardly less trivial than Midwinter's and, here again, we can hardly be said to be in the presence of working-class culture as a total way of life. There is no indication that the working-class sense of community which inspires the management of 'the cooperative societies for buying and selling beer' has also created the Labour Movement, the instrument of working-class social, economic and political amelioration and of working-class engagement with central economic and political institutions.

However, though oddly neglecting distinctively working-class institutions like trade unions, friendly societies, consumer cooperatives and the complex of political groups which constituted the Labour Party, Jackson's intended, if misconceived, lauding of working-class sense of community does hint at what is probably the distinctive working-class contribution to Western civilization. Raymond Williams has argued that it is mistaken to define working-class culture by reference to pastimes and recreations — pigeon fancying, whippet racing, brass bands, etc. In his view, the key lies in the notion of working-class solidarity which gave birth to that complex of political, economic and educational institutions which constitute 'the Labour Movement': but *solidarity*, not that amiable sociability which is popularly supposed to characterize working-class culture. It is, indeed, odd that anyone who (in Jackson's own phrase) is impressed with 'the fact that industrial workers over ten generations made so much out of such squalor and indignity' should see the acme of working-class culture in brass bands, beer cooperatives and jazz clubs, exciting as these may be as recreations and pastimes. And in the search for miracles it is surprising that Jackson ignores what Thompson (1968 : 13) has called 'the agency of working people, the degree to which they contributed by conscious efforts to the making of history.' The class consciousness which Thompson discerned as the outcome of 'the making of the English working class' was, above all, a political consciousness; 'consciousness of their interests and of their predicaments as a class' which, in the century following the period covered by Thompson's study, forged the institutions of the Labour Movement. Hurt argues (1972 : 13-14) that the very coinage of the term 'working class' was to substitute an active, positive conception of class for the connotations of patient, uncomplaining deference and acceptance of the *status quo* implied in earlier notions like 'the lower orders' and 'the poor'. In view of the historical evidence of an active working class in pursuit of political rights and economic amelioration, it is interesting that Jackson should see nothing incongruous in the fact that his search for the source and inspiration of working-class leadership should merely take him into social clubs, sporting clubs and brass band contests, and nowhere near political parties, trade union branches or WEA classes. Perhaps such a search would discover only empty halls, evidence of a heroic working class in sad decline. But to pretend that thriving recreational associations are the 'bounty' from a 'wretched industrial past' which 'could give the lead in the quality of living possible within the new urban life' (Jackson 1968 : Ch.11) is to make light of the social, economic and political problems facing modern urban societies.

Although he does not trivialize working-class culture in the fashion of Midwinter or Jackson, Hoggart's richer and more comprehensive account of working-class life also neglects its political culture. With a wealth of concrete detail, Hoggart does evoke working-class life at its grass roots, in the vivid metaphorical tone of its speech, its entertainments, its rituals associated with birth, marriage and death, illness and misfortune. But his account is also curiously lacking with reference to working-class political perceptions. In his conclusion, some half-dozen pages are devoted to acknowledgement of what he calls the 'earnest minority' or the 'saving remnant' which is to be found active in trade unions, political parties or adult education. It is also interesting that this brusque dismissal of the active minority is lacking the concrete texture of the remainder of the book; the 'earnest minority' remains an abstraction. To be sure, Hoggart does conclude that 'it is difficult to overstress the importance to a society of people like this', but it is difficult to grasp what this importance might be if it is not in some interaction with the majority. Yet Hoggart cautions circumspection in reading working-class histories which implies that the activities of minorities are characteristic of an entire class. For him, since this minority 'would be exceptional in any class, they reveal less about their class than about themselves'.

Hoggart is taking the view, which others have held in relation to working-class participation in culture (C3), that unless the majority of a class is involved in a particular activity it is inappropriate to include such activity in accounts of the culture of that class (A.E. Green quoted in Elbourne 1974). Yet, as a cultural phenomenon, it is odd if the working-class movement has to be excluded from an account of working-class culture. To bring it within such a description there are two possibilities. One could attempt to show a larger participation in the working-class movement than is allowed by terms like 'earnest minority' or 'saving remnant'. Or one might argue that notwithstanding its active pursuit only by a minority, an activity has such repercussions upon the perceptions of the majority that it can properly be categorized as an aspect of the culture of an entire class.

To take this second point first: one account which sets the political culture at the centre of working-class culture is Thompson's *The Making of the English Working Class* (1968). Thompson defines class as what happens 'when some men, as a result of common experiences (inherited or shared), feel and articulate the identity of their interests as between themselves, and as against other men whose interests are different from (and usually opposed to) theirs' (p.10). As this kind of psychological phenomenon, 'class is defined by men as they live their own history, and, in the end, this is the only definition' (p.11). But, on Thompson's account of it, this self-definition of the working class is not in terms of a peculiar complex of recreations and pastimes (C4), nor in terms of folk art (C3), nor as the kind of cultural totality which Hoggart describes, characterized by fatalism, 'the lack in most people of any feeling that some change can, or indeed ought to be, made in the general pattern of life' (1968 : 70). The class consciousness of which Thompson writes is 'embodied in traditions, value-systems, ideas and institutional forms' as the cultural expression of 'the productive relations into which men are born'. That is, working-class culture is an aspect of political economy; the making of the working class is in its political response to economic exploitation: 'Thus working men formed a picture of the organization of society, out of their own experience and with the help of their hard-won and erratic education, which was above all a political picture' (p.792). And, in contrast with the view that fatalism is the characteristic working-class response to the facts of the social universe, Thompson sees working-class consciousness in more dynamic terms. He insists on the importance of *making* because his is the account of 'an active process, which owes as much to agency as conditioning'. The working class 'contributed by conscious efforts to the making of history'. Moreover, these conscious efforts were political initiatives: working-class consciousness is, above all, political consciousness, 'consciousness of their interests and of their predicaments as a class', which issued in political and economic institutions — trade unions, consumer cooperatives, friendly societies and political movements — that complex of sects which ultimately chrystallized into the Labour Party. On the view that the distinctive consciousness of a class is manifest in the institutions it creates and sustains to further its interests and resolve its predicaments, it is difficult to see how any plausible account of working-class culture can assign to the Labour Movement anything but a central position.

From the point of view of a modern curriculum which attempts to relate to working-class culture, Thompson's account may seem so remotely historical as to be of only academic interest. Arguably, how the working class was *made* a century and a half ago has little relevance for the working class today. For on one interpretation, its classic institutions are either in sad decline or their continued existence is a threat to modern social needs: the cooperative movement is but a shadow of its heyday, friendly societies seem redundant in the Welfare State, and trade unions, once a necessary instrument for defence of the standard of life, now threaten to grind economies to a standstill. Whatever one's response to this last judgement, it is probably true that these working-class institutions are not what they were. However, especially from an educational point of view, a vital part of any culture is its history. In the United States it is increasingly taken for granted that the necessary development of a positive self-concept by disadvantaged Blacks requires reference to Black history, not only in the Americas, but also in its African origins. In this connection, whatever its factual accuracy, Alex Haley's *Roots* has become a potent cultural symbol in the mid-1970s. Similarly, the history of the working class seems a necessary point of reference in a curriculum devised to develop human initiatives towards the resolution of our contemporary working-class predicaments. For although nineteenth-century working-class institutions may be obsolete and irrelevant to late twentieth-century needs, it is not clear how modern disadvantaged groups could liberate themselves without similar, if different, socio-political initiatives. Political knowledge of this sort is clearly seen as a necessary curricular component by some advocates of Black libera-tion for example (Seasholes 1965).

However, with reference to the first question posed above ('How far is working-class political culture a minority preoccupation?') the history of the working class is problematic. In the later edition of his book, Thompson acknowledges critical response to his thesis that hundreds of thousands, not minorities, were involved. Against the criticism that he attributes 'to the apathetic and silent masses those views that only some of the minority are demonstrated to have held', he adduces evidence to the contrary. He claims 'massive support' for their leaders at the peaks of political agitation: 'not scores, but hundreds and sometimes thousands were prepared to walk many miles to hear an orator' (1968 : 936). But, as Thompson also insists, questions about the magnitude of political participation cannot be resolved merely by counting those who hold 'some card-of-member-ship of a class' (1968 : 937). With reference to the political culture, as with the arts, it is necessary to make distinctions (elaborated below) between different kinds of relationship to cultural artefacts, distinc-tions implied in the categories of creator, critic and appreciator or spectator. Just as readers and listeners are multitudes by comparison with the few who are authors or composers, so are the activities of voting and conversation about politics widespread in relation to the minority who generate political theories or actively seek political office. But this is true of any social class and it does not give any warrant for concluding that the majority is politically apathetic or its culture bereft of political interest. The term 'silent majority' was coined precisely to make the point that it is not an *indifferent* majority. From a childhood roughly concurrent with Hoggart's and separated geographically only by the Pennines, his account evokes sympathetic memories; but although one's parents and relatives were anything but members of his 'earnest minority' (as defined by participation in adult education or active membership of trade unions or the Labour Party), conversation about politics was far from infrequent. Voting in local and national elections was discussed in terms of what the various candidates had done with respect to the social and economic predicaments of a working-class family in the 1930s, and it is difficult to recall the near universal political fatalism assumed by Hoggart. Indeed, his concession that the political activity of the minority has 'valuable consequences for almost every member of the working class' must require that there be more of interest and support from the majority than that it is just prepared to benefit from the social change engineered by a minority whilst seeking diversion from the circuses of popular culture. Hoggart concluded that 'people are not living lives which are imaginatively as poor as a mere reading of their literature would suggest'. But nor is their culture as bereft of political interest and commitment as his own account would have us believe.

If the totality (C1) of working-class culture includes a political culture in the sense required by Thompson, how is this component to be characterized with reference the categories C2, C3 and C4? Although the working-class political culture has elements of art and recreation (folk song associated with work and protest, for example, and the rituals and recreations of the miners' galas) it is obviously neither a manifestation of C3 nor C4. Nor, at first sight, does it seem to be an aspect of C2, especially of C2n, the best that has been thought and said, since it is often argued that the Labour Movement is essentially a practical phenomenon, largely devoid of theory. Either it is attributable to a further cultural category, or C2 requires some redefinition in order to accommodate it. Superficially, characterization of C2 as the arts, sciences and philosophy would seem to exclude the *practice* of politics. No doubt political theory is part of culture in this sense. But whatever theoretical underpinning the Labour Movement has (in abstract theories of socialism, equality, etc.) seems to be the creation of middle-class intellectuals (Kautsky quoted in Parkin 1972 : 101; see also 61):

> The vehicle of science is not the proletariat, but the *bourgeois intelligentsia*: it was in the minds of individual members of this stratum that modern socialism originated, and it was they who communicated it to the more intellectually developed proletarians who, in their turn, introduce it into the proletarian class struggle

where conditions allow that to be done. Thus, socialist consciousness is something introduced into the class struggle from without and not something that arose in it spontaneously.

This is to claim that the working class has not contributed to culture through reasoned and systematic analysis of social institutions.

But perhaps culture in the sense of C2 can be widened to include not merely the theoretical mode, but also practical responses to the environment. Though it has been criticized for its exclusive literary, non-practical tone, Arnold himself insisted that his notion of the best culture was a 'social idea' (1960 : 70). Culture was to be the remedy for anarchy: it had a 'special utility for the circumstances in which we find ourselves, and the confusion which environs us. Through culture seems to be our way, not only to perfection, but even to safety' (Arnold 1960 : 202). Culture was, ultimately, for action, 'to get men to allow their thought and consciousness to play on their stock notions and habits disinterestedly and freely; to get men to try, in preference to staunchly acting with imperfect knowledge, to obtain some sounder basis of knowledge on which to act' (Arnold 1960 : 205-6). Though Arnold went on to hope that the inspiration of culture would be towards less action, in the interests of less confused action, his formulation of the relationship between culture and action foreshadows recent revival of the notion of *praxis*. Through culture, he hoped for a fusing of Hebraism and Hellenism: Hebraism, the energetic driving at practice; Hellenism, the tendency towards reflection. Arnold saw the two more often than not presented as opposites and incompatible (1960 : 207): the task of culture was to see that these, 'man's two great natural forces ... will no longer be dissociated and rival, but will be a joint force of right thinking and strong doing to carry him on towards perfection'. No doubt modern praxical theorists take a more radical view of the social change required for human perfection than did Arnold, but *praxis*, the notion of theory fused with practice, is clearly implicit in his formulation of the relationship between culture and action.[5]

The notion of *praxis*, then, points to the reformulation of the conception of culture (C2n) as the best that has been thought, said and *done*, where what is done is the dialectical outcome of a juxtaposition of 'the predicament' with some conception of the good life.

Thompson argues that the radical political culture of the early nineteenth century, out of which working-class consciousness and its political initiatives (its *praxis*) were forged, was an intellectual culture (1968 : 781-820). More, it was a literary culture. On the one hand, working-class autodidacts put their literacy to work in study of mainstream Western culture, especially its political philosophy. On the other hand, there was literature addressed to the worker himself in radical newspapers and pamphlets, of which the *Black Dwarf*, the *Republican* and Cobbett's *Register* are the best known examples. Thompson claims that Cobbett created a radical intellectual culture in producing 'imaginative writing of genius ... part of the English political tradition', prose that is 'more than polemic: it is also political theory'. Thompson is also clear about Cobbett's limitations. As theory, his was 'ephemeral political writing', not, perhaps, literature to be relished in tranquility a century later. Its importance lay in its contribution to *praxis*; it 'nourished the culture of a class' and, with other radical literature, it generated working-class political activity in pursuit of working-class betterment (Thompson 1968 : 820-37).

Our conclusion is that working-class culture, as a political culture, is intimately related to C2n. It is nourished by mainstream Western culture, and it is the best expression in thought, word and action of aspirations of the disadvantaged towards the good life. In terms of the three tasks already outlined in order to give curricular expression to an educationally relevant, normative conception of culture, the history and present preoccupations of the Labour Movement seem a necessary point of reference in order to concretize the principles and modes of social action available to the disadvantaged. The third of our suggested tasks is also relevant here. Does this distinctively political culture have any relevance for the cultural mainstream, and as a contribution towards a common curriculum?

Working-class culture and the cultural mainstream

In earlier dismissing the notion that working-class culture can be sensibly circumscribed in isolation from the cultural mainstream, it was suggested that sub-cultures are more profitably seen as overlapping in areas of common culture. This area of shared culture is variously referred to as the central or dominant culture, or the cultural mainstream. The idea of a cultural mainstream suggests the possibility of tributary cultures, both feeding the mainstream and existing as currents mingled within it. The alternative formulation with reference to cultural centres and peripheries allows for a geometrical representation of cultural overlap as in the accompanying diagrams. Diagram (a) is an attempt to draw a cultural map

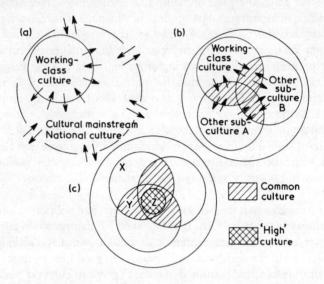

Fig. 4.1 *Working-class culture in relation to common culture, mainstream culture, high culture*

which indicates the relationship of working-class (or any other) culture to the cultural centre or mainstream, whether this is conceived as a national culture or, more widely, as Western culture. (The bi-directional arrows of the gaps in the outer circle represent the relationship of a national culture to mainstream Western culture for example.)

Diagram (b) points to the considerable and growing overlap with other sub-cultures. This overlap may be understood as constituting the common culture.

If only at the level of daily life in the market place there is common involvement in large numbers of economic, social and political institutions. One of the problems which is raised both by emphasis upon the exclusiveness of different sub-cultures, and discontinuity of meanings between different social groups, is the denial of the possibility of a common life, and of the interdependence of individuals and groups within the community. Any conception of community which transcends the small locality requires some conception of a common culture. Those ideologies which emphasize the desirability of classlessness take it as axiomatic that the quality of life would be improved if the conflicts which seem implicit in class differences were replaced by cooperation arising out of recognition of the common human attributes which individuals or groups share. And even if one is sceptical about the possibility of disinterested dissolution of sectional interests into common interests, prudence at least would seem to call for recognition that without shared meanings about large areas of experience, social life would be impossible. Indeed, the explicit assumptions by conservative educationists about the impossibility of shared meanings between groups ignores the sense in which the existing social hegemony depends upon acceptance of the notion of common interests across social groupings. But even aside from this kind of ideological point, it is evident that daily life in the market place depends upon common acceptance of conventions and institutions of many kinds. There we exchange the products of our work and, however tacitly, subscribe to an ethic which takes for granted a responsibility to those who consume the goods and services we make. The conventions of measurements are shared in common (monetary, weight, length, time, etc.). The law is commonly understood and largely accepted across social class, as are the moral norms which give the law its acceptance. Much the same is true of the political culture, especially with reference to electoral practices, public finance (taxation) and so on. There are common emotional dispositions which make appeals to patriotism possible and which, at times of external threat, are an impetus towards the closing of class ranks in the name of national unity. Thus, over a wide range of human activity there is widely understood everyday knowledge which is the necessary basis of life in the community for individuals and groups with differing interests and talents in other respects.

Moreover, it is arguable that the area of overlap representing the common culture is a growing phenomenon. The bi-directional arrows of diagram (b) illustrate this trend towards 'normative convergence' which seems evident in the apparently contradictory thrusts towards bourgeoisification and proletarianization (Goldthorpe *et al.*

1969 : Vol.III, 163). Bourgeoisification of the working class is the more familiar notion.[7] The twin effects of affluence and technological change seem to make for the withering of the working class. Growing affluence encourages the adoption of a middle-class life-style as measured by the increase in working-class ownership of houses and of consumer durables (especially cars) which, a quarter-century ago, were beyond the reach of most working-class families. It seems that supermarkets are full of people buying foods which only the rich could once afford: with reference to patterns of consumption it certainly does look as though 'we are all middle-class now'. It is this sort of apparent identity of consumer habits across social class which probably accounts for American claims that the notion of a working class no longer has any relevance in the United States.

However, this assumption of working-class bourgeoisification is frequently questioned by industrial sociologists who point to the persistence of political radicalism and support of trade unions amongst affluent workers, and argue that beneath the economic veneer of affluence there has been no value shift which would indicate the erosion of the working class (Goldthorpe *et al.* 1969 : Vol.III, 162):

> We must be sceptical of the reliance that is placed on rising affluence, advances in technical knowledge in industry and changing patterns of urban residence as forces likely in themselves to bring about a radical restructuring of the stratification hierarchy. [8]

This rejection of the bourgeoisification thesis is based upon the assumption that the essence of working-class culture lies in working-class solidarity and the persistence of those institutions of a distinctive economic and political kind which have been its outcome. The strength of the Labour Movement seems undiminished and working-class culture conceived *as* the Labour Movement flourishes, even it sometimes seems *because of* affluence.

Paradoxically, however, it is arguable that the withering of class is also implicit in the counter-process, the proletarianization of the middle class, through the tendency of the middle classes to assimilate the economic, political and educational institutions of the Labour Movement. Shorter (1973 : 24) notes the growing tendency of white-collar workers 'to forge themselves militant labour unions, along the lines of industrial worker unions'.[9] In Britain there is the growing phenomenon of professional and proto-professional groups seeking affiliation to the Trades Union Congress. In 1976, the decision of the Association of University Teachers to affiliate to the TUC prompted discussion of whether university professors can properly be regarded as working class. This movement of professional groups towards affiliation with an organization traditionally the preserve of blue-collar, manual workers has encountered resistance within these professions precisely because it appears to subject to the norms of the industrial working class, occupations which it is believed cannot properly be conducted under conditions of industrialism. Eric Ashby has argued (1976) that university teachers are not employees but, by royal charter, 'members of the university'. He finds the functions of the AUT and of the TUC incompatible, the former concerned with academics' responsibilities to their students, to their peers within the same discipline and to 'the guild which is the university they serve'. By contrast, he sees the TUC concerned with pay, pensions and working conditions, with rights rather than responsibilities.[10]

Proletarianization is also implicit in middle-class infiltration of the Labour Party and its participation in the institutions of the Welfare State. The degree of middle-class takeover can be seen in the recent composition of Labour Cabinets, now drawn almost entirely from those with a university education and in professional rather than manual occupations. Similarly, there is a declining percentage of Labour MPs who can be designated 'rank and file' workers, and an increase in those who are professional workers, especially in the period 1935-51.[11] A similar trend is also discernable in the staffing of Trade Union administrations. The Vice-Chancellor of the University of Warwick is reported as claiming that 'trade union head offices would be wholly populated by Warwick graduates in the 1980s'.[12] Of course, it is arguable that the virtual middle-class takeover of the Labour Party constitutes not so much the proletarianization of the middle class as the bourgeoisification of the Labour Party. On this view, the affluent worker's continued support of Labour would only underline his bourgeoisification, not the persistence of working-class consciousness. Nevertheless, the Labour Party remains committed to support and extension of the Welfare State. And whilst supposedly hostile to the erosion of individual initiatives by socialized public services, the middle class itself is a significant beneficiary of the

Welfare State. Indeed, it was his assumption that the middle class exploits public educational provision (for example, through its over-representation in higher educational institutions) at the expense of the poor which constituted Illich's most cogent advocacy of de-schooling (1971).[13] Moreover, the new middle class which has emerged as a consequence of the continuing shift from industrial to service occupations and the enlargement of the traditional profes-sions is substantially dependent upon salaries from occupations remunerated through taxation revenue. We argued above that as against fee earners and those whose salary derives from private industry, these professionals and para-professionals in the public service have a vested interest in the maintenance and growth of the public sector, the Welfare State and 'socialist' forms of employment (see Ch.2). The middle class has also had a tendency to take over educational institutions designed for the working class, from the Mechanics' Institutes of the nineteenth century, through the Workers' Educational Association of the early twentieth, to the Open University, a creation of the Labour administration of the mid-1960s as a second-chance institution for the working class, but largely enrolling middle-class students (Draffan 1973).

The bi-directional arrows of diagram (b) represent, amongst other aspects of cultural cross-fertilization, these contrary processes of bourgeoisification and proletarianization. From the point of view of the working class, the proletarianization of other classes represents its most important contribution to the cultural mainstream.

One further distinction is of importance in attempting to assess the nature of working-class culture and its relationship to the cultural mainstream. Any discussion of culture in class terms and with reference to cultural overlap has to mark a distinction between objective and subjective conceptions of culture. In sociological theory, culture is conceived objectively as a totality of artefacts and values 'out there', as in the notions 'Western culture', 'high culture', 'working-class culture'. The familiar anthropological con-ception of culture (C1 — as well as the totalities C2 to C4) is an objective view of culture in this sense. But, subjectively, we also speak of personal culture, having reference to that part of the totality which a single individual internalizes. In this sense, cultural horizons or boundaries differ between individuals and no two people, even from the same social class or family, will have identical cultural perspectives. This is as true of members of the working class as any other group. Subjectively, therefore, with reference to individual or personal culture, to say that a person is a member of the working class does not comprehensively define what his personal culture complex will be. Diagram (c) (where 'high culture' has been represented within the common overlap of all sub-cultures) indicates possible locations of members of the working class from this subjective point of view. Person X is in such a marginal position that he participates hardly at all in the central or dominant culture: life in the so-called cultures of poverty seems to have this very marginal relationship to anything which could be described as a common culture. On the other hand, person Z is centrally located such that he participates fully in the high culture. Social and educational history is full of examples of working-class intellectuals (often autodidacts) utterly committed to the kind of cultural activity which is usually encapsulated within the notion of high culture. The curricula of distinctively working-class adult schools rarely consisted of something which could be described as working-class culture or 'a culture of the folk'. The curriculum of Chartist schools, for example, was devoted to 'the knowledge of the time', including the work of Shakespeare, Milton, Byron, Shelley, Keats, Spencer, Hume, Gibbon, Rousseau, Voltaire; working men devoted their spare time to learning Latin, Hebrew and Greek, science, political economy, philosophy and history.[14] In taking the mainstream culture as its educational point of reference, the working class has been partly in pursuit of distinctively working-class aims — knowledge of those institutions which were the instruments of its exploitation, and knowledge and skill appropriate to the creation of counter-institutions for its own economic amelioration and political liberation. But part of its aim was also the pursuit of personal culture and enrichment. A recent study of Lancashire weavers in the nineteenth century has found them performing the works of Haydn, Mozart, Handel and Beethoven (Elbourne 1974). As Thomas Burt, the first Labour MP, insisted (quoted in Simon 1960 : Vol.I, 367): 'We say educate a man not simply because he has got political power, and simply to make him a good workman; but educate him because he is a man.' In passing, and with reference to the notion that the school should be regarded as an instrument of social change, it is interesting that political education for the working class has largely been a function of adult education. Whatever the contribution of schooling to 'political literacy', it is likely that one only ultimately learns to speak the language of politics, as an adult, when functioning maturely in a socio-economic role.

It seems that in the subjective sense of culture, the culture of working people often cannot be defined without reference to the high culture; and, paradoxically, to include the high culture in working-class culture (as defined by what some working people may enjoy) is to de-classify it. But not quite: commenting on the Lancashire weavers described by Elbourne, Martin described them as participating in the high culture of Salzburg and Esterhazy (1975). Elbourne's riposte was (1975): 'This area of Lancashire produced what might almost be called "popular art music" '.[15] The Larks of Dean played and sang established art composition but with a make-shift approach and enthusiasm far removed from "the high culture of Salzburg and Esterhazy". This implies that singing the Messiah in Huddersfield is not quite the same as singing it in Salzburg. It means something different, as a reading of any of the items in the above list of cultural works may mean something different to members of the working class. This raises a point which is sometimes made against the notion that a common curriculum in the school can open the way to a common culture. That is, even where different people seem to be attending to the same object, they inevitably invest it with a different meaning such that it functions as a different object. In a sense this is an obvious point, as we have just argued with reference to the notion of personal culture. The call to individualize instruction stems, in part, from a recognition that no two learners (however similar they appear in terms of their interests, intelligence, social background) have similar life histories; hence, their perceptions of objects will be dissimilar, however slightly. But opponents of the notion of a common culture believe that whilst, on the whole, people similarly circumstanced will attach common meanings to the same cultural artefact, marked differences in intelligence or in social perspective will call forth different perceptions of things. The next chapter examines criticism of the common curriculum from this point of view and attempts to relate the notion of high culture to common everyday experience.

5

Culture and
the curriculum

Common culture and the curriculum

With the growing persistence of demands for a common curriculum
within the framework of the comprehensive school, the claims of a
gifted minority are also vigorously promoted as part of the educational dialectic. For however adventitiously, as Vaizey observes (1975
: 123), there is the belief (noted in Ch. 1) that comprehensive schools
should promote a less intellectually oriented curriculum since
'academic education in itself is anti-egalitarian and, therefore, the
comprehensive school ought not to be particularly attached to
academic values'. It is this kind of assumption which prompts
objection to notions of a common culture from educationists who
believe that the quality of a civilization derives from its high culture
— culture in Arnold's sense of 'the best that has been thought and
said in the world' (C2n). It is in its threat to the integrity of this best
culture that a common culture seems undesirable. It is taken for
granted that a common culture must refer to the lowest common
denominator of intelligence and taste. On this view, logically, the
only common meaning which could attach to a cultural artefact

would be folly, not wisdom, though it is also usually taken for granted that whilst the foolish cannot understand the wisdom of the wise, the contrary is not the case.

Hence, opposition to the notion of a comprehensive school's transmitting a common culture comes from those who see in it inevitable implications of anti-intellectualism and philistinism. If the common culture is something which is to be shared in every respect by everyone, then the content of such a culture (and its related curriculum) can only be at a very modest intellectual level. As James, a persistent critic of comprehensive schooling has put it, the notion of a common culture which unites carpenters, factory workers, bishops, lawyers, doctors, sales managers, professors and garage mechanics 'rests either on an over optimistic belief in the educability of the majority that is certainly not justified by experience or on a willingness to surrender the highest standards of taste and judgement to the incessant demands of mediocrity' (1951 : 106). Implicit in this quotation is the assumption that it is democratization of education — in the sense that equality of cultural outcomes is sought through a compulsory common curriculum — which threatens civilization. This is to believe that only a minority has the capacity for becoming cultured in our sense of C2n. We have already discussed Bantock's repeated polemic in this strain through his affirmation that 'the wise man and the fool see not the same tree'. He stands in a tradition of literary critics and educationists who have questioned the wisdom of a democratization of culture. Leavis, one of the better known of these, is categorical about the cultural disintegration entailed by making it widely available (1930): 'It is impossible to question the clear fact; only a minority is capable of advanced intellectual culture ... It is disastrous to let a country's educational arrangements be determined, or even be affected, by the assumption that a high intellectual standard can be attained by more than a small minority'. A common culture, then, is seen as a debased culture, inevitably at odds with culture conceived as 'the best' of which human creativity and ingenuity is capable.

The debasement appears twofold. Corruption of the existing cultural stock is assumed to be a consequence of its popularization. Coleridge argued that the attempt to popularize science would only result in 'plebification' (in Kirk 1973 : 146). Bantock (1976) argues that Deweyan cultural collectivism represents a form of 'regression from full cultural maturity' and that 'the assimilation of high and popular culture (the latter largely based on the findings of the media)' leads to 'manifestations of "élite" avant-gardism', again a pejorative judgement. But not only is corruption of existing culture threatened by the search for common meanings; the conservative case is that there is also a danger that future cultural creativity will be condemned to mediocrity. In part this is fear of the operation of a cultural Gresham's Law; that is, that the mediocre will drive out the best culture because a majority of people lack the intellectual capacity for understanding it. But there is also the assumption that, as Plato held, the intellect is threatened by the appetites (MacIntyre 1970 : 44, summarizing Freud):

> Civilization is founded on this very process of repression. It is by an ascetic renunciation of instinctual pleasures that the libido is made available in sublimated forms for the task of creating high culture. Only a minority élite are able to engage in those tasks. Were they to lose this control of the social order the blind instinctual passions of the masses would destroy civilization.

To these psychological arguments that high culture is inconsistent with the democratic conception of culture as a common heritage, there is sometimes added a sociological point. Even if its preservation and renewal did not require high intelligence or capacity for emotional discipline, high culture requires the existence of a leisured class, 'certain sophisticated social groups who lift themselves beyond the immediate cares and pressures of everyday life in order to contemplate the deeper realities of human existence' (Bantock 1963 : 23).[2]

The psychological and sociological arguments about the inevitable minority reference of culture fuse, especially when one thinks in terms of the *creation* of cultural artefacts and values. Indeed, the minority argument is more cogent when we move from the area of understanding to that of creation. It does seem true that civilized culture (C2n and C3n) is the product of a small minority blessed with creativity. From this evident truth it is then argued that unless this minority is nurtured in conditions where high ability is recognized and stimulated by a curriculum which would be beyond the comprehension of most children in schools, the continued vitality of our culture is threatened. A number of points are relevant in evaluating this point of view.

It is, indeed, difficult to conceive of seminal work in modern science and mathematics which did not grow out of formal training in a school of mathematics or science. And whilst the early technologists of industrialism were sometimes ill-educated, even illiterate, in the age of cybernetic and electronic technology, an academic grounding would also seem imperative for the creative technologist. But creative activity in the arts seems another matter. It is by no means clear that this is always or even frequently nurtured by a school curriculum focused upon conventional disciplines. An honours degree in English is not obviously the best preparation for the novelist, poet or dramatist: it is interesting that Auden took 'the function of the Honours school of English language and literature [to be] to train future teachers of English for all levels from elementary school to university' — not, that is, to train poets (Entwistle 1970b : 28).

A second reason for calling in question the value of segregated academic schooling for the creative person has reference to the fact that in those areas of culture with a distinctively human reference, it is not clear that anything seminal could be created without knowledge of and reference to the mainstream of life. Philosophers of the stature of Kant, Hume, Locke and Marx have taken the view that their work would be pointless if not capable of being understood by the public at large, and Bernard Crick has recently noted (1975 : 154-5) that Rawls's theory of justice hinges upon the commonly understood notion of fairness.[3] This would seem to imply that major philosophers have themselves accepted a need for understanding of the common life in the mainstream of civilization. Indeed, it is not clear what would be the point of defending civilization if it were not, in some sense, the concern of the entire community. For nothing follows for civilization or education (except, perhaps, decadence) from the spectre of an exclusive coterie cultivating each other, whilst the rest of us is distracted by a culture of the folk. The notion of saving civilization through an educationally and socially privileged minority would only make sense if, in some way, everyone would suffer from its destruction. Leavis (1930) seems to imply this universal relevance of a minority culture when he writes, 'upon this minority depends our power of profiting by the finest human experience of the past'. Implicitly, we, the crowd, benefit from them, the minority. But if this is the justification of minority privilege, it needs to be made explicit how the majority benefits from the civilization which only a minority can understand and defend. Either this would be through a demonstration that the majority *recognizes* the benefits of civilization, a conclusion surely entailing some notion of a common culture; or one needs to be shown how the majority just does benefit, in ignorance, without either contributing to civilization or understanding what it is. This second possibility seems highly implausible, not promising very much for the health of civilization. But, in fact, Western civilization (i.e. Western culture in our sense of C2n) has always been a search for the best possible articulation of 'meanings' in relation to the common life: 'the best that has been thought and said' was (as Arnold himself made clear in *Culture and Anarchy*)[4] articulated in exploration of the meanings of daily social experience. Western civilization cannot mean the support of a cultivated élite for its own (or culture's or civilization's) sake. That kind of self-indulgence is itself corrupting of culture: there is something effete, if not corrupt, about a 'best' culture which is there merely for the private edification of the few who contrive, through their manipulation of the educational system, to keep it to themselves. The only valid defence of a minority charged with the responsibility of being creative and enjoying privileged educational provision at public expense, is that the minority creates and defends cultural values on behalf of all, including future generations. In this sense, at least, culture is a common possession. Even on prudential grounds, the integrity of the high culture hardly seems likely to be successfully maintained so long as it remains the possession of a minority under siege. In some sense, the majority must understand and value high culture if the 'halls of culture' (libraries, museums, galleries, concert halls, universities) are to be maintained by subsidy from the public purse. It is no doubt possible to envisage an exclusive minority simply 'talking' to itself, without threat to its own position and without consequences for the rest of us, the folk, in pursuit of our utterly different concerns with art and recreation (C3 and C4) at a quite unrelated level. But outside the library or study, and away from the concert hall or picture gallery, the folk stand in the market place at least as an irritant, if not as a threat to the clerisy: unless, that is, we have a notion of common citizenship which makes it impossible to ignore the imperatives of a common culture if only with reference to the necessary relationships between individuals from different social groups. Hence, a sense of common culture (and its curricular implications) needs exploration which is relevant to notions like citizenship, civility, everyday life and knowledge. In this context one cannot escape consideration of shared values, experiences, artefacts and the common meaning which has to be attached to these. This is especially true with regard to moral issues as James recognized, notwithstanding his rejection of the possibility of a common culture (1951 : 111). In crucial areas of human interaction we take it for granted that standards of morality, judgement and social responsibility will be widely accepted and understood by the majority of people.

This is to say that failure to recognize the importance of the shared area of daily experience also tends towards a simplistic conception of leadership. English educational theorists committed to minority culture tend to lack any social theory which accounts for the relationship of different groups in society, and, especially, for the role of the minority as leaders, persuaders, teachers, rulers, communicators. James, for example, has written at length about education for leadership. This turns out to be a plea for the schooling of the nation's top people in segregated secondary schools and institutions of higher education. But an adequate theory of leadership would entail both a theory of the nature of those who are followers and some notion of how leaders communicate with followers. Aside from a very derisory view of the ability of the mass, James has no conception of how it might be led — even as sheep. One could understand an élitist conception of leadership which focused upon techniques of manipulation. But James does not even do this. His leaders are simply experts rather than leaders and, typically, these spend a great deal of time bemoaning that their expertise is neither understood nor valued and that the ill-educated and ill-informed mass is disruptive of social order because it fails to understand what is in its own best interests. At the same time, given democrative imperatives, experts are impotent since they have been trained, in isolation, only to speak to one another. So communication is a dialogue of the deaf. And yet, it is important to stress, this very impotence is a consequence of the ideology of leadership which underpins a segregated school system.

Given the assumption that, in some sense, leadership requires communication, it is odd that in discussions of common culture recourse is not had to what is evidently a simple fact of life in relation to created artefacts. It may always be true that the creators of culturally valuable artefacts are a small minority, but those who are destined to appreciate the work of others are legion in comparison with those who will be innovative in any field of human endeavour, and the somewhat larger number who are trained as critics or performers in the arts and in those corresponding interpretative roles in the sciences. This suggests the need for a stance in relation to culture which distinguishes the categories 'creative', 'interpretative' and 'appreciative'. In relation to cultural objects there are the creators — writers, composers, dramatists, painters, philosophers and scientists. Presumably one dimension of understanding which is exclusive to these innovators is the knowledge (however tacit) of what it means to be creative; what the creation of a particular kind of artefact requires in terms of experience, discipline, knowledge, skill and even drudgery. Secondly, there are interpreters: performers (actors, musicians, dancers); critics, not only in relation to the arts, but also to philosophy and science; teachers also fall into this category, their characteristic grasp of an aspect of the culture being partly critical, partly in terms of what it means to communicate the culture to learners at different levels of maturity. Thirdly, in a sense not entailed by the activities of creation or interpretation, there are appreciators — readers (including the readers of criticism), listeners, spectators. This category is compounded of those whose appreciation is informed by some technical knowledge and those whose stance is simply aesthetic, those, for example, who can enjoy music but can neither play an instrument nor read a score. And as well as there being different levels of appreciation, depending upon having or lacking technical knowledge, appreciation depends upon intensity of interest and, perhaps, upon differential intellectual or emotional capacity. Gramsci calls attention to a familiar, minimal sense of appreciation represented by the ability to follow an argument without being able to reproduce it: the man of the people, he argued, 'has no concrete memory of the reasons (i.e. for accepting a conclusion) and could not reproduce them, but he knows that reasons exist, because he has heard them expounded, and was convinced by them' (1971 : 339). Ayer noted that this kind of experience is not unfamiliar in academic life when an argument is accepted as valid on the authority of one's peers, which one follows but has not the technical resources to verify in detail (1956 : 39). A similar kind of distinction can obviously be employed to distinguish between the creation of an artefact and its use: one can make use of a map without knowing anything of the principles and procedures which the cartographer employs in mapping a terrain.

In terms of this spectrum from creativity through to simple appreciation, it is by no means clear that the highly intelligent and well educated must always be located at the innovative pole, even with respect to an area in which they are specialized or trained. Evidently many of the products of privileged schooling display a penchant for convergent thinking and the implications of this for their influence upon the creation and conservation of the culture is by no means clear.

So far two considerations have been presented which point to the desirability of searching for common cultural experiences as the basis for a common curriculum: the large area of experience members of a community share within the marketplace and as citizens; and the fact that different levels of understanding of cultural artefacts are implied in the distinctions just drawn between those who create and those who interpret their creations or simply understand at the various levels of appreciation. Thus, there is a central area of culture whose assimilation is universally necessary if any meaning is to be attached at all to notions of community or citizenship and, with reference to any particular cultural artefact, there is inevitably a wide range of understanding attaching to different roles we occupy as creators, interpreters or spectators.

However, one has little difficulty in agreeing that the notion of a common culture is educationally inappropriate if this means that every student in every grade has to be brought to exactly the same level of understanding of everything that is taught. One does not have to distinguish between students in terms of social class, or with reference to intellectual categories like gifted, able, average, dull or stupid, in order to conclude that the realities of the educational process require that teachers should discriminate amongst students. For example, beyond the required minimum, a university teacher rarely expects all students in a class to read precisely the same texts. Individual students are recommended different reading on the basis of their expressed interests, the difficulties they experience with a particular discipline or aspects of it, and their willingness to read beyond what the course requires. Nor is this fact about differential performance and understanding by university students simply a consequence of the recent expansion of higher education and the possibility that 'more means worse'. Universities have always classified their awards in recognition that differential examination performance means that some students have worked harder, read more, read more perceptively and reached a subtler understanding of the curriculum content. But students differently classified have often followed a common curriculum although, evidently, its meaning has differed between individuals. Disciplines are also studied to varying depth in institutions at different levels within the educational hierarchy. As well as there being university history, physics and French, these things are part of the secondary school curriculum. Yet it is not expected that they will be understood by students at these different levels to the same degree (i.e. have the same meaning), nor by students in different years within the same institution. Thus, it is simply a fact of academic life that similar curriculum content evokes different meanings and different understanding from students at different levels of maturity.

It is also evident that if the notion of a common culture is to remain intact, it must be capable of interpretation in a sense other than that everyone in a community can be, or would want to be, initiated into the total culture. This point has already been made in drawing a distinction between objective and subjective conceptions of culture. But in advanced technological societies, it is not simply that differences in intellectual capacity, emotional disposition, personal interest, talent and taste make for uniquely individual cultural configurations. What has already been said about the educational philosopher's tendency to universalize the concept of education is subject to the proviso that, concretely, education is manifest in '"educated men" with various stresses, various tendencies towards specialization' (Bantock 1963 : 177). The two cultures debate — whatever the validity of the dichotomies upon which it was based — was a reminder that with a high degree of academic and technological specialization, the total high culture itself is not a common property of intellectuals.

Apart from this obvious fact that there will be specialized

individual competencies for vocational reasons, there is nothing undemocratic about the notion of there being minority tastes and interests, provided we acknowledge that the mass-minority distinction (usually words carrying, respectively, pejorative and approving overtones) is not crudely applied to a fixed minority group against the remainder who always and irredeemably constitute the mass. As Williams insists (1961a), who constitutes the mass happens to be a function of where one happens to be standing at a particular time. As Ortega y Gasset put it (1957): 'The minorities are individuals or groups of individuals which are specially qualified. The mass is the assemblage of persons not specially qualified'. But special qualification may refer to a vast range of human accomplishments — literary criticism, teaching philosophy or physics, mountaineering, yoga, judo, pitching a baseball, wine making, rose growing or cultivating prize marrows, writing novels, coarse or fly fishing, breeding whippets or pigeons as well as racehorses, and so on almost indefinitely. Some of the more specially qualified members of society are *amateurs* of various sports and pastimes:

> The phrase 'mass culture' conveys emotional overtones of passivity: it suggests someone eating peanuts at a baseball game, and thereby contrasting himself to someone eating canapés at the opening of a sculpture exhibition. The trouble with this picture is that the former is probably part of a better educated audience, in the sense that he is likely to know more about baseball than his counterpart knows about sculpture.

Frye concludes (1967 : 20, 188): '... in a democracy everybody belongs to some kind of élite, which derives from its social function a particular knowledge or skill that no other group has'. From this point of view it is interesting that Eliot's familiar list of characteristic activities of English culture includes a number which are minority tastes.[5] Only one of them — the music of Elgar — could be considered part of the high minority culture and Elgar even is a man to suit all tastes. His 'Pomp and Circumstance' marches do not attract the same concert audiences as the symphonies, the concertos and the oratorios. Other items in Eliot's list are upper-class minority tastes — Henley, Cowes and the 12th of August — none of them demanding great intellectual subtlety or aesthetic sensibility. And though the 'respectable' classes have an image of the working class perpetually

going to the dogs, those mainly working-class activities in Eliot's list
— the dog races, pin tables, darts — are practised regularly and
skilfully only by minorities.

It is thus a mistake to equate 'minority' with 'highbrow',
'intellectual' or 'cultured' in the senses of C2 and C3 above. Ortega
Y Gasset (1957) further observed that

> the select man is not the petulant person who thinks himself
> superior to the rest, but the man who demands more of himself
> than the rest ... For there is no doubt that the most radical division
> that it is possible to make of humanity is that which splits it into
> two classes of creatures: those who make great demands on them-
> selves, piling up difficulties and duties; and those who demand
> nothing special of themselves, but for whom to live is to be every
> moment what they already are, without imposing upon them-
> selves any effort towards perfection; mere buoys that float on the
> waves.

This is to the point to a mass-minority distinction on grounds other
than those of social class or formal educational achievement. To be a
member of a minority group is to pursue a special interest with as
much commitment as one's ability and circumstances permit.
Lawton argues (1975 : 45) that although some cultural activities may
have an almost exclusive middle-class clientele — opera, for instance
— the majority of middle-class people are no more likely to be
involved in these than the majority of the working class. Indeed, as
minority specialized competencies there are activities which, from
the viewpoint of the initiated, put even the most self-conscious élitist
squarely in the middle of the mass. Jazz, which Bantock took to
characterize a popular culture is, in fact, a minority taste. Indeed,
there are different schools of jazz, some of them quite esoteric, and
their adherents probably regard the cultivated 'highbrow' as no less a
part of the indifferent mass than those in thrall to commercial pop. It
is not only 'highbrow' tastes and interests which are threatened by
the growth of mass media of communication. The tabloid press and
the mass television programmes, so far as these pursue circulation
and ratings by appeal to the lowest common denominator of taste,
constitute a threat to the adequate coverage of minority interests in
things like gardening and 'minor' sports and recreations, no less than
to minority interests in books, music or the theatre.

But Eliot's list also includes mass activities in a sense which is not exclusive of minorities and individuals but comprehends them. A Cup Final, Derby Day and, by extension, a world series, the Olympic Games, a Coronation or Presidential Inauguration, Concorde and its problems are cultural artefacts which command the attention of entire nations. From an obstinate highbrowism some individuals may display no interest in these, but this tells us more about their own cultural limitations than the activities they despise. There is something pathetic about the man who knows every minor Elizabethan poet or composer but who does not know what it is that made Stanley Matthews or Babe Ruth into household names. A popular national event, even a Cup Final or World Series, will evoke appreciation at many different levels. Pace Bantock and Blake, the literary critic and the garbage collector may not be seeing the same game. But if the subtleties of the strategy elude one of them (one won't say which), both are obviously enjoying a common experience. It is not clear why Bantock should want to insist that the conditions for a common culture are not met because the meanings derived from such an experience are not identical. Because an activity has a mass following in appealing to a universal audience, this tells us nothing about its quality or the kind of individual response it might evoke. Nor have we any right to assume, for example, that classical oratorios sung by weavers in Burnley or Huddersfield or miners in Merthyr Tydfil become a trivialized Handel or Mozart, in a way that does not happen when they are performed by choirs drawn from the professional middle class from the Home Counties when they are sung in London's Albert Hall. As Elbourne implies (1974),[6] the former do something with this musical culture which is not in its performances in Salzburg or Esterhazy, but it would be presumptuous to conclude that this transition means that it has become diluted in its performance by singers of an impoverished sensibility, such that the different meanings in the one case are subtle, sensitive and 'educated', in the other superficial or crude.

It is not clear why, because different groups of people may read different meanings into commonly enjoyed activities, one group should be excluded from the possibility of appreciation on its own terms. One might argue, for example, that neither Handel nor Mozart imagined themselves composing for industrial artisans in the North of England and that, therefore, wide dissemination of their works somehow frustrates the artist's intention. But then, nor did Mozart or Handel compose for the modern industrial and commercial middle class, which is largely the concert-going public for their works as performed today. Apart from matters of copyright, an artist has no rights over his works, especially over who has access to them as readers or listeners. To publish means to make one's work publicly available and it is not clear what licence an educationist has to protect an artist from his public. Indeed, it is an odd view of education which is deliberately conceived, thus, in restrictive terms. And discussion of the possibility or desirability of a common culture does not depend upon present facts about the class profile of different cultural activities. The question, rather, is of the possibility of widening access to various cultural artefacts (in relation to conceptions C2n to C4n) and deepening, through schooling, the meanings which people are able to perceive in them. This is not a question of whether schools can *create* a common culture, but whether better educational provision can widen access to the best culture our civilization has to offer. This raises the question of how far the best culture can be equated with 'high culture' and what relevance, if any, this has for common everyday experience.

High culture and the curriculum

It is a frequent criticism of the school curriculum that it is a misconceived attempt to transmit a diluted form of the high culture. This is taken to be the hangover from an earlier age when the school served the distinctive interests of an upper, leisured class: when schooling becomes universal, the curriculum of upper-class secondary schools is taken over wholesale, albeit in a watered down form, and to some educationists the working class 'seems particularly at risk in handling this curriculum which constitutes the former high culture' (Bantock 1976 : 49).[7]

However, it remains an unexamined myth that schools have transmitted a high culture. Part of the difficulty in validating this claim lies in the vagueness of the notion of high culture itself. It is one of those terms which is freely used, but which usually functions as nothing better than a cliché or slogan for polemical purposes. It is rarely defined or given concrete reference; in particular, it is not clear what it is about high culture which makes it high. Usually the reference seems, tacitly, to include the great traditions (in Leavis's sense) of literature, music, painting, sculpture and, perhaps, philosophy. In this sense, high culture has figured hardly at all in the curricula of publicly provided schools. Except for literature (including classical literatures) the high culture of the arts has had only a small place in the curriculum of secondary schools, even of academic secondary schools. In terms of the plastic arts there has been little attention to the great tradition of Western art and much the same has been true of music in the curriculum. From personal experience one knows that it was possible to go through some dozen years of schooling in both English elementary and grammar school without learning (from the school itself) of the existence of Haydn, Mozart, Handel, Beethoven, Tchaikovsky, not to mention less popular composers from the musical high culture. Music was the singing of folk songs, if this is an accurate description of 'Lass of Richmond Hill', 'The British Grenadiers', 'The Harp that once through Tara's Halls', 'Marching through Georgia' and 'Polly Wolly Doodle'. Similarly, pictorial art was drawing still-life objects in perspective (with the occasional 'treat' of painting from the imagination). So far as school was concerned, Michelangelo, Leonardo, Raphael, Hals and the Impressionists were as non-existent as the great composers.

Far from being even a watered down encounter with the high culture as art (C3n), the school curriculum is usually an aggregation of subjects of which only one, the national literature, comes near to fitting this description. If the rest — mathematics, science, history, geography, craft, civics and religious knowledge — are high culture, this must be in a different sense; perhaps in the sense that they are the preoccupation of institutions of higher education. That is, the notion of high culture may be extended to cover the systematized, 'scientific' organization of knowledge as it exists in the product of scholarly research. On this view there are several great traditions (constitutive of what we have called C2n) other than those in the arts, especially literature. High culture then becomes synonymous with intellectual life. But unless we make the kind of assumption to which some élitist educational theory comes perilously close — that intellectualism has no function except as a game played for its own sake — this wider concept of high culture has to be examined for its relationship to the common life. As we hinted earlier, this conception of their work as necessarily related to common experience has been accepted by seminal thinkers in the history of philosophy. It has been especially true of linguistic analytical philosophy which has taken ordinary language as its data on the assumption that, as Austin put it (1970 : 182),

> our common stock of words embodies all the distinctions men have found worth drawing, and the connexions they have found worth making, in the lifetimes of many generations: these surely are likely to be more numerous, more sound, since they have stood up to the long test of the survival of the fittest, and more subtle, at least in all ordinary and reasonably practical matters, than any that you or I are likely to think up in our arm-chairs of an afternoon — the most favoured alternative method.

High culture may not be popular culture in the sense that many people read philosophy and the like, but it has a popular reference in the sense that people are interested in the contributions of 'high' philosophy to the cultural mainstream. Few, other than philosophers (and not all of those), may be interested in the hundreds of pages of subtle nuances by which Rawls legitimizes his principle of justice. But everyone is interested in justice and, in his own way, is capable of arriving at not dissimilar conclusions.

Leading scholars in other disciplines have also made this kind of assumption about the mundane reference of their work. Economists have taken it for granted that fundamental economic principles are few and simple. Addressing fellow economists, Robbins wrote (1949): 'I do think that it is important that we should not undervalue the simpler truths of the subject; they may seem trite and obvious to us, but they are not necessarily so to the rest of the world'. Devons made a similar point when he concluded that as an applied economist he was rarely applying complex theoretical analysis or complicated statistical techniques to the problems on which he was asked for advice (1961):

> In so far as economic theory is useful in enabling us to understand the real world and in helping us to take decisions on policy, it is the simple, most elementary and, in some ways, the most obvious propositions that matter ... Two of the most important sets of theoretical models are those of a price system and those of the relation between income, production, employment and expenditure.

In both of them it is the elementary propositions conveyed by the models that I find relevant and usable.[8]

And Lipsey has concluded (1963): 'At the beginning economics consists largely of making explicit ideas which appeal strongly to commonsense and which are already held in a vague sort of way'. A similar point about the simple mundane origins of science has been made by Harré (1960 : 7):

> A study of the working of science must begin with a study of the language of description and explanation. We must begin with the logically simplest kinds of descriptions and explanations — those we formulate in everyday language to deal with everyday situations. In a way the study of the logical gradation from everyday to technical language parallels the study of the historical development of science, for it was out of untechnical descriptions and explanations that the technical language of science grew.

These scholarly claims for the essential simplicity of economics and natural science underline Bruner's general thesis (1963 : 12, 33) that 'the basic ideas that lie at the heart of all science and mathematics and the basic themes that give form to life and literature are as simple as they are powerful'. As Hirst puts it (1965): 'the various forms of knowledge can be seen in low level development within the common area of our knowledge of the everyday world'. From this kind of assumption it is possible to see the traditional curriculum, not as a watering down of the incomprehensible for the benefit of the stupid, nor as a device for alienating the school from life, but as a valid instrument for cultivating rational, informed, intelligent awareness of human nature, society and the natural universe.

However, the assumption dies hard that this 'scientific',[8] structured view of the universe in all its diverse manifestations is really irrelevant for most children. As we have seen, at least one version of the community school option sees the traditional curriculum as encouraging irrelevant escapism, whilst from the educational Right it is believed fitting only for intellectuals, experts or teachers. 'Scientific' knowledge from the various subject areas may be all right for the upwardly mobile working-class child who sees himself destined for one of the learned professions. But, this argument continues, for everyday purposes most people need something else: not mathematics, for example, but the few scraps of arithmetical knowledge which enable one to function effectively in the super-market and the post office. Arguably, the market-place requires little more than the capacity to count, together with the skills of simple addition and subtraction, possibly multiplication and division — the sort of skills which, if the teaching of them were sufficiently long deferred, could be acquired by anyone in a period of a few weeks. The point is sometimes put as follows, as if to startle us at the enormity of what we really do in schools in passing on a mountain of useless intellectual garbage: 'Suppose we wiped the curricular slate clean and began to rethink it from scratch in terms of people's daily life needs, would we not be left with only a tiny fraction of the baggage which now serves as the curriculum?' Though this is rarely added (since those educationists who pose the question presumably do have a vested interest in the continued institutionalization of education in schools), the question which must follow is whether these minimum skills and knowledge could not be adequately acquired in the marketplace itself without the expense of schooling.

But the proposition that our daily life really only makes minimal demands on the traditional curriculum seems predicated upon the assumption that the average man and his wife need know only enough to do the shopping, pay the rent, buy the furniture, hire the television, pick up the newspaper, place a bet, teach the children reasonable manners and so on. Academic disciplines may represent refined, structured comment on daily experience but most people can manage well enough without it. However, this really is a prescription for the training of helots. It assumes that there are no questions to be asked about what is in the shops and what is not, and why what is there should cost what it does; no question about who owns the newspapers and the source of their revenues; or about who decides what is on the television; why some people find it impossible to get a mortgage, or by whom and by how much is the rent subsidized; what is it that makes children difficult to socialize, and so on. No doubt critics of the traditional curriculum would agree that these are important questions; their point would be that they are usually ignored in schools. However, as I have argued elsewhere (Entwistle, 1970a ; 137-9), it is not clear that we really equip people with a lifelong capacity to grapple with personal daily problems by focusing entirely on their own and society's current dilemmas when they are children. When they are pensioners (or senior citizens as the current euphemism has it), their personal problems will be quite different and, if social and technological change is only half as radical and persistent as the futurists claim, the problems likely to confront individuals and societies a quarter-century hence are, as yet, undreamed of. If this is so, the most relevant education we can offer any child is one which introduces him to fundamental modes of thought in relation to human experience and the natural universe. This is the only safeguard against learning becoming obsolete as the environment changes and the person ages. Moral education, for example, may well use the drug problem or the local example of racial intolerance to concretize the perennial problems of personal discipline and social justice which confront human beings irrespect-ive of place and time. But it is the capacity to relate one's experience to moral principles, and not merely the learning of current problems and their proposed solutions, which constitutes a moral education.

Much the same is true of those other areas of life for which the academic disciplines attempt to formulate fundamental concepts and principles. As Robbins made explicit and Devons implied, although fundamental economic principles may be few and simple, 'trite and obvious', they can nevertheless 'have all the bewildering and irritating properties of new truth'. But if the obvious can also be bewildering and irritating, this would imply that, paradoxically, grasp of the obvious has to be by a process of systematic exploration of complex relationships. The answers to apparently simple econo-mic questions do not simply lie on the surface of common sense. Indeed, commonsense economics is as replete with folklore and superstition as commonsense politics, science or history. People may be content to live their lives at this commonsense level of the half truth, whether they know or not what it implies for them personally in loss of power, efficiency and insight, or what their ignorance means for their neighbours in its potential for intolerance and prejudice. But it is no part of an educationist's business to decide that anyone must remain in the grip of ignorance, irrationality or superstition, much less to decide exactly which particular children are to be denied opportunity for enlightenment.

Bantock faulted the elementary school tradition for transmitting a *watered down* version of the high culture. It is true that blueprints for elementary school curricula did draw upon academic disciplines, but the intention was to educate children in order to assist in bringing coherence and principle to their daily experience. Elementary education has been dismissed as 'educational shoddy' and, as part of the polemic to win secondary education for all, this was understandable. It is also sometimes dismissed as a process of control of the working class. But perhaps this elementary school tradition is due for re-appraisal: for one thing, it was itself a developing tradition.[9] It was possible, for example, for an English elementary school between the wars to employ methods which are now taken to be typical of 'open' schools or 'progressive education'. Writing at that time, Gramsci also saw Italian elementary education as having potential as an instrument for establishing working-class hegemony. It was in its cultivation of literacy, its teaching of literature, history, science and social science (though Gramsci did not use that term) that its radical educational potential lay. For Gramsci drew an interesting distinction between commonsense and good sense. Commonsense he saw as an amalgam of good sense, folklore and superstition. The educational task was to enlarge the component of good sense within commonsense, exposing folklore and superstition to the critical light of historical and scientific knowledge. This constituted a relevant education for the working class and peasantry (Gramsci, 1971 : 323ff.)

Gramsci also took it as axiomatic that there is no disadvantage in being well informed from the culture's stock of received truth. There is a school of thought which has it that learning how to learn is what is really important and that the well stocked mind is a liability. Dismissed pejoratively as 'the banking theory' of education,[10] learning subjects for their substantive content is assumed to add nothing to daily experience and is seen as inconsistent with learning how to learn. Knowledge, as product, gets in the way of learning, as process. But it is not clear how one learns how to learn in the sense of mastering general principles of thinking for application to life situations without also learning something concrete. At least, the much despised factual content of the curriculum must exist as scaffolding for the building of intellectual structures and skills.

Of course, it is another of our educational myths that one can live one's daily life without a vast store of factual information. But without such a stock life would be insupportable. Common, everyday activities like watching television or reading newspapers with intelligent comprehension depends upon having a considerable cognitive repertoire; upon remembering (either at the level of recognition or recall) a great deal of information. To watch an evening's television is to be bombarded with a vast array of information whose significance one must understand to make sense of even the simplest of programmes. The news, for example, is often presented in terms of oblique geographical reference: Peking snubs Moscow; Moscow warns Prague; Paris mistrusts London; Washington faces Hanoi across the table, and so on. Not only are items of a geographical, scientific, historical or literary nature the meat of the mass media, but such concepts are often used metaphorically requiring some cognitive sophistication from even the modestly educated viewer or reader. Either one already knows what is being referred to in a television programme or one misses the point. An entire accessible library of works of reference is of little relevance to the problem of having in mind the information which is essential to following a play or television documentary, or to reading a newspaper without constant interruption in order to look things up. And it is not an unfamiliar experience that one misses the opportunity of getting the most from a visit to a strange place because one lacks relevant background information. Being in a position to seize opportunities before they pass requires that one has a considerable repertoire of information which is sometimes a condition not merely for extracting the most from an experience but for having the experience at all. Bourdieu stresses the importance of the 'pre-knowledge that individuals owe to the school', particularly for having experiences in the cultural realms we have designated C2n and C3n. He records the complaints of French workingmen when faced with cultural artefacts in galleries and museums: 'When you don't know anything about it, it's difficult to get the hang of it ... Everything seems the same to me ... beautiful pictures, beautiful paintings, but it's difficult to make out one thing from another ... It's difficult for someone who wants to take an interest in it'. Bourdieu concludes, 'Without this principle of separation and the art of applying it that the school teaches, the natural world is merely an indeterminate, undifferentiated chaos'; and lacking this cultural information one is 'condemned to the monotonous diversity of meaningless sensations' (1973 : 195-6). My argument has been that English schools have rarely provided this necessary guide to the plastic arts and music. But the argument is capable of extension to the more commonplace routines of daily life, especially watching, reading and talking about the news and other featured content of the media. Daily experiences of this kind would also be indeterminate and undifferentiated chaos, without the historical, geographical, political and scientific 'pre-knowledge' we acquired at school.

In passing it is worth noting that 'the news' itself is largely information acquired simply for its own sake. No doubt one does occasionally 'use' the news — the weather forecast, for example, or the item focusing upon a local or national cultural event — but, for the most part, the news is a series of unrelated items of information which it is just interesting to know. And, without conscious intention, the news is banked up — as a store of knowledge which provides individuals with a context for subsequent experience. Indeed, having an experience in the future is often contingent upon already having information — acquired in school or from the news — available at least in recognition memory, if not always readily available for reproduction (or testing) on demand. Unless one's own experience is utterly idiosyncratic, it is simply not true that most of what was learned at school is completely and irretrievably lost. Those educationists who wish to divert schools from their traditional role as transmitters of the cultural stock ignore their own dependence upon this cultural capital, just as they forget that whatever innovative resources they themselves have were also acquired whilst in receipt of the 'traditional' schooling they denounce. Somehow, though not surprisingly, they learned how to learn in the process of becoming *learned*. Education involves learning which is anticipatory to ensure response to experience as it happens, and the learning-how-to-learn account of education, so far as it dismisses the implications of *being learned*, is much like closing the stable door after the horse has bolted.

However, one of the reasons for insisting upon the value of a process-oriented, or what Freire calls a 'problem-posing', education rather than a banking or product view of learning, is that the former seems more fruitful for achieving the object of creativity as an outcome of schooling. But aside from the question of how far creativity or problem solving is possible without first, as Dewey (1958) insisted, 'taking a tradition into oneself', there is the question of how far, and in what sense, creativity is a realistic possibility for most of us who pass through the educational system. Most of us are not destined to be creative except in the diluted sense of being 'adaptable' or capable of working independently and without supervision;[11] or in that minimal sense of creativity as novelty exemplified in the fact that the letter I write to the insurance company this time, having stove in the wing of my car on the gatepost, has to be different from the one I wrote last time when I backed it into a tree. And, to continue to be autobiographical about the matter of creativity, I am sure that I shall never be creative in physics after the fashion of Rutherford, but I am also quite convinced that occasionally I make sense of an experience in terms of the physics I learned at school and the bits and pieces of scientific information I have picked up since; and that much the same is true of the history, geography, mathematics and poetry that I have 'banked up' over the years.

Yet general knowledge of this kind which contributes towards the quality of living in a modern community has often been dismissed by educationists as of little importance through their too ready characterization of it as 'inert ideas'. But if the metaphor of education as banking is differently applied it does, paradoxically, emphasize the importance of memorized information. Education as banking is usually applied to the notion of a learner banking up information in his own memory. But the learning-how-to-learn, research-oriented concept of education can also be seen as advocacy of intellectual banking of another sort, where the learner merely learns how to draw cheques upon data banks. This ignores our common experience that the cognitive coinage of daily life must often be ready at hand. As with our financial resources, some of our cognitive assets must be liquid if we are to make the most of life's fortuitous encounters with the environment. Indeed, a more serious objection to the concept of education as primarily concerned with learning how to draw upon the data banks — libraries, computers, resource centres — is that there is a danger of people learning to write cheques on accounts which are empty: the data banks may be full of cognitive coins but this is unhelpful if there is nothing in one's own personal account.

The assumption that common daily experience does not suffer and, indeed, is enriched by systematic study and memorization of traditional subjects requires two provisos. First, the 'high culture' of the university — if that is what teaching and research in higher education produces — must not be watered down for use in schools in the sense of becoming a recital of abstractions emptied of all concrete reference to the human, social and natural universes. Provided that 'concrete' has reference to more than mere physical objects, the developmental stages of Piagetian psychology are suggestive of the way in which the learning of abstractions grows out of reference to the concrete: the implication is that simple material suitable for grasping by the immature does not entail dilution from the complex but, rather, is a point of departure in the concrete facts from which complex abstractions are derived (literally from which they are abstracted): the 'simple' can be conceived as concrete phenomena, spontaneously encountered in daily life or presented deliberately in the classroom, which the child learns to complicate as he acquires a capacity for formal operations. I have elaborated this argument elsewhere (Entwistle 1970b : 89-92).

It is possible to regard subjects at the formal operational stage as the high culture and, in Piagetan terminology, what is being claimed in saying that the curriculum is a watered down high culture is that teaching often begins and ends and is saturated throughout with formal operations. However, when the learner has properly progressed to the stage of formal operational thought, he has reached the stage at which appreciation of the high culture in one or more of its traditions is possible. But on the Piagetian account of it, capacity for formal operational thought is the culmination of a developmental process, beginning in preoperational thinking and, necessarily, taking in a concrete operational stage.

A second proviso is that the high culture (whether conceived either as C2n or C3n) must be accepted as a developing culture. It has its classical forms — the best that *has been* thought and said. It also has a modern reference — the best that *is being* thought and said. A relevant curriculum keeps up-to-date by incorporating new forms of knowledge. Though the mundane reference of high culture has been illustrated by reference to economics, this (and other social disciplines) figures hardly at all in the school curriculum. Mention of economics is also a reminder that the classical and modern components of high culture are not unrelated, the former being a cultural dinosaur, the latter a cultural man in space.

Modern economics can be neo-classical, and new departures are sometimes no more aptly described than in terms of what they displace — post-Keynsianism, for example — implying the debt of the new even to what it replaces. So curriculum modernization will probably be a process of addition rather than subtraction, though *reorganization* of the old with the new will almost certainly be necessary to accommodate this modernization.

Notwithstanding the undoubted truth that daily experience (in the market-place, reading newspapers, watching television, participating in the democratic political process at various levels, making the best of one's income, having conversation with friends and in the commerce of family life) can be enriched by what has traditionally passed for school knowledge, it seems evident that many students in school do not accept this account of its relevance. One explanation of this is to be found in the assumption that culture (in any of its senses) appears enervated and irrelevant because it becomes divorced from the experience of work: in these circumstances it 'becomes gratuitous and socially divisive, a luxury for the happy few' (Meakin 1976 : 197). We turn now to examine this hypothesis by considering some of the cultural and educational correlates of work and leisure.

6

Leisure and
vocational education

Introduction

In the total or anthropological conception of culture (C1), the
activities and artefacts of both work and leisure are obviously
cultural phenomena. However, educational theorists have frequently taken the view that vocational or technical knowledge and
skills are not the proper concern of the educational system: to
speak, as we commonly do, of technical or vocational education
seems to many a contradiction in terms. Implicitly, culture, when
conceived normatively (C1n), cannot include work, and all its
attributes, much as crime, drug addiction, political corruption and
so on, must also be excluded. But leisure seems a different matter.
Indeed, it has been argued that leisure *is* the basis of culture. An
alternative view, however, is that vocation should be a central
educational concern, a conclusion which requires resolution of some
of the conceptual ambiguities in notions like 'technical', 'vocational', 'training', 'liberal'. In particular, it is arguable that
technical, vocational, liberal and general education are related, not
exclusive or dichotomous terms,[1] and much the same is true of

the relationship between education and training. And it is evident that some of the connections between education and social stratification can only be understood when the vocational relevance of education is underlined and some of the myths about the future of leisure are subjected to critical examination.

Technological innovation and the withering of class

Earlier we noted two conceptions of classlessness, the Marxist and the social democratic, the former entailing the assimilation of other classes to the working class, the latter requiring that class distinctions should dissolve into more fundamental conceptions of humanity or individual uniqueness. However, it is not absolutely clear from Marxist theory how far the withering of the state associated with the dictatorship of the proletariat also entails the withering of the working class in its historical sense. Marxian men who fish, hunt, philosophize and criticize at will, bear little resemblance to the working classes observed by Marx and Engels in the 1840s and whose exploitation and alienation were the impetus to socialism. And in the mid-twentieth century, the withering of the traditional working class has seemed more a consequence of the success of capitalism, than of revolutionary socialism (Bottomore 1974 : 110-13). As was earlier observed, two related phenomena seem to have been at work in expanding the middle class at the expense of the working class: the apparent conquest of poverty in so-called affluent societies, and the technological changes ushering in the 'post-industrial society'. Whilst this thesis of bourgeoisification has been called into question in view of persisting radicalism and union membership amongst affluent manual workers, and in view of the apparent proletarianization of the middle class,[2] there is evidence that technical innovation does operate to diminish the proportion of blue-collar manual workers in the economy relative to an expanding sector of professional and proto-professional occupations calling upon symbolic knowledge rather than manual skill (Bottomore 1974 : see also Thompson 1973).

Notwithstanding that liberal educationists have often been hostile towards a vocational bias in schools, it is evident that this transformation of the occupational structure of advanced industrial societies is a bonus to the educational system. Knowledge becomes

the major technical resource of increasing numbers of workers
(Drucker 1969 : Part 4) and it appears that the only impediment to
a general upgrading of knowledge and skill could be inherent
stupidity in a residue of the population. We have noted the
assumptions of conservative educational theorists that a substantial
minority, if not the majority, of the population is incapable of
responding to the demands of a culture conceived in cognitive-
rational terms. On the other hand, it has been argued that an
individual's perception of what, for him, is a realistic aspiration in
occupational and domestic terms is likely to colour his acceptance of
the value of schooling. Not unexpectedly in a Marxist, Gramsci
asked (1971 : 133), 'Can there be cultural reform and can the
position of the depressed strata of society be improved culturally
without a previous economic reform and a change in their position
in the social and economic fields?' He concluded: 'Intellectual and
moral reform has to be linked with a programme of economic
reforms — indeed the programme of economic reform is precisely
the concrete form in which every intellectual and moral reform
presents itself'. Halsey (1972a : 19) cites the view that expectation
of 'high achievement and performance on the part of the sub-
working class would be irrational until the structure of opportunities for jobs, and indeed all the other elements of citizenship in the
afluent society, are provided equally for all, independently of their
social, familial and racial origins'. Similarly, Quine (1974) has
argued that educationists 'will have little success unless they
understand and alter the fundamental social and economic reality
which underpins the entirely realistic social and expressive values of
children and parents on these (i.e. working-class) housing estates'.
American educationists (Cloward and Jones 1963 : 215)[3] concerned with disadvantaged groups have drawn similar conclusions
about the relationship between personal aspiration (especially the
desire to seize educational opportunity) and 'appraisal of reality':

> Evaluation of the importance of education in the lower and work-
> ing classes appears to be influenced by occupational aspirations.
> The point is not, as has been so often suggested, that low income
> people fail to perceive the importance of education as a channel
> of mobility, but rather that their level of occupational aspiration
> influences their evaluation of education much more than is
> characteristic of the middle class person.

These largely theoretical assumptions have recently received empirical support in Britain from a survey, *Attitudes of Young People to School, Work and Higher Education*: 'In general there is evidence that perceptions of earnings and career opportunities do influence the educational decisions of many students'.[4]

The cultural relevance of these assumptions about the relationship between educational aspiration and a realistic appraisal of what the future holds in occupational terms, is that transmission of a quality culture depends upon the learner's perception that such a culture may have meaning with reference to the social and economic realities of his daily life. Exhortation to live by reference to the best that has been thought and said is unlikely to be persuasive where socio-economic realities remain what they are for many persons in an industrial society. The wider dissemination of those qualitatively valuable cultural activities and preoccupations is likely to be associated with an intensification of the shift towards occupations requiring improved educational standards in the work force. That is, the cause or condition of class, of disadvantagedness or privilege, of one quality of culture or another, is the economic-technological structure of a society: people are privileged or disadvantaged, first, in the satisfactions they derive from work or through the brutalizing and monotonous discipline which it imposes on them. And if one's future seems destined to be unemployed, or spent in routine unskilled labour, one probably cultivates a life-style appropriate to this condition.

In Britain, this reversal of the conventional wisdom that education is an independent variable (or, as in Helvetius' phrase, 'L'education peut tout') was sanctioned by the Newsom Report (Central Advisory Council for Education 1963 : introduction). Its review of the educational needs of the below average child began from the assumption that the educability of a population is a function of the demands made upon it by the level of technological development. In support it quoted Lord Macaulay's belief that 'Genius is subject to the same laws which regulate the supply of cotton and molasses. The supply adjusts itself to the demand. The quantity may be diminished by restrictions and multiplied by bounties.' The view of those we have just quoted who see a person's valuation of education as a function of his occupational aspiration, amounts to the claim that almost two centuries of mechanized industrial technology has imposed a restriction upon the aspirations and, hence, upon the educational achievements of large sections of the working class in industrial societies. Arguably, the indifference to the school curriculum displayed by many working-class children results from the perception (fostered, in part, by attitudes they encounter in familiar adults, often teachers as well as neighbours and relatives) that work will probably demand far less of them in terms of knowledge and skill than the modest academic competencies which even the least able acquire in school. Even 'backward' children attain levels of literacy and numeracy far higher than is required by a good deal of industrial work. Much industrial activity is counter-educational: it is a graveyard of literacy and skill.

In face of this kind of occupational reality a not uncommon reaction is to assume that people really enjoy undemanding work which leaves them free to daydream (Castle 1961 : 200). Paradoxically, it seems, their 'job satisfaction' depends upon being able to forget the job even whilst they are doing it. Empirical evidence varies on how far people look for satisfaction in their jobs (Weir 1976; Argyle 1972 : Chs 4 and 5). Evidently in this respect, one man's meat is another man's poison: this individual couldn't stand being cooped up in an office; that one volunteers for service in submarines.[5] But whatever people's preferences, the conventional wisdom has it that soul-destroying work is inescapable and that schooling ought to be tailored to this fact (Wilson 1975 : 20-4): 'The canvas of equality of opportunity cannot be pressed too vigorously in case the result turns out to be some sort of Dodo race in which everybody wins and vital services are left to be done by those too over-educated to undertake them.' Given the implication here that people are capable of better (i.e. are capable of being 'over-educated'), what is ignored by people who adopt this position is how one justifies, morally, selection which restricts some people to the modest educational achievements necessary for the performance of vital, but menial, services. For it is one thing to argue that justice requires treating unequals unequally and the making of special educational provision for the cultivation of excellence; it is quite something else to believe that justice is served when the personal development of some is deliberately restricted to make them willing lackeys for the rest. Faced with this dilemma, the best liberal response seems to be that we should revalue social roles so that we attach new importance to menial tasks. On the necessary assumption that some people really enjoy this kind of work, the only problem seems to be to ensure that it is well remunerated and that social status or esteem should attach to those who perform it. But, especially with reference to status and esteem, this is easier said than done. It is not that we fail to recognize the importance of menial work and, even if we do forget, a grim reminder of the importance of such work occurs when, occasionally, strikes of garbage workers in New York or of snow removal crews in Montreal rapidly bring entire metropolises to a halt. Clearly, it is not a lack of recognition of its social utility which prevents our attaching esteem to conventionally low status employment. Indeed, since such employment is often relatively well paid, it is not clear how a widespread change of attitude to the existing occupational hierarchy could be engineered. The only answer would seem to lie in the elimination of such jobs altogether. If an appetite for education does seem to be whetted by perceptions of the economic and social roles one seems destined to fulfil, then the bounty which calls forth 'genius' and releases that potential for intelligence, skill and sensibility which humanistic educational philosophy believes to be the distinguishing mark of men *as* men, would seem to lie in technological innovation towards increasing automation. A civilization capable of colonizing outer space should not find it beyond its technological resources to make low status, low skilled, monotonous, soul-destroying occupations obsolete.

However, such is the received view that education ought to be liberal — in the sense which precludes it from being vocational — that the educational bounty potentially available from technological innovation is itself assumed to be destructive of educational values. Anti-vocationalism in education poses itself in terms of variations on the theme that life is really for leisure. Work and leisure are conceived as autonomous and discontinuous entities, each existing necessarily only at the expense of the other: time at work seems time lost to leisure, and leisure time, apparently by definition, is not available for work. Those educational slogans which dichotomize living and earning a living derive from the notion that work is a curse, an economic imperative for provision of life's material requirements but, in itself, alienating, tedious, soul-destroying, instrumental. Leisure is viewed as compensation for having to live with the curse of Adam, and the opportunity presented by automation is assumed to lie in its potential for freeing men from the need to work at all and in liberating the school from its prostitution to the economic system (Faunce in Parker 1971 : 140): 'In the long run the primary responsibilty of the school may well become that of instilling certain kinds of values and interests which permit the creative use of leisure and, in general, the teaching not of vocational but of leisure skills.' This is a not uncommon conclusion amongst educationists who find in leisure, not in work, the conditions of human happiness and personal fulfilment. If technological innovation puts us on the threshold of a Golden Age of Leisure, this has seemed to offer peculiar opportunities to education. As an instrumental activity, work seems a necessary evil to which education, when properly conceived, has nothing to contribute. When oriented towards work, education seems destined to degenerate into mere training. From this standpoint, vocational education is, at best, a device for socializing the young into acceptance of the economic imperatives and disciplines of the world of work. At worst, it sells out education to the values of the affluent society, the rat race, the military-industrial complex and so on. Hence, when the economic imperative to work is diminished, this seems to point up the importance of that very thing — leisure — to which education seems peculiarly relevant.

However, this assumption of a dramatic reduction in work and the availability of vastly increased free time is based upon a misunderstanding of the nature of automated technology, as well as of the economic imperatives of free enterprise economic systems and of the nature of leisure itself (Entwistle 1970b : Ch.3). Economically, it remains a fact that in capitalist societies unemployment is the only device we know for creating mass 'leisure', and the dole or welfare the only fiscal devices for putting purchasing power into the pockets of these 'leisured'. In the depression of the mid-1970s, the Golden Age of Leisure begins to look like a Fool's Paradise.

But unemployment is not part of the logic of automation. The fact that automated processes nudge workers off the direct production line only means that productive effort is removed to the processes of planning, design and maintenance. The lengthy and costly gestation periods of industrial prototypes — Concorde was conceived some fifteen years before its first commercial flight — consumes considerable manpower. Moreover, the tertiary or service sector of the economy is, in principle, capable of almost indefinite expansion so long as the good society remains only an aspiration, whilst industrial slums and polluted nature disfigure the earth and disease afflicts mankind.

Leisure education and the notion of a leisured class

Falsification of the leisure myth in its recent form does not render education for leisure inapposite. But the problem of education for leisure will be solved neither by repudiation of vocational education, nor in curricular provision for training in spare-time activities. This last is frequently a preferred solution for modern leisure theorists. Leisure is taken to be time spent in play: the 'leisure skills' are those required for the performance of varied kinds of recreational pastime — games, sports, arts and crafts and holiday pursuits.

Parker shows how in the hands of a growing body of 'professional recreation workers, recreationists, leisurists and even recreators', this recreational view of leisure becomes an élitist conception. He quotes an apologist for the professional recreational movement: 'Since the average citizen is unable to invent new uses for his leisure, a professional élite shares a heavy responsibility for discovering criteria for ways of employing leisure and creating enthusiasms for common ends within the moral ends of the community.' As Parker observes (1971 : 128-9), 'this implies a situation in which only a cultivated few know how to use leisure ... The "moral aims" to be pursued emphasize that only certain kinds of leisure are to be promoted and that they are intended as a means of social control'. This is obviously the twentieth-century version of early nineteenth-century schooling and religion conceived as a 'gentling of the masses'. In fact, it is not clear that the equation of leisure with play or recreation takes any account of the preferences of most laymen. In a survey of blue- and white-collar Civil Service employees at all status levels, Friedlander (1966 : 441) found that 'recreational activities were perceived as having the least value for potential stimulation, particularly when compared with work related activities'. He concluded that 'one may well question the extent to which recreation will prove an even partial substitute for work as an opportunity for a meaningful environment'. Nevertheless, it is also possible to interpret this sort of data as evidence of the incapacity of most people to discover, learn and enjoy leisure activities of a life-enhancing kind. Indeed, the stress on education for leisure as initiation into various forms of recreational play activity does assume this incapacity for leisure to be a cultural disability which has to be overcome. But it is unnecessarily crude to dismiss a preference for work-related, spare-time activities as an inability to escape the moral limitations of the Protestant work ethic. To the contrary, perhaps most people correctly perceive leisure as a unitary conception such that work time cannot profitably be dichotomized with spare time. Indeed, such a conclusion that leisure is a quality of which all life's activities may partake would be in line with historical conceptions of leisure.

It is most fruitful to conceive of leisure, not as a residue which remains when economic obligations have been fulfilled, but rather as a way of life, indeed, as life itself. The conventional wisdom has it that leisure is that period of time which is distinct from time spent at work: in relation to 'life space' — 'the total of activities or ways of spending time that people have' (Parker 1971 : 25) — the relationship between work and leisure is taken to be as in Fig. 6.1.

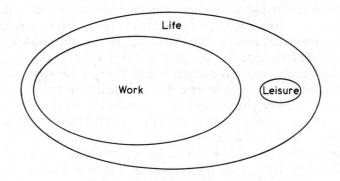

Fig 6.1

The unfilled portions of the large oval represent other 'obligatory' biological claims like sleep, eating, cleansing and other non-work duties or obligations. No doubt, in the above diagram, the proportion of leisure to work is more favourable than in the early period of industrialism when spare time barely existed. On the other hand, the notion of a Golden Age of Leisure implies a distribution somewhat as in Fig. 6.2.

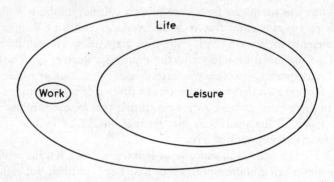

Fig. 6.2

I have already suggested that current economic problems are likely to be unfavourable to the assumption of leisure-in-affluence upon which this conception is predicated. But even if problems of economic production and distribution were solved, such that material affluence were possible without the imperative to work, this would have little to do with leisure. The fact that people have unlimited free time does not mean that they will have anything at all of leisure. It is this realization that prompts the view that if increasing free time is to have the characteristic marks of leisure people must be taught how to use it profitably.

However, in the examples of Figs 6.1 and 6.2, where work and leisure are sharply differentiated, the relevant educational task is conceived as one of how to teach people to use their spare time profitably. But education for leisure in this sense seems misconceived. It is appropriate to conceive leisure neither as a residue left over from time not consumed by work, nor as a condition upon which work merely intrudes. Leisure is a whole, total life-style: for those who have it, leisure *is* life. The appropriate diagramatic representation is as follows:

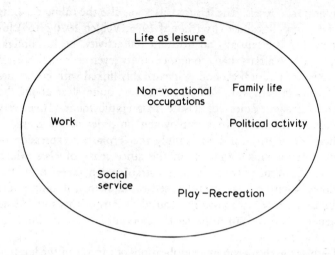

Fig. 6.3

Unlike in Figs 6.1 and 6.2, the various life activities have not been sharply circumscribed: there is assumed a good deal of interpenetration or overlap; for example, from work there is a good deal of overspill into political activity, social service, recreational activity with friendly colleagues and so on.

Whatever the size of the work component in this last conception of leisure, its presence in the schema is essential. It is a myth that historically the leisured class had no work to do (Veblen 1970 : 33): 'An habitual neglect of work does not constitute a leisure class.' This class was *free*, as distinct from slave or serf, in that it worked for itself or for the state, especially in 'honourable employments'. In what he called the 'best development' of the institution of a leisured class in feudal Japan and feudal Europe, Veblen saw the class distinctions in these societies, not as between 'working and non-working classes, but in terms of employments *proper* to the several classes' (my italics). The upper or leisured classes were not idle; they were occupied in 'employments to which a degree of honour attaches' (Veblen 1970 : 19). Above all, they were landowners who managed their own estates (thus providing work for others) (Kirk 1973 : 316; Gretton 1917 : 109-10; Veblen 1970 : 55) and, arising from their concern with property, provided government at appropriate levels. The leisured class was also the ruling class: its work lay in political activity (Kampf 1973; Veblen 1970 : 165).[6] But politics is essentially an instrumental activity, no less obligatory in human affairs than economic activity (even as in the classical discipline of political economy, inextricably linked with economics as a social imperative). Veblen (1970) was quite clear about the 'economic significance' of leisure class employment. Their very exemption from industrial employment in order to fill political, military or priestly roles was simply the '*economic* expression of their superior rank'. Indeed, in the strict sense of class which applies the term only to economic stratification (See Ch.2), the notion of a leisured class would be self-contradictory, if leisure were to be understood as non-work. Considerations of this sort led de Grazia (1973 : 377-80) to prefer the notion of 'a leisure kind' to that of a leisure class.

Despite the clear economic implications of the role of the leisured class in history, there persists the Aristotelian notion that a qualitative difference remains between the occupations of the free man of leisure and those of other workers. For example, de Grazia, who is categorical that leisure is related to neither work nor play, eventually enters the disclaimer that he has had in mind the modern sense of work which does not apply to aristocratic occupations. His concept of leisure derives from Aristotle (1962 edition : 300-7) who distinguished between degrading or servile occupations and those which are 'proper' to a free man:

> ... then as to useful things — there are obviously certain
> essentials which the young must learn, but they do not have to
> learn all useful things, since we distinguish those that are proper
> for a free man and those that are not. The citizen must take part
> only in those useful occupations which do not degrade the doer.
> Among degrading activities and vulgar pursuits we must reckon
> all those which render the body or soul or intellect of free men
> unserviceable for the demands and activities of virtue. We there-
> fore call degrading those occupations which have a deleterious
> effect on the body's condition and all work that is paid for these
> make a mind preoccupied and unable to rise above menial things
> ... it is proper for a free man to do something for himself or for
> his friends on account of its value in itself, but he that does the

same action on others' account may on occasion be regarded as doing something paid for or servile.

The interesting point about Aristotle's conception of degrading work is that few occupations in the modern world escape this taint of servility. Most professional workers, as well as manual labourers, would have to be excluded from Aristotle's category of free men. For it is not simply occupations that have a deleterious effect on the body's condition which are degrading, but also work which attracts remuneration. That is, it is not the task itself which is crucial to the distinction between servile and free, but whether it is paid for. Nowadays, most members of the learned professions are either salaried or in receipt of fees for their services.

Some modern Aristotelians reject this notion that the activites of intellectuals and members of the learned professions should be designated as work and subject to the same economic and moral evaluation as manual work. Pieper (1964 : 123), for example, objects to the implications of the terms 'intellectual work' and 'intellectual worker' which reduce the educated man, the scholar, to the level of 'functionary', indistinguishable from the wage earner and, hence, a practitioner of the 'servile arts, essentially utilitarian in purpose'. Similarly, de Grazia believes (1973 : 386) that 'if a doctrine of equality is extended to work it stunts the growth of a life of leisure'. In this context he notes the existence of 'a rudimentary' leisure class — philosophers who out of economic necessity have to become professors, for example. No doubt these modern apologists for the leisured classes are contending, defensively, that the health of a society depends upon its willingness to support those who choose the contemplative life. Pieper quotes Aquinas' view that 'it is necessary for the perfection of human society that there should be men who devote their lives to contemplation'. And immediately to underline the moral basis of that claim he observes, '*nota bene*, necessary not only for the good of the individual who devotes himself, but for the good of human society'. But, however legitimate this assertion of our need for intellectuals, scholars and sages against a climate of opinion where immediate utility is a major criterion of value, the logic of Aristotelian leisure must not be forgotten. That modern Aristotelians do not dwell upon it does not alter the fact that Aristotle's conception of the good and virtuous life depends upon the institution of slavery. And however legitimate this may have seemed at that point in the evolution of human society, modern man finds repugnant any notion of the good life which is lived at the expense of others. Current notions of social justice find it abhorrent that anyone should live on unearned income which derives from the labour of others. To modern man, analysis of the good life in Aristotelian terms must be unacceptable because of its failure to incorporate a conception of social justice applicable to all men. Such a conception demands that we all work to live and, for most of us, this means being employed by someone else and being in receipt of a wage or a salary. This is especially true of employment in government, that characteristic occupation of the leisured classes. In modern legislatures the amateur of private means gives way to the professional politician. And although we are occasionally disturbed at the thought of men making a living out of politics, adequate payment of members of legislatures is accepted as an essential measure of social justice, especially in pursuit of the notion of political equality between social classes.

Some contemporary social and educational theorists attempt to abstract Aristotle's concept of the good life of leisure from its sociological context, arguing that the Aristotelian concept of leisure is no less relevant for a society with quite different economic and moral imperatives. But Aristotle's notions of slavery and leisure hang quite logically together and either confusion or hypocrisy results from attempting their separation. In fact, all kind of ambiguity is built into the Aristotelian concept of leisure and its historical successors. A close examination of the tradition of 'liberal' citizenship reveals that this leisured, cultivated existence is only 'allowed' because the life of the Aristotelian citizen, the Platonic Guardian, the Renaissance *cortigione*, the English or American country gentleman, was essentially a function which had political and, hence, economic value. Mass discontent, if not revolt, destructive of privilege tends to follow when the leisured class ceases to be identified with good government or the provision of adequate employment. As Veblen put it (1970 : 144), through its acquisitive, pecuniary, non-productive role, 'the bent given to the growth of economic institutions by the leisure-class influence is of very considerable consequence'. Thus, because leisure was contingent upon the performance of tangible economic functions, education of the leisured class could never simply be characterized as 'for its own sake'. Classic statements of liberal education from Plato on are concerned with training for the performance of economic and political roles which constituted work in any meaningful sense and for which the material standard of life can only be adequately conceived as a reward for services rendered.

For leisure today the Aristotelian model only has relevance if two conditions are met: first, if we are able to divest it of the notion that the leisured class was under no imperative to work or render service to the community by the provision of good government or adequate employment; secondly, if we are able to find a substitute for slavery or serfdom, that is, if we can demonstrate that the total life-style which characterizes leisure can be widely available. It is clear that the classical model can only take us so far. Today's leisure class (whether a minority or, according to the utopianism of the Golden Age of Leisure dream, the mass of men) can no longer fit the Aristotelian model of a class which works for itself and is, thus, able to delude itself that it is neither servile in the sense of receiving an income, nor in the sense of being under an obligation or compulsion to work.

However, perhaps we can capture the essence of Aristotelian leisure in the notion of freedom. If only under the pressure to provide good government and work for others, the leisured classes were obliged to work, but had considerable choice about the timing and conditions of their work. Though Marx's ideal work situation may sound fanciful to modern ears (in respect of its concrete particulars), it is essentially a description of the life-style of the leisured classes (Marx and Engels 1967 : 110-11):

> In Communist society, where nobody has one exclusive sphere of activity but each can become accomplished in any branch he wishes, production as a whole is regulated by society, thus making it possible for me to do one thing today and another tomorrow, to hunt in the morning, fish in the afternoon, rear cattle in the evening, criticize after dinner, in accordance with my inclination, without ever becoming hunter, fisherman, shepherd or critic.[7]

The essence of all this, anachronistic though its details may seem, is freedom to choose. That is, leisure has two characteristics in relation to work. There is room for manoeuvre in terms of *when* the work is done, and there is choice amongst a variety of work roles and activities. Lanfant notes (1972 : 22-3) that the French equivalent, *loisir*, is etymologically related to the Latin *licet* — 'il est permis'. Hence, l'expression ''je travail à loisir'' n'est pas contradictoire ... le loisir est liberté, autonomie, libération, temps a soi, etc.' It is clear that these criteria of 'leisure-in-work', especially those relating to timing, were also substantially satisfied by the work patterns of traditional artisans (Shorter 1973 : 3)[8].

In modern economies, it is this condition of freedom, the ability to exercise discretion and choice of time and place where one fulfils one's occupational obligations, which characterizes the professional and, increasingly, the para-professional worker. The morning at golf, the afternoon at the races, the lengthy coffee and luncheon break are all either themselves occasions where a good deal of work allegedly gets done or, as relaxation, they have to be paid for with work done at times when other people are relaxing. This interpenetration of work and recreational activity has been noted in a number of studies (Parker 1971 : Ch.6). The fact that many business executives seem to enjoy less free time than manual workers evokes less sympathy when we recognize this fusion of work and nonwork activities: '... in cases where their work embodies many of the values normally associated with leisure, a separate period of time labelled leisure appears to be necessary neither to their own happiness nor to their creative function in society' (Parker 1971 : 38). It is also frequently ignored by professional middle-class people who criticize slackness and laziness in industrial workers that their own work usually affords ample opportunity for social relationships; and that the 'tea break mentality' of factory operatives probably represents a search for sociability at work (rather than a simple disinclination to work) where personal interaction is not intrinsic to the industrial process. Riesman implied that this search for companionship at work represents something other than a desire to escape from unsatisfying work routines. He believed that workers may want to be at work without working (1964 : 146): 'At a certain point ... workers seem to want to buy leisure inside rather than outside the plant.'

On the view of leisure as a total life-style which embraces work, play, political obligation, social service, family life and friendship, education for leisure is simply what was traditionally conceived as liberal education. In a modern democratic society of working men (whether of hand or brain, professional and highly skilled or unskilled) where the Aristotelian distinction between free men and servile men is inapplicable, the only sense in which education can be liberal is in freeing all men from whatever constraints may happen to bind them, especially the limitations imposed by inhuman discipline at work. For in modern industrial societies most people need to be freed from the tyranny of routine, monotonous, brutalizing and soul-destroying toil. One of the first economic historians understood that the greatest restriction upon the intellectual and aesthetic sensibilities of a great many workers is imposed by the work they do (Adam Smith quoted in Meakin 1976 : 11):

> The understandings of the greater part of men are necessarily forced by their ordinary employments. The man whose life is spent in performing a few simple operations of which the efforts are the same or very nearly the same, has no occasion to assert his understanding or to exercise his invention in finding out expedients for removing difficulties that never occur. He naturally loses, therefore, the habit of such exertion and generally becomes as stupid and ignorant as it is possible for a human creature to become.

But a man is not delivered from the tyranny of routine, monotonous, industrial processes by the pretence that he need not work at all, or by attempting merely to 'liven up' his spare time whilst he continues in a soul-destroying occupation. We delude ourselves that we can correct the ill-effects of work which alienates the worker by provision of compensatory spare-time activity of a 'life-enhancing' kind. The preferred spare-time activity of those who work mechanically is likely to be as undemanding and mechanical as their work: 'The hypothesis that a low self investment in one's job is associated with higher self investments in other parts of life is so far only weakly demonstrated. Indeed, support is forthcoming for the opposite view' (Cherus 1976 : 45).[9] Durkheim observed the futility of trying to redeem the worker from the ill-effects of extreme division of labour by compensatory spare-time activity (1964 : 370). In this connection:

Suppose that we can relieve some of the bad effects that are attributed to the division of labour: that is not a means of preventing them. The division does not change its nature because it has been preceded by general culture. No doubt it is good for the worker to be interested in art, literature, etc, but it is nonetheless bad that he should be treated as a machine all day long.

He concluded however:

Who cannot see that two such existences are too opposed to be reconciled, and cannot be led by the same man? If a person has become accustomed to vast horizons, total views, broad generalizations, he cannot be confined, without impatience, within the strict limits of a special task.[10]

There is undoubtedly a want of realism about a concept of education for leisure which assumes that you can educate a man whose work is trivial and repetitive out of the pursuit of trivial, mechanical spare-time activities. Engels's view of what has been called 'the compensatory leisure hypothesis' was that the mechanical brutalizing work he witnessed was more likely to be compensated for by spare time spent in drunkardness than in a search for 'vast horizons' (Wilensky 1961-2; Engels 1958 : 45-6). As Lawton shows, a number of historians, including some actively involved in the working-class movement, have insisted that industrialism impoverishes popular culture and turns the working class to irrational, escapist solutions to the problems of life. Similarly, industrial sociologists point to the alienating effect of treadmill occupations and the non-rational responses they induce (Lawton 1975 : 48). So far as the cruder, bestial manifestations of industrialism persist in soul-destroying work and the prevalence of slum housing, it may be too much to expect there the refinement of sensibility which is implicit in being educated. As was suggested earlier, the dynamic of technological innovation has its own implication for the development of knowledge and skill.

This dismissal of other people's work and recreations in unflattering terms is sometimes seen as the patronizing stance of the middle class. However, a number of studies have found job satisfaction to be highest amongst professional and skilled manual workers, lowest amongst the unskilled and semi-skilled (Lockwood 1975 : 18, 29n; Cousins and Brown 1975; Parker 1971 : Ch.5, 20n, 21n). Others point to evidence for concluding that 'those who find work more demanding are more likely to be socially or intellectually active in their spare time than those who find work less demanding' (Parker 1971). Work satisfaction seems to relate to having a sense that one has skill which can be employed creatively, that there is opportunity to exercise initiative and responsibility, that there is a social dimension to one's work and that a task can be seen through from its beginning to completion. On the other hand, work which is repetitive, apparently useless, done under close supervision and in conditions of extreme division of labour — what Berger calls work 'in the basement' of the industrial system — is 'apprehended as a direct threat to self-identification, an indignity, an oppression' (Parker 1971 : 51). Work is much more likely to be perceived as a 'central life interest' by professional and para-professional workers than by manual industrial workers (Parker 1971 : 69).

No doubt it was the compulsion of this sort of logic which led Riesman to reverse a judgement from *The Lonely Crowd* and concluded in *Abundance for What?* (1964 : 166) that 'we cannot take advantage of what remains of our pre-industrial heritage to make leisure more creative, individually and socially, if work is not creative too'. Other sociologists of work and leisure have also concluded with Aron that 'the meaning of leisure in a given civilization depends upon the meaning given to work' (Parker 1971 : 61-2). W.E. Moore (1963 : 38) argued that 'leisure is a problem where work is a problem and probably proportionately. The "constructive" use of leisure is likely to depend in considerable measure on the constructive definition of jobs.' Perhaps it could not be otherwise. Howe emphasizes that mass commercialized culture is functional to the existing economic system: 'Whatever its manifest content, mass culture must not subvert the basic patterns of industrial life ... It must provide relief from work monotony without making the return to work too unbearable' (cited in Parker 1971 : 82). Picking up this notion that 'the nature of work and its status in any given culture affords us an invaluable key to the understanding of that culture as a whole', Meakin (1976 : 13) concludes that 'the impoverishment of popular culture is inextricably linked with the impoverishment of work in our society, and if we wish to change the one we must change the other as well'.

If it is unrealistic to expect that interesting and creative spare-time pursuits can compensate for soul-destroying work, there is a similar want of realism about the conclusion that we are all about to experience a considerably diminished work week (except in the cruel context of economic depression) and almost unlimited spare time. From the example of a traditional leisured class, if leisure in modern society is to have any meaning, it is in the conception of a total life-style, compounded no less of economic and political activity than of recreative play, and it is this reality with which any conception of education for leisure must come to grips. Indeed, given this conception of leisure as a total, inclusive life-style, characterized by a good deal of choice and freedom of manoeuvre in relation to all life's activities — work, play, political activity, social service — the notion of education for leisure which focuses merely upon playful, spare-time activities is mistaken, even trivial. This is not to say that activities designed to interest students in a variety of recreational pursuits have no place in the curriculum: a rich and varied play life is as essential to leisure as is a work life where initiative, choice, skill and responsibility have the fullest possible rein. However, the inadequacy of a concept of education for leisure which is exclusively concerned with recreation is that it leaves life's major tyranny — the tyranny of unpleasant, monotonous toil — untouched. It also fails to offer insight into those other activities — political and economic management — which were as much the preoccupation of the traditional leisured class as was sport and recreation or mere idleness. For education of the leisured class was, above all, political education. It follows that a modern education which liberates must embrace technical or professional education which is necessary to pursue occupations requiring skill, intelligence, judgement and specialized knowledge. Such education has a vocational element also in showing how occupations relate to a wider cultural context, especially to the political culture. For there are political implications in having no work at all. Those condemned to idleness in being cut off from the economic system are also politically impotent: a good deal of power is exercized through the major economic institutions, whether of capital or labour. As well as the teaching and learning of technical competence, vocational education implies imparting an awareness of moral, social, economic, political and aesthetic dimensions of work (Thompson 1973; Entwistle 1970b : 55-9).[12]

Although in educational history 'vocational' has often referred specifically to craft or manual training, in Western culture the word also has reference to an attitude of mind, and the sort of moral commitment a man brings to his work. Even within living memory, people spoke of having a vocation to teach, to the ministry, to law, to medicine and so on. And whilst the word was less likely to be used in connection with craft and manual occupations, the sort of pride and commitment which a skilled artisan had in his work was indicative of a sense of vocation. This commitment to a job well done entails some sense of a close connection between technical skill, personal taste, citizenship and morality. When related to this wider sense of vocation, vocational education is a genuine educational experience in that it mediates knowledge, skills and attitudes which lift the worker's perspective beyond the technical demands which the job itself imposes. Historically, apprenticeship involved this kind of cultural orientation through the teaching of moral and social obligation to the community of one's craft, to the customer, and to the society beyond, as well as initiation into the mysteries of the craft. From this point of view, the free man is not one who is relieved from the obligation of earning a living, but one who understands the implications for his work of economic and political decision-making (including the political decisions of his own union or professional association) and who has a sense of responsibility for the quality of his work. It is in this sense that vocational education is a liberal education and, together with political and aesthetic education, an essential component of education for leisure.

Conclusion

On a number of occasions above it has been noted that the philosophical perspective in education seemingly stands in conflict with the sociological. The former is essentially humanist in conceptualizing education without reference to limiting social categories like nationality, religion, race, and especially, class. But from a sociological point of view this appears naively oblivious to the facts of the socio-educational universe. It was Durkheim who first criticized the philosophical perspective in educational theory when insisting that it is society which determines educational ends. In his view, the philosopher, using a psychological model of human nature, conceives of the individual learner in a sociological vacuum (1956 : 115):

> For Kant as for Mill, for Herbart as for Spencer, the object of education would be above all to realize, in each individual, carrying them to their highest point of perfection, the attributes of the human species in general. They stated as a truism that there is one education and one alone, which, to the exclusion of any other, is suitable for all men indiscriminately, whatever may be

the historical and social conditions on which they depend — and that it is this abstract and unique ideal that the theorists of education propose to determine.

In his introduction to the original edition of *Educational Sociology*, Fauconnet underlined this as follows (Durkheim 1956 : 31): '... we know that classical philosophy has almost always failed to consider the real man of a given time and place, the only one that is observable, in favour of speculating on human nature ... it often sets up laws for an artificial man, independent of any social milieu.'

As we have argued in Chapter 3, our reason for emphasizing *man* is to avoid the conservatism entailed in the view that a given sub-culture represents an adequate or valid way of life, simply following from the social fact of its existence. The humanistic reference is necessary for the dialectic of social change. Indeed, what strikes the reader of Durkheim's sociological account of education is its conservative conception with reference to any given society. Societies are hierarchically structured with reference to the specialization of functions and Durkheim cannot envisage education which is not governed by this fact. Education is for our 'station in life', in accordance with the rule of human behaviour that we 'concentrate on a specific limited task. We cannot and we must not all be devoted to the same kind of life; we have, according to our aptitudes, different functions to fulfil, and we must adapt ourselves to what we must do' (Durkheim 1956 : 63). Durkheim drew support for this conclusion from historic societies since Ancient Greece and concluded, with reference to the possibility that there is 'an ideal, perfect education, which applies to all men indiscriminately', that it is useless to imagine 'a kind of education that would be fatal for the society that put it into practice' (1956 : 65).

Unfortunately, with reference to the industrial society at the time when Durkheim was writing, another conclusion of his which we accepted earlier seems fatal to the possibility that there can be anything worthy of the name of education for many future workers in an industrial society. It will be recalled that Durkheim rejected the compensatory view of leisure, arguing that the monotonous toil characteristic of minute, 'anomic' division of labour could not coexist in the same person with 'wide horizons'. Together with his conclusion that schooling has to be tailored to fit society's needs for a hierarchy of tasks — some mundanely practical, others highly theoretical — this makes the educational prospect for many future workers bleak indeed. But it is also possible to take the view that human ingenuity can itself be enlisted to develop a technology which diminishes the need for servile occupations and increases the demand for those requiring knowledge, skill, intelligence and taste. Such has been the expectation of technology from Aristotle, through Marx to the present day. Hence, the view that education is inextricably linked to the economy, necessarily leads to the conservative conclusion that a majority has to be socialized into roles as 'hewers of wood and drawers of water', only from 'a failure of imagination. Obviously, this metaphor in which we characterize 'degrading' toil is quite anachronistic in its application to modern society. But that other forms of servility exist does not require that they be with us forever. In one sense, the view that education is inevitably vocational is deterministic, and we have argued that a young person's perception of his likely future role will probably affect his motivation to learning. But this notion is not deterministic in the sense of assuming the socio-economic structure at any time to be natural, therefore unalterable. Durkheim's appeal to history in order to establish the social determination of education only underlines that the educational system of Rome was not that of Greece and that neither was that of the Middle Ages or the Renaissance. And he went on to argue that the socio-educational imperative of the modern nation was towards a broadly human culture: because of the extreme division of labour, 'the individuals who compose it are so different from one another that there remains hardly anything in common among them, except their human quality in general ... In other words, in society so differentiated, there can hardly be any collective type other than the generic type of man'. However, Durkheim still insisted that this modern educational importance of a humanistic culture is not derived from philosophical assumptions about human nature, in the abstract. It remains a sociological imperative for prevention of the decomposition of modern societies (1956 : 121-2): 'our pedagogic ideal is explained by our social structure, just as that of the Greeks and the Romans could be understood only through the organization of the society'. But however it is justified — from the sociological or the philosophical perspective — a humanistic education requires the assumption that the creation of a different economic system depends not merely upon man's technological ingenuity but also upon political, social, moral and aesthetic decisions relating to things like environmental (especially urban) renewal, the conquest of poverty and different priorities with reference to the consumption of goods and the demand for services. This is to say that the social needs which colour the complexion of the educational system are not independent of human calculation and decision.

One difficulty with the 'social needs' account of education is that without some concept of the good life or the good society, derived from a universal concept of man, there is no reason why a society should not condemn some of its citizens to roles which are injurious to their health and morals, as well as intellectually stifling and blunting to aesthetic sensibility. Given our existing expectations, we do put some of our fellow men at risk in these respects. To argue that no one should knowingly be put in an occupational role which is injurious to his health and morals, or which encourages intellectual atrophy, is to appeal to some universally valid principle of human nature. It is a common property of civilized societies that they generate protests against the exploitation on which they are based, by reference to some concept of *man*, i.e. universal principles which ought to apply to everyone. This dialectic within societies between the imperatives of the *status quo* and some ideal moral principle is one condition for necessary social change. The specialization and cultural heterogeneity which Durkheim saw as characteristic of modern societies does not have to be hierarchical. Conceivably, societies could be pluralistic without distinctions of status and power, and technologically specialized without committing citizens to work-roles of undiminished monotony and brutality.

But the notion that education must be, thus, incorrigibly vocational requires another assumption in order to be humanistic. This is that man realizes himself through work; that the cliché 'education is for living not learning a living' makes nonsense where work is seen as a defining characteristic of man. In Chapter 6 it was suggested that a conception of leisure which fails to accommodate work is culturally irrelevant. On this view, vocational education cannot be dismissed as instrumental. It is, rather, a necessary curricular component of any education conceived in terms of personal, human development. It may appear extrinsic or instrumental from the point of view of national economies, but from an individual's viewpoint it can be an intrinsically satisfying educational experience making the difference between skilled, knowledgeable personal growth, or a life spent in rote, unskilled toil. Humanistic educational conceptions like 'full personal development', 'realization of individual potential' and 'education of the whole man' cannot be unpacked, concretely, in a way which excludes man the worker. For even social change radical enough to prevent alienation by transforming the productive relationships in society would not make work redundant. On the contrary, in the words of *The Communist Manifesto* (Marx and Engels 1967 : 87 and 163), it would herald the day when work once again has '*charm* for the worker'; the time 'when labour is no longer a means to life but has become life's principal need'. One of Marx's criticisms of the Gotha programme was its failure to demand technical schools in combination with elementary schools (Cosin 1972 : 171). He did not look for the abolition of technical education but to the takeover of technical schools by the working class.

If social change is to be in a direction which is liberating for human beings, a normative dimension is inescapable in educational theory. But this conclusion has to be set within the context of two further facts. First, to insist upon humanism as the basis of educational theory does not deny the possibility of pluralism with reference to an educationally relevant concept of man. All it denies is the adequacy of any educational norm which diminishes for any category of learner the value of essential human qualities like rationality, or envisages them consigned to economic roles which inhibit the development of intelligence, sensibility and skill. If some social roles are demonstrably servile, dehumanizing and 'anomic', our obligation is not to find good reasons for condemning some of our fellow men to their performance but rather, by technological innovation or a redefinition of our social and personal needs, to do away with such roles.

Secondly, the sociological categories of nationality, religion or social class are important points of reference so far as these exemplify, concretely, distinctive contributions to human culture. This point was argued in Chapter 4 with special reference to working-class contributions to the cultural mainstream. Moreover, a child's own culture is an essential educational point of departure and an object of continuous reference for exemplification of the knowledge, values and skills to be learned from the various arts and sciences. But nowadays, and increasingly, the cultures of all modern industrial societies are multicultures, and talk of teaching a child from a particular class or ethnic group to value its own culture is mischievous if it does not recognize this fact. It is also educationally inadequate to fail to look for the outcome of schooling in a personal culture in the sense defined in Chapter 4. Whatever the pride which can properly derive from nationlity, ethnic origin, social class or religious affiliation, it is blind if it discourages the individual learner's search for knowledge, insights and values in the cultures of other social groups as they mingle within the cultural mainstream. The social history of the working class is full of evidence that individual pursuit of personal culture in the mainstream of Western culture is rarely an escape from the realities and predicaments of working-class life but, on the contrary, is an essential contribution to the making of working-class consciousness. As was argued in Chapter 3 with reference to advocacy of a locally oriented curriculum for the community school, it is not clear that educationists perform any service to underprivileged children by pretending that social amelioration can derive from anything other than the acquisition of knowledge of institutions, ideas and ways of life which transcend their immediate physical and cultural environments. A curriculum may be irrelevant in neglecting the concrete concerns of daily life or in failing to assimilate modern as well as classical forms of knowledge (Ch.5). But it cannot be judged irrelevant simply in focusing upon subject matter which transcends children's spontaneously perceived needs in this place and at this time.

to expect people to view common curriculum differently.

Notes

Notes to Chapter 1

1 See Harrington (1973), Tumin (1967), Kolko (1962) and Parker (1974).

2 Tawney (1974 : 26) wrote of the 'disease of inequality'.

3 See also Wilson (1966 : 173). Even Tawney (1974 : 112-13), who attacked what he called 'the religion of inequality' — i.e. attempts to find functional justifications for inequality — nevertheless insisted that 'inequality of power is inherent in the nature of organized society'. As he put it, concretely, 'No one complains that captains give orders and that crews obey them, or that drivers must work to a timetable laid down by railway managers'.

4 Jencks (1972 : 3) underlined this point with reference to the social values of Americans: '... they have no commitment to ensuring that everyone's job is equally desirable, that everyone exercises the same amount of political power, or that everyone receives the same income'. However they do believe 'that rules determining who succeeds and who fails should be fair'.

5 Hindess also draws attention to evidence that workers perceive deprivation and inequality not by reference to upper- and upper-middle-class norms, but in relation to circumstances of other workers who are only slightly better off than themselves. That is, their conception of equality does not stretch across the entire range of human circumstances. See also Parkin (1972 : 61).

6 In the event, of course, it is far from clear what do constitute relevant reasons for educational discrimination. It depends upon one's concep-

tion of what constitutes an education. For example, those religious denominations which take religion to be at the root of education believe that religious affiliation is especially relevant as a discriminator in the provision of schooling. It even seems that some modern radicals make a similar assumption about the relevance of social class, on the grounds that any class sub-culture constitutes a valid and adequate way of life. (See below, Ch.3)

7 The evidence on how far there has been a working-class access to institutions of secondary and higher education is conflicting. A decade ago, an OECD (1967) report demonstrated that despite considerable expansion of facilities for secondary and higher education, the social composition of the student body had changed very little since the 1920s. However, more recent OECD statistics suggest that despite the persistence of social selectivity in access to higher education, there has been a more rapid decline in inequality of access than seemed likely at the end of the 1960s (*The Times Higher Education Supplement*, 24 January 1975). Westergaard and Little (1964), whilst insisting that expanded provision for secondary and higher education has benefited lower-class children only minimally, do show that as between the top and lowest special groups entering grammar school, the ratio fell from 37:1 for the generation born before 1910, to only 6:1 for the generation born in the late 1930s. Obviously, much depends upon the time scale with which one is operating. A more dramatic increase in working-class access would be evident over the first quarter of this century than through the middle half of the century. With reference to this evidence, Littlejohn (1972) concludes that in the UK 'there is a long term trend towards increasing equality of oppor-

tunity in all sectors of education. What people disagree about is whether it proceeds at a satisfactory rate or not.'

8 Tawney (1974 : 105) called this the Tadpole Philosophy of Equality:
'It is possible that intelligent tadpoles reconcile themselves to the inconvenience of their position, by reflecting that, though most of them will live and die as tadpoles and nothing more, the more fortunate of the species will one day shed their tails, distend their mouths and stomachs, hop nimbly on to dry land, and croak addresses to their former friends on the virtues of the means by which tadpoles of character and capacity can rise to be frogs.'
See also Parkin (1972 : 49)

9 The Coleman Report concluded that statistical comparisons showed:
'... Whites attending schools with greater resources, although this is not uniformly true, *and perhaps the most striking point is the small size of the differences.* The differences between locales (in particular, north-south differences, and to a lesser extent, metropolitan-nonmetropolitan differences) are for most resources greater than within-locale or national differences between schools attended by minority students and those attended by Whites.' (Coleman 1969 : 256)
See also Coleman (1973 : 20): '... the examination of school inputs to effects on achievement showed that those input characteristics of schools that are most alike for Negroes and Whites have least effect on their achievement.'

10 The notion of equality of results does not render the concept of equality of opportunity redundant. Because equality of opportunity is an instrumental notion — neutral as to ends — it does not follow that its application will necessarily underpin the established social order. In terms of the intentions of those reformers who

first emphasized equality of opportunity, the notion is quite relevant to a belief in the importance of equal outcomes. Fair chances for all and the removal of irrelevant impediments to schooling are especially important when equality of outcomes is the objective.

11 Green explores several politically acceptable options for approaching the problem of securing equality of educational results, including raising the learning rate of the disadvantaged without depressing that of the advantaged. His assumption — reinforcing his conclusion that the prospects of achieving this equality are indeed dismal — is that whatever teaching strategies might be developed to accelerate the learning of the less able would also be available to the middle class. It is difficult to conceive of any pedagogical device which would benefit the former but leave the latter untouched. Such provision would either not have to affect the middle class one way or the other, or its application to its own children would have to be repugnant to the middle class. Such a pedagogical device which improved lower-class performance in school whilst leaving the middle class indifferent or revolted (but did not put its children at a disadvantage) is difficult to envisage.

12 Some support for the notion of group rather than individual equality is in Hobsbawm (1975): '... the idea of equality was always a notion of equality between classes rather than between individuals'. However, for Hobsbawm this notion of class equality is a good deal more radical than Coleman's and Green's conclusion that the principle of equality is satisfied when there is proportional distribution of benefits amongst students from different groups or classes. For this leaves the system of social stratification essentially intact: it is simply that the economic and social strata become peopled with different individuals. But, for Hobsbawm, the point of stressing equality between groups was to achieve 'the abolition of class privileges and distinctions'. He had in mind the socialist belief that 'the group as a whole, the class as a whole had to be improved rather than simply the individual himself.' This kind of class equality is not consistent with the meritocratic notion of there being equal opportunity to become unequal, a notion which is quite consistent with the idea that 'the range of distribution of benefits and their distribution within that range is approximately the same for each relevant social group'.

13 Wilson argues that 'all human beings have the same status as choosers and creators of value'. Hence '... if one's morality pays any attention at all to the facts of human nature, to the actual powers and capacities of men, and also to the principle that similar cases demand similar treatment, then this particular similarity amongst men is plainly one of the most important. It will be the most reasonable basis for the belief that men have the equal right to decide their own destinies since they have an equal capacity to do so: and for the belief that they have an equal right to make their wills and purposes felt — to actualize them in the world — since the will and purposes of each man are ultimately as valid as those of his neighbours.' (Wilson 1966 : 95)

14 Largely, but not completely; this is not to argue, for example, that motivation of demand may not be attributable to factors over which teachers have some control.

15 However, it was argued at a recent OECD conference that perhaps undue attention has been paid to psychological reasons for dropping out of school and that financial impediments to continued education should receive more consideration

(*The Times Higher Education Supplement*, 24 January 1975). This is an attempt to link equality and education from the side of demand, not supply, where lack of demand is attributed to economic constraints rather than a distaste for schooling.

16 This is the view taken by Holt (1967 : 281-6), for example.

17 The current tendency amongst radicals to categorize schools as 'hegemonic' derives from interest in the work of the Italian Marxist, Antonio Gramsci. Briefly, Gramsci uses the concept to refer to the relationship between social classes where one class (the bourgeoisie in capitalist society) exercises control over other classes. This control is not coercive, i.e. by police, military and legal constraints, but moral and intellectual. The hegemonic class exercises control through power founded 'upon wide ranging consent and acquiescence ... Every relationship of hegemony is necessarily an educational relationship' (Gramsci 1971 : 350). Hegemony is exercised through civil institutions like the church, school and the media of communication. Hence, substitution of proletarian for bourgeois hegemony requires reform of the school system, in Gramsci's view, mainly by reorganization along comprehensive lines.

18 As Tawney put it (1974 : 108):
'... individual happiness does not only require that men should be free to rise to new positions of comfort and distinction; it also requires that they should be able to lead a life of dignity and culture, whether they rise or not, and that, whatever their position on the economic scale may be, it shall be such as if fit to be occupied by men.'

Notes to Chapter 2

1 The reference here is to classics of educational literature such as Plato's *Republic*, Aristotle's *Politics*, Quintillian's *Orators*, Castiglione's *The Book of the Courtier*, Elyot's *Governer*.

2 Here I have in mind texts like T.P. Nunn's *Education: its Data and First Principles* (1920), A.N. Whitehead's *Aims of Education* (1932), Hughes and Hughes's *Learning and Teaching* (1937), and their later *Education* (1960).

3 See Banks (1965 : 53-65) for discussion of the relationship between educability and social class (as an economic category) with reference to various national contexts. See also Porter (1965 : Ch.7) for similar data on Canada; Husén and Boalt (1976 : Chs 5-7) on Sweden; Natanson and Prost (1973 : Ch.2) on France.

4 See Bernstein 1971, Vol.1, especially his essay 'Social class and linguistic development'. Labov (1973) offers a radical criticism of Bernstein. See also Lawton's (1975) sympathetic critique.

5 Aron quoting unnamed American.

6 Cf. Meyer and Buckley's point that 'individual Protestant churches are often class churches. Episcopalians, Presbyterians, Congregationalists and Unitarians tend to be upper and upper-middle class and Methodists and Lutherans tend to be middle class and Baptists, Evangelicals and Revivalists tend to be lower class.

7 It is a sociological commonplace that Americans, for example, are loath to categorize themselves in public as anything less than middle class; cf. Parker (1974); Lewis and Maude (1949) note that whilst 46 per cent of British respondents to a 1948 Gallup Poll were prepared to categorize themselves as working class, at about the same time 65 per cent of

Canadians and 88 per cent of Americans claimed middle-class status.

8 Banks and Finlayson have recently produced evidence suggesting that explanations of the success of working-class boys in all types of secondary school may be found in emotional relationships between parent and child which bear little relationship to socio-economic status. Miller (1971) goes further in claiming 'that social and emotional interaction which goes on between parents and children is critical to the problem of using educational opportunity, for middle-class as well as working-class families.'

9 Gretton (1917 : 7-8): '... the middle class is that portion of the community to which money is the primary condition and the primary instrument of life'; see also 12, 139 and 205ff.

10 See note 17 to Ch.1.

11 Gramsci, for example, was urging comprehensive reorganization of the school system in Italy half a century ago.

12 See Floud and Scott's evidence on the relationship between the social-class origins of teachers and the social-class complexion of the schools in which they teach (1965 : 539-

43). That this is not simply a Western phenomenon has been observed by Margaret Mead (1973): '... in present day Bali, the high castes are sending their daughters to the Dutch schools to be trained as teachers because it is pre-eminently important that learning should be kept in the hands of high castes and profoundly inappropriate that low caste teachers should teach high caste children.'

13 Klein (1965 : 401) notes that Willmott and Young found that 'the bitterest attacks on the way of life of the working-class seemed to come from people who were close to the boundary between working and middle class, whose own job had dropped in status or financial reward or whose own future was insecure ... the teacher who said "I suppose before the war I'd be middle class. Teachers had a high social standing then, but now professional people are now the lowest." '

14 It should be noted, however, that part of Bernstein's intention in relating different conceptions of schooling to different middle-class groups is to discover how far either conception might be inimical to the education of working-class children.

Notes to Chapter 3

1 Both theoreticians and practising politicians in the British Labour Party, for example, have taken the view that, in Attlee's words, 'the abolition of social class is fundamental to the socialist conception of society'; see also Crosland (1963) and Tawney (1974).

2 In fact, Williams's position with reference to Marxism has been ambivalent. In *Culture and Society* he wrote of 'a recent controversy among English Marxists', that 'this is a quarrel which one who is not a Marxist will not attempt to resolve'. But in a recent essay he has expressed

sympathy with Marxists like Goldmann, Lukacs and Gramsci; see also his essay in Parakh (1975).

3 This, for example, was Gramsci's view of technical education; see also Hodgen (1925 : 268).

4 See, for example, Halsey (1972a : Ch.10)

5 See Kozol (1972), for example.

6 See Labov (1973), for example.

7 See below for discussion of the view that elementary education was a diluted form of high culture.

8 It is beyond my scope here to examine this claim for emotional education as, peculiarly, a function of

movement and dance. However, Redfern has analysed this claim in detail, throwing doubt upon Bantock's claims. He is critical of Bantock's reliance upon Laban's work as a theoretical underpinning for his own views.

9 See also Leavis's essay, 'Literature and-society' in *The Common Pursuit* (1952).

10 See Allcorn and Marsh for importance of this distinction between sociability (1975 : 211-13).

11 As a supervisor and examiner of teachers in training, most of the good and excellent teaching I have seen has been in the teaching of history to classes of less able children; see also Redfern (1976):

'This consideration of skilful teaching raises the more fundamental issue of whether the traditional curriculum, if it has failed for a large percentage of secondary school children, as Professor Bantock claims, may have done so not so much from what it consists of, as on account of inappropriate methods and unimaginative presentation.'

12 See also R.S. Moore (1975); Taylor and Ayres (1973 : 267); Bergel (1962 : 366); Lipset (1960 : Ch.4); Parkin (1973 : 52) also cites a Czechoslovakian social scientist's similar observations on the less skilled working man.

13 'This *sort* of élitism': putting it this way does not rule out a consideration of the proper role of élites and experts in any society.

14 See, for example, the essays in Keddie (1973) by Mead, Gladwin and Frake.

15 See Kucynski (1967), the Appendix titled 'Historiography of the origins of the working class'.

16 Klein (1965 : 88n.) also concedes the existence of cognitive poverty in other social classes.

17 In fact, Midwinter does occasionally make sympathetic gestures towards history and geography, but these are as parochial as the rest of his pro-

posals. In the case of history, for example, there must be no giant strides into the distant past, but modest steps into the children's immediate ancestry. It is claimed for these modest steps that they might take us to the more distant past. But there is nothing to show how this backward movement is to be achieved: for example, whether it is always laboriously, through generation by generation connections, or whether at some point there has to be a 'schizophrenic' leap across time and place. The fact is that in the real world the social environment does not methodically unfold for us, gradually, year by year or mile by mile.

18 Grambs (1965 : 25) refers to evidence of the motivating effect of the study of Black history upon the learning of Black children. He cites Lewin's claim (with particular reference to Jews) that the child who is aware of the history of his social group is better able to cope with the problems of being in a disadvantaged position.

19 Since no other authors are cited for this text, further citations will be credited to the editor as Halsey (1972a).

20 In response to a critic, Halsey (1972b) emphasizes that he does not believe that the schools unaided can bring about the social transformation he desires. No doubt he believes that both cause and cure of local ills lie in the wider community. What is doubtful is whether the proposed EPA curriculum is adequate for bringing this fact home to children in these areas.

21 Cf. Midwinter (1972b : 24): '... if they are disadvantaged and unhappy the hope is that they may be on the way to *rationalizing* their dissatisfaction creatively rather than expressing it incoherently and perhaps violently' (my italics).

22 There is a curious ambivalence towards television amongst advocates of community education. Halsey (1972a) uses the fact that children

watch television as a disclaimer that their perceptions 'are not simply focused on the local environment'. But Midwinter takes television's zooming us away to far off places as especially irrelevant for EPA children.

23 For other radical criticism of the school's insistence on literacy see two essays by Graff (1972 and 1973); also Young (1971 : 37-8); Leach (1972) and Folley (1975).

24 See Melnik and Merrit's introduction for an outline of the conventional arguments for literacy (1972). Most of the other contributors to this text also take the case for literacy to be axiomatic.

25 Miller argues in his critique of McLuhan (1971 : 112-13):
'... it seems unlikely that literacy would, by its very nature, have impoverished the richness of spoken language. Quite the reverse. The expressive possibilities offered by being able to write thoughts down after mature consideration would seem, on first principles at least, to be a friendly condition for linguistic innovation. In fact the advent of literacy, far from extinguishing the imagination, has vastly increased the number of its expressive options. Indeed, it is hard to overestimate the subtle reflexive effects of literacy upon the creative imagination, providing as it does a cumulative deposit of ideas, images and idioms upon whose rich and appreciating funds every artist enjoys an unlimited right of withdrawal.'

26 In terms of the point I am making that what is true of print can be no less true of other media, it is interesting that Postman (1973 : 95) looks to increased use of electronic communications technology in schools in order to provide students with computerized individual programmes. If anything, this would intensify privacy in the process and as the product of schooling.

27 For a variety of reasons to do with economics, status, taste or convenience, people find themselves well served by the use of obsolete machinery. They fly in obsolete aeroplanes (indeed, on the 'obsolete as soon as it leaves the drawing board' view of obsolescence, every aircraft in commercial service is obsolete), they drive obsolete cars (the more obsolete the car the more prestige there is in owning it), they ride bicycles increasingly (an obsolete piece of technology if ever there was one) and, paradoxically, find that these get them to places that more sophisticated machinery cannot.

28 For an extended critique of McLuhan's work see Miller (1971 : 76), especially Ch.5. With references to the dogma that the medium is the message, Miller concludes: 'Doubtless the various media *have* had their characteristic effects, but in acknowledging such influences there is no need to emphasize them to the exclusion of everything else — especially not with reference to epistemological theory which has no foundation in neuro-psychological reality.' He further argues that McLuhan's persistence in ignoring the content of the media and concentrating instead upon 'their abstract form' amounts to the 'abdication of political intelligence'.

29 Wellek points out that 'the political attack on literature amounts to an attack on conservative ideology, which necessarily has been expressed in print, just as revolutionary ideology has found expression in print, struggling, no doubt, with the obstacles of censorship and government monopoly of print long before the advent of modern totalitarian right or left' (1973 : 128-9).

30 See, for example, Marx; Gramsci.

31 See *The Times Educational Supplement*, 8 October 1971.

Notes to Chapter 4

1 I have elsewhere developed some educational implications of this distinction. See Entwistle (1970 : 131-6).

2 For elaboration of this distinction between socialization and education with reference to political culture, see Entwistle (1971 : Ch.2).

3 See Parkin (1973 : 79-80) on alternative views of the existence of an American working class.

4 My own experience in parking my own car at Maine Road, Manchester (where children may be less 'cute' than in Liverpool) is that I am never approached for the 'fee' until I have parked the car myself. I recall asking one of these small youngsters what exactly he meant by offering to 'mind' my car. Clearly, he was not accustomed to being asked that sort of question but, after several second's pause, he replied, 'We'll stop fellas from jumpin' on 'em'.

5 For discussions of the concept of *Praxis* see Richard Bernstein (1971) and Hoffman (1975).

6 See also Simon (1972) for examples of exponents of the radical culture with reference to education.

7 Cf. Engels's letter to Marx in 1858: '... the English proletariat is fast becoming more and more bourgeois. The most bourgeois of all nations seems to have finally reached a point where it has a bourgeois aristocracy and a bourgeois proletariat alongside the bourgeoisie. In a nation which exploits the whole world that is, to some extent, understandable.' Quoted by Harrington (1973 : 179-80).

8 Each of the volumes of the *Cambridge Studies in Sociology* (Goldthorpe *et al.*) is relevant to this theme. See also Hamilton (1967); Salaman (1975 : 220); Parker (1974 : 148-50); Shorter (1973); Vaizey (1975 : 103-4).

9 Harrington argues that this is a consequence of their being 'subjected to a productive discipline like that of the workers', despite having 'middle-class' education and income (1973 : 439ff.). As Davis and Cousins put it (1975 : 203); 'to be a proletarian is not to be pauperized but to be a commodity'.

10 See also the contrary viewpoint expressed by Marshall and Moody on the advantages to be gained by affiliation to the TUC, *The Times Higher Education Supplement*, 27 February 1976; also Marshall, 'Are university teachers members of the working class?', *The Times Higher Education Supplement*, 21 November 1976.

11 See tables 8.6, 8.7 and 8.10 in Ch.8 of A.H. Halsey (ed.) (1972) *Trends in British Society since 1900*. London and New York: Macmillan.

12 *The Times Higher Education Supplement*, 26 March 1976.

13 Gretton noted that the 'peculiar genius' of the middle class was 'not to attack institutions, but to handle them in such a manner as to find a sheltered area for personal profit under them' (1917 : 127).

14 See Simon (1960 : 200-1); Silver (1973 : xix) and (1975 : 84).

15 See Elbourne's letter to *The Times Higher Education Supplement*, 28 February 1975.

Notes to Chapter 5

1 Other literary critics in this tradition have been Coleridge, T.S. Eliot, William Walsh: see also Annan (1975 : 102).

2 This conception of leisure as the basis of culture is especially associated with Pieper and Eliot.

3 This point is elaborated further

below (pp.149-50) with reference to the views of academic economists on the essential simplicity of economic theory.

4 For Arnold, reflection on the best that has been thought and said was for the pursuit if personal perfection as a means towards the perfecting of society: 'Culture leads us to conceive of true human perfection as a harmonious perfection, developing all parts of our society.' That is culture was not to be thought of as an esoteric, private possession; it stimulates social criticism aimed at social reform.

5 According to Eliot, a characteristic list of English cultural artefacts includes: 'Derby Day, Henley Regatta, Cowes, the twelfth of August, a cup final, the dog races, the dart board, Wensleydale cheese, boiled cabbage cut in sections, beetroot in vinegar, nineteenth-century Gothic churches and the music of Elgar.'

6 Elbourne cites a *Manchester Guardian* report of a working-class concert in 1839: 'I do not believe that the well-educated portion of the public are aware of the real character of these concerts. They take it for granted that it is music for the mob, cheap and worthless.'

7 See also Stenhouse (1967 : 10) for the view that the components of the traditional curriculum, '... the great cultural traditions of the humanities and the sciences are essentially élite cultures, inaccessible to many people.'

8 Here one is using 'scientific' in a special, but historically familiar sense, with reference to any organized body of knowledge; see Collingwood (1963).

9 See, for example, Hurt (1972 : 75).

10 The banking theory of education has most recently been dismissed by Freire (1971) as 'necrophilic' and serving the interests of oppressors. One trouble with educational metaphors is that they obscure the complexity of the educational experiences they aim to clarify (see Entwistle 1970 : Ch.9). Freire does, indeed, imply that the dialectic of education requires both banking and problem-posing approaches (see p.72). In a forthcoming paper, 'Political education and the works of Antonio Gramsci' (to be published in *Teaching Politics*), I have suggested that Gramsci saw schooling as banking with reference to the education of children and that one must look for the radical component of his educational theory in the education of adults. For the latter he clearly sees a crucial place in education for dialogue, as does Friere whose 'pedagogy of the oppressed' is essentially adult education.

11 I find that my own students, when pressed about what they mean by creativity, tend to fall back on the notions of adaptability and ability to work independently.

Notes to Chapter 6

1 I have attempted a clarification of these related notions elsewhere, see Entwistle (1970b : Ch.5). Other issues dealt with only summarily in the present context are also examined there in detail. Since one of the criticisms levelled against that text was that, despite its title, it had nothing to say about leisure, the present discussion examines the relationship between education, work and leisure largely from the perspective of the latter.

2 For criticism of the bourgeoisification thesis see Westergaard (1972); Parker (1974) and Halsey (1976 : 112). Halsey rejects what he calls 'the liberal theory of necessitous history',

the belief that equality and the withering away of class is, amongst other things, a function of the unionization of the middle class and the privatization of the working class. Though he concedes that it remains an open question whether it would succeed, he prefers the less deterministic device 'in which choice is to be made about the structures of inequality, which can be channelled through the political process, and in which the role of political leadership and political will are absolutely central'. This view requires a questionable assumption about the autonomies of politics, economics and culture.

3 Cloward and Jones (1963 : 215); see also Hyman (1953 : 495); Entwistle (1970 : Ch.7) and Barrow (1975 : 190).

4 Reported in *The Times Higher Education Supplement*, 27 February 1976.

5 The importance of allowing for personality differences when attempting to humanize work by increasing variety and responsibility has recently been underlined by findings of the Institute for Social Research in Ann Arbor: 'Without allowances for individual differences in personality such initiatives could be counterproductive.' Reported in *New Behaviour*, 2 October 1975.

6 See also Hexter (1961 : 67):
'... one of the most impressive and universal traits in the complex of writings about the education of the aristocracy for service to the Commonwealth is the subordination of questions of right and privilege to questions of responsibility. Something is made of the rights of the aristocrats to office, more of their responsibility through education to prepare themselves for office, and most of their responsibility to turn the education they get to the service of the public weal.'

7 Dahrendorf (1975 : 76) updates this Marxian notion of freedom in work by asking, why not 'collect people's taxes in the morning and repair their cars in the afternoon, assemble television sets in the morning and go to a polytechnic in the afternoon'? Though it does not offer this kind of variety in work, there is a growing tendency in continental Europe for firms to adopt variable work schedules which give employees some latitude in arrival and departure times from work. See Dumas (1973).

8 See also Cousins and Brown (1975) who found some two-thirds of the respondents in their survey of shipbuilding workers enjoying autonomy, lack of supervision, finding their work skilful and enjoyable, committed to the maintenance of high standards of workmanship — the characteristics of leisure-in-work. See Parker (1971 : 31) for the notion of leisure-in-work.

9 One study recently confirmed that this greater investment of self in spare-time activities by those with professional-level occupations extends to sport and physical recreation as well as to intellectual and artistic activity; see the *Sunday Times* reporting a survey by the National Opinion Polls, 8 June 1975.

10 Bryan Wilson who, we have just noted, believes in restricting educational opportunity to prevent people becoming over-educated for the jobs they have to do, is also a modern exponent of the work-leisure compensation fallacy (1975 : 73). Simon notes that Adam Smith believed that education could mitigate the brutalizing effects of the minute division of labour (1960 : Vol.1., 139).

11 See also Dumazadier and Latouche for French evidence on this point (1961).

12 See also Meakin (1976 : 8), quoting Ruskin: 'Industry without art is brutalizing'; this is Meakin's own theme throughout.

References

Aiach, P. and Willmott, P. (1975) Inequality and education in the East End of Paris. *New Society*, 9 October.

Allcorn, D.H. and Marsh, C.M. (1975) Occupational communities — communities of what? *in* Bulmer, M. *Working Class Images of Society*. London and Boston; Routledge and Kegan Paul.

Allen, J.E. (1972) The right to read — target for the '70s, *in* Melnik, A. and Merrit, J. (eds) *Reading: Today and Tomorrow*. London: University of London Press.

Annan, N. (1975) Equality in the schools, *in* Vaizey, J. (ed.) *Whatever Happened to Equality?* London: BBC.

Archambault, R.D. (1965) *Philosophical Analysis and Education*. London: Routledge and Kegan Paul.

Argyle, M. (1972) *The Social Psychology of Work*. London and Harmondsworth: Allen Lane and Penguin Books.

Aristotle (1962) *The Politics*. Harmondsworth: Penguin Books.

Arnold, M. (1960) *Culture and Anarchy*. Cambridge: Cambridge University Press.

Aron, R. (1969) Two definitions of class, *in* Béteille, A. (ed.) *Social Inequality*. Harmondsworth: Penguin Books.

Ashby, E. (1976) Why the AUT was wrong to join the TUC. *The Times Higher Education Supplement*, 30 April.

Attlee, C.R. (1937) *The Labour Party in Perspective*. London: Gollancz.

Austin, J.L. (1970) *Philosophical Papers* (second edition). London: Oxford University Press.

Ayer, A.J. (1956) *The Problem of Knowledge*. Harmondsworth: Penguin Books.

Baernreither, J.M. (1889) *English Associations of Working Men*. London: Sonnenschein.

Banks, O. (1965) *The Sociology of Education*. New York: Schocken Books.

Banks, O. and Finlayson, D. (1973) *Success and Failure in the Secondary School*. London: Methuen.

Bantock, G.H. (1952) *Freedom and Authority in Education*. London: Faber and Faber.

Bantock, G.H. (1963) *Education in an Industrial Society*. London: Faber and Faber.

Bantock, G.H. (1966) *The Implications of Literacy*. Leicester: Leicester University Press.

Bantock, G.H. (1968) *Culture, Industrialisation and Education*. London: Routledge and Kegan Paul.

Bantock, G.H. (1969) Social and cultural values in the seventies, *in* Garforth, F.W. (ed.) *Aspects of Education*. Hull: Institute of Education.

Bantock, G.H. (1970) *T.S. Eliot and Education*. London: Faber and Faber.

Bantock, G.H. (1975a) Equality and education, *in* Wilson, B. (ed.) *Education, Equality and Society*. London: Allen and Unwin.

Bantock, G.H. (1975b) Towards a theory of popular education, *in* Golby *et al.* (eds) *Curriculum Design*. London: Croom Helm.

Bantock, G.H. (1976) Quality and equality in curricular provision, *in* Skilbeck, M. and Harris, A. (eds) *Culture, Ideology and Knowledge*. Milton Keynes: Open University Press.

Barrow, R. (1975) *Moral Philosophy and Education*. London: Allen and Unwin.

Bell, R.B. (1962a) Social-class values and the teacher, *in* Bell, R.B. (ed.) *The Sociology of Education*. Homewood, Ill.: Dorsey Press.

Bell, R.B. (ed.) (1962b) *The Sociology of Education*. Homewood, Ill.: Dorsey Press.

Bendix, R. and Lipset, S.M. (eds) (1953) *Class, Status and Power*. Glencoe, Ill.: Free Press.

Bergel, E.E. (1962) *Social Stratification*. New York: McGraw-Hill.

Bernstein, B.B. (1971-3) *Class Codes and Control*, 3 vols. London and Boston: Routledge and Kegan Paul.

Bernstein, R. (1971) *Praxis and Action*. Philadelphia: University of Pennsylvania Press.

Bestor, A.E. (1952) 'Life-adjustment' education: a critique. *Bulletin of the American Association of University Professors*, 38 (Autumn).

Bestor, A.E. (1955) *The Restoration of Learning*. New York: Knopf.

Béteille, A. (ed) (1969) *Social Inequality*. Harmondsworth: Penguin Books.

Blackburn, R. (1972) *Ideology in Social Science*. London: Fontana Books.

Bottomore, T.B. (1974) *Sociology as Social Criticism*. London: Allen and Unwin.

Bottomore, T.B. and Rubel, M. (eds) (1963) *Karl Marx: Selected Writings*. Harmondsworth: Penguin Books.

Bourdieu, P. (1971a) Intellectual field and creative project, *in* Young, M.F.D. (ed.) *Knowledge and Control*. London: Collier-Macmillan.

Bourdieu, P. (1971b) Systems of education and systems of thought, *in* Young, M.F.D., as above.

Bourdieu, P. (1973) Cultural reproduction and social reproduction, *in* Brown, R. (ed.) *Knowledge, Education and Cultural Change*. London: Tavistock Publications.

Brown, R. (ed.) (1973) *Knowledge, Education and Cultural Change*. London: Tavistock Publications.

Bruner, J. (1963) *The Process of Education*. Cambridge, Mass.: Harvard University Press.

Bulmer, M. (ed.) (1975a) *Working Class Images of Society*. London and Boston: Routledge and Kegan Paul.

Bulmer, M. (1975b) Some problems of research in class imagery, *in* Bulmer, M., as above.

Burgess, T. (ed.) (1971) *Dear Lord James*. Harmondsworth: Penguin Books.

Castle, E.B. (1961) *Ancient Education and Today*. Harmondsworth: Penguin Books.

Central Advisory Council for Education (1963) *Half our Future*. London: HMSO.

Central Advisory Council for Education (1967) *Children and their Primary Schools*. London: HMSO.

Charbonnier, G. (1973) 'Primitive' and 'the civilized' peoples: a conversation with Levi-Strauss, *in* Disch, R. (ed.) *The Future of Literacy*. Englewood Cliffs, NJ: Prentice-Hall.

Cherus, A. (1976) Better working lives — a social scientist's view, *in* Weir, M. (ed.) *Job Satisfaction*. London: Fontana Books.

Clark, C. (n.d.) *Black studies or the study of Black people*. Publication of the Department of Psychology, Communications and Afro-American Studies, Stanford University.

Cloward, R.A. and Jones, J.A. (1963) Social class: educational attitudes and participation, *in* Passow, A.H. *Education in Depressed Areas*. New York: Teachers College Press.

Cohen, A.K. (1955) *Delinquent Boys*. New York: Free Press.

Cole, W.E. and Cox, R.L. (1968) *Social Foundations of Education*. New York: American Book Company.

Coleman, J.S. (1969) A brief summary of the Coleman Report, *in Equal Educational Opportunity*. Cambridge, Mass.: Harvard University Press.

Coleman, J.S. (1973) Equality of opportunity and equality of results. *Harvard Educational Review*, Vol. 43, No.1.

Collingwood, R.G. (1963) *The Principles of Art*. London: Oxford University Press.

Cook, L.A. and Cook, E.F. (1960) *A Sociological Approach to Education*. New York: McGraw-Hill.

Corwin, R.G. (1965) *A Sociology of Education*. New York: Appleton-Century-Crofts.

Cosin, B.R. (1972) *Education: Structure and Society*. Harmondsworth: Penguin Books.

Cousins, J. and Brown, R. (1975) Patterns of paradox: shipbuilding workers' images of society, *in* Bulmer, M. (ed.) *Working Class Images of Society*. London and Boston: Routledge and Kegan Paul.

Cox, C.B. and Dyson, A.E. (1969a) *Fight for Education* (Black Paper). London: The Critical Quarterly Society.

Cox, C.B. and Dyson, A.E. (1969b) *The Crisis in Education* (Black Paper). London: The Critical Quarterly Society.

Cox, C.B. and Dyson, A.E. (1970) *Goodbye Mr Short* (Black Paper). London: The Critical Quarterly Society.

Crick, B. (1975) Basic concepts for political education, *in Teaching Politics*, September.

Crittenden, B. (1973) *Education and Social Ideals*. Don Mills, Ont.: Longman Canada Ltd.

Crosland, C.A.R. (1963) *The Future of Socialism*. New York: Schocken Books.

Dahrendorf, R. (1969) On the origin of inequality among men, *in* Béteille, A. (ed.) *Social Inequality*. Harmondsworth: Penguin Books.

Dahrendorf, R. (1975) *The New Liberty*. London and Boston: Routledge and Kegan Paul.

Davis, R.L. and Cousins, J. (1975) The 'new working class' and the old, *in* Bulmer, M. (ed.) *Working Class Images of Society*. London and Boston: Routledge and Kegan Paul.

Dearden, R. (ed.) (1972) *Education and the Development of Reason*. London and Boston: Routledge and Kegan Paul.

Devons, E. (1961) *Essays in Economics*. London: Allen and Unwin.

Dewey, J. (1958) *Art as Experience*. New York: Capricorn Books.

Disch, R. (ed.) (1973) *The Future of Literacy*. Englewood Cliffs, NJ: Prentice-Hall.

Draffan, R.A. (1973) Working-class students still too rare. *The Times Higher Education Supplement*, 23 February.

Drucker, P. (1969) *The Age of Discontinuity*. London: Pan Books.

Dumas, E. (1973) Variable work schedules. *Montreal Star*, 20 January.

Dumazedier, J. and Latouche, N. (1961-2) Work and leisure in French sociology. *Industrial Relations*, Vol. 1.

Duncan, B. (1973) Comments on *Inequality*. *Harvard Educational Review*, Vol. 43, No. 1.

Durkheim, E. (1956) *Education and Sociology*. London: Collier-Macmillan.

Durkheim, E. (1964) *The Division of Labour in Society*. London: Routledge and Kegan Paul.

Easthorpe, G. (1975) *Community, Hierarchy and Open Education*. London and Boston: Routledge and Kegan Paul.

Elbourne, R.P. (1974) *Industrialization and Popular Culture*. M.Phil. thesis, University of London.

Eliot, T.S. (1948) *Notes towards a Definition of Culture*. London: Faber and Faber.

Engels, F. (1958) *The Condition of the Working-Class in England*. Oxford: Blackwell.

Entwistle, H. (1970a) *Child-Centred Education*. London: Methuen.

Entwistle, H. (1970b) *Education, Work and Leisure*. London: Routledge and Kegan Paul; New York: Humanities Press.

Entwistle, H. (1971) *Political Education in a Democracy*. London and Boston: Routledge and Kegan Paul.

Floud, J. and Scott, W. (1965) Recruitment to teaching in England and Wales, *in* Halsey, A.H., Floud, J. and Anderson, P.A., *Education, Economy and Society*. New York: Free Press.

Folley, B. (1975) Why be literate? *Sunday Times*, 7 December.

Freire, P. (1971) *Pedagogy of the Oppressed*. New York: Herder and Herder.

Friedlander, I. (1966) The importance of work versus nonwork among socially and occupationally stratified groups. *Journal of Applied Psychology*, Vol. 50, No.6 (December).

Friedman, M. (1975) Rich and poor, *in* Vaizey, J. (ed.) *Whatever happened to equality?* London: BBC.

Frye, N. (1967) *The Modern Century*. Toronto: Oxford University Press.

Gans, H.J. (1967) *Levittowners*. New York: Pantheon Books.

Glazer, N. (1976) 'Equal opportunity' gone wrong. *New Society*, 22 January.

Golby, M., Greenwald, J. and West, R. (eds) (1975) *Curriculum Design*. London: Croom Helm.

Goldthorpe, J.H. *et al.* (1968) *The Affluent Worker: Industrial Attitudes and Behaviour*; (1968) *The Affluent Worker: Political Attitudes and Behaviour*; (1969) *The Affluent Worker in the Class Structure*. Cambridge: Cambridge University Press.

Goody, J. (1973) Literacy and the non-literate in Ghana, *in* Disch, R. (ed.) *The Future of Literacy*. Englewood Cliffs, NJ: Prentice-Hall.

Goody, J. and Watt, I. (1962-3) The consequences of literacy. *Comparative Studies in Society and History*, Vol. V.

Graff, H.J. (1972) Towards a meaning of literacy. *History of Education Quarterly* (Fall).

Graff, H.J. (1973) Literacy and social structure in Elgin County, Canada West, 1861. *Histoire Sociale*, Vol. VI, No. 11.

Grambs, J.D. (1965) The Self-Concept: Basis for re-education of Negro youth *in* Lincoln Filene Centre for Citizenship and Public Affairs, *Negro Self Concept*. New York: McGraw-Hill.

Gramsci, A. (1971) Prison Notebooks (ed. by Q. Hoare and G. Nowell Smith.) London: Lawrence and Wishart; New York: International Publishers.

Grazia, S. de (1973) *Of Time, Work and Leisure*. New York: Kraus Reprint Co.

Green, T. (ed.) (1971) *Educational Planning in Perspective: Forecasting and Policy-making*. Guildford: Futuros/Iliffe Science & Technology Publications.

Green, T. (1971) The dismal future of equal educational opportunity, *in* Green, T. (ed.) above.

Gretton, R.H. (1917) *The English Middle Class*. London: G. Bell and Sons.

Gross, N. (1961) A critique of 'social class structure and American education', *in* Bell, R.B. (ed.) *The Sociology of Education*. Homewood, Ill.: Dorsey Press.

Halsey, A.H. (1972a) *Educational Priority*, Vol. 1. London: HMSO.

Halsey, A.H. (1972b) Attending to Robert Jackson. *The Times Higher Education Supplement*, 1 December.

Halsey, A.H. (1975) Class, status and power, *in* Vaizey, J. (ed.) *Whatever Happened to Equality?* London: BBC.

Halsey, A.H., Floud, J. and Anderson, P.A. (1965) *Education, Economy and Society*. New York: Free Press.

Hamilton, R.F. (1967) *Affluence and the French Worker in the Fourth Republic*. Princeton, NJ: Princeton University Press.

Harman, D. (1972) Illiteracy: an overview, *in* Melnik, A. and Merritt, J. (eds) *Reading: Today and Tomorrow*. London: University of London Press.

Harré, R. (1960) *The Logic of the Sciences*. London: Macmillan.

Harrington, M. (1973) *Socialism*. New York: Bantam Books.

Havelock, E. (1973) Poetry as preserved communication, *in* Disch, R. (ed.) *The Future of Literacy*. Englewood Cliffs, NJ: Prentice-Hall.

Hexter, J.H. (1961) *Reappraisals in History*. New York: Harper Torchbooks.

Hindess, B. (1971) *The Decline of Working-Class Politics*. London: Paladin Books.

Hirst, P.H. (1965) Liberal education and the nature of knowledge, *in* Archambault, R.D. (ed.) *Philosophical Analysis and Education*. London and Boston: Routledge and Kegan Paul.

Hobsbawn, E.J. (1975) Equality in the past, *in* Vaizey, J. (ed.) *Whatever Happened to Equality?* London: BBC.

Hodgen, M.T. (1925) *Workers' Education in England and the United States*. London: Kegan Paul, Trench Trubner and Co. Ltd.

Hoffman, J. (1975) *Marxism and the Theory of Praxis*. London: Lawrence and Wishart.

Hofstadter, R. (1963) *Anti-Intellectualism in American Life*. New York: Knopf.
Hoggart, R. (1968) *The Uses of Literacy*. Harmondsworth: Pelican Books.
Holly, D. (1971) *Society, Schools and Humanity*. London: Paladin Books.
Holt, J. (1967) *How Children Learn*. London: Pitman.
Howe, G. (1975) Equality and party politics, *in* Vaizey, J. (ed.) *Whatever Happened to Equality?* London: BBC.
Hurt, J. (1972) *Education in Evolution*. St Albans: Paladin Books.
Husén, T. and Boalt, G. (1967) *Educational Research and Educational Change*. New York: John Wilson.
Hyman, H. (1953) The value systems of different classes, *in* Bendix, R. and Lipset, S.M. (eds) *Class, Status and Power*. Glencoe, Ill.: Free Press.

Illich, I. (1971) *Deschooling Society*. London: Calder and Boyars.
Inglis, F. (1975) *Ideology and the Imagination*. Cambridge: Cambridge University Press.

Jackson, B. (1968) *Working-Class Community*. London: Routledge and Kegan Paul; New York: Humanities Press.
Jackson, B. and Marsden, D. (1962) *Education and the Working Class*. London: Routledge and Kegan Paul.
James, E. (1951) *Education for Leadership*. London: Harrap.
Jarvie, I.C. (1972) *Concepts and Society*. London and Boston: Routledge and Kegan Paul.
Jencks, C. (1972) *Inequality*. New York: Harper and Row.
Jencks, C. (1973) Inequality in retrospect. *Harvard Educational Review*, Vol. 43, No. 1.

Kampf, L. (1973) The humanities and inhumanities, *in* Disch, R. (ed.) *The Future of Literacy*. Englewood Cliffs, NJ: Prentice-Hall.
Katz, M.B. (1971) *Class, Bureaucracy and Schools*. New York and London: Praeger.
Katz, M.B. (1973) *Class, bureaucracy and schools*, *in* Myers, D. (ed.) *The Failure of Educational Reform in Canada*. Toronto: McLelland and Stewart Ltd.
Keddie, N. (1971) Classroom knowledge, *in* Young, M.F.D. (ed.) *Knowledge and Control*. London: Collier-Macmillan.
Keddie, N. (ed.) (1973) *Tinker, Tailor ... The Myth of Cultural Deprivation*. Harmondsworth: Penguin Books.
Kirk, R. (1973) *The Conservative Mind*. New York: Equinox Books.
Klein, J. (1965) *Samples from English Cultures*. 2 vols. London: Routledge and Kegan Paul.
Kohlberg, L. (1971) Stages of moral development as a basis for moral action, *in* Beck, C.M., Crittenden, B.S., Sullivan E.V. (eds), *Moral Education*. Toronto: University of Toronto Press.
Kolko, G. (1962) *Wealth and Power in America*. New York: Praeger.
Kozol, J. (1972) *Free Schools*. New York: Bantam Books.
Kuczynski, J. (1967) *The Rise of the Working Class*. New York: McGraw-Hill.
Kvaraceus, W.C. (1965) Negro youth and social adaptation, *in* Lincoln Filene Centre for Citizenship and Public Affairs, *Negro Self Concept*. New York: McGraw-Hill.

Labov, W. (1973) The logic of nonstandard English, *in* Keddie, N. (ed.) *Tinker, Tailor ... The Myth of Cultural Deprivation*. Harmondsworth: Penguin Books.
Lanfant, M.F. (1972) *Les Théories du Loisir*. Paris: Presses Universitaires de France.

Lawton, D. (1968) *Social Class Language and Education*. London: Routledge and Kegan Paul.

Lawton, D. (1975) *Class, Culture and the Curriculum*. London and Boston: Routledge and Kegan Paul.

Leach, E. (1977) Literacy be damned. *Observer*, 20 February.

Leavis, F.R. (1930) *Mass Civilization and Minority Culture*. Cambridge, Mass.: Minority Press.

Leavis, F.R. (1952) *The Common Pursuit*. London: Chatto and Windus.

Lewis, O. (1970) The culture of poverty, *in* his *Anthropological Essays*. New York: Random House.

Lewis, R. and Maude, A. (1949) *The English Middle Class*. London: Phoenix House.

Lincoln Filene Centre for Citizenship and Public Affairs (1965) *Negro Self Concept*. New York: McGraw-Hill.

Lipset, S.M. (1960) *Political Man*. New York: Doubleday.

Lipsey, R.G. (1963) *An Introduction to Positive Economics*. London: Weidenfeld and Nicolson.

Littlejohn, J. (1972) *Social Stratification*. London: Allen and Unwin.

Lockwood, D. (1975) Sources in variation in working-class images of society, *in* Bulmer, M. (ed.) *Working Class Images of Society*. London and Boston: Routledge and Kegan Paul.

Lomax, D. (1971) Focus on the student teachers, *in* Burgess, T. (ed.) *Dear Lord James*. Harmondsworth: Penguin Books.

Lucas, J.R. (1975) Equality in education, *in* Wilson, B. (ed.) *Education, Equality and Society*. London: Allen and Unwin.

McBride, F. (1972) Reading — is there such a thing? *in* Melnik, A. and Merrit, J. (eds) *Reading: Today and Tomorrow*. London: London University Press.

Mace, F.B. (1971) The book in an audio-visual world. *Icographic* (October).

MacIntyre, A. (1970) *Marcuse*. London: Fontana Books.

Malmquist, E. (1972) Reading: a human right and a human problem, *in* Melnik, A. and Merrit, J. (eds) *Reading: Today and Tomorrow*. London: London University Press.

Marcus, S. (1974) *Engels, Manchester and the Working Class*. New York: Weidenfeld and Nicolson.

Marsden, T.H. (1953) Social selections in the Welfare State, *in* Bendix, R. and Lipset, S.M. (eds) *Class, Status and Power*. Glencoe, Ill.: Free Press.

Marshall, T. (1975) Are university teachers members of the working class? *The Times Higher Education Supplement*, 21 November.

Martin, D. (1975) The road from Rochdale to Rome. *The Times Higher Education Supplement*, 21 February.

Marx, K. and Engels, F. (1967) *The Communist Manifesto*. Harmondsworth: Penguin Books.

Mead, M. (1973) On educational emphases in primitive perspective, *in* Keddie, N. (ed.) *Tinker, Tailor ... The Myth of Cultural Deprivation*. Harmondsworth: Penguin Books.

Meakin, D. (1976) *Man and Work*. London: Methuen.

Melnik, A. and Merrit, J. (eds) (1972) *Reading: Today and Tomorrow*. London: London University Press.

Meyer, K.B. and Buckley, W. (1969) *Class and Society*. New York: Random House.

Midwinter, E. (1972a) *Projections*. London: Ward Lock.

Midwinter, E. (1972b) *Social Environment and the Urban School*. London: Ward Lock.

Midwinter, E. (1975) *Education and the Community*. London: Allen and Unwin.

Miller, G. (1971) Moves for equal opportunity. *The Times Educational Supplement*, 8 October.

Miller, J. (1971) *McLuhan*. London: Fontana Books.

Moore, R.S. (1975) Religion as a source of variation in working-class images of society, *in* Bulmer, M. (ed.) *Working Class Images of Society*. London and Boston: Routledge and Kegan Paul.

Moore, W.E. (1963) *Man, Time and Society*. New York: John Wiley.

Moyle, D. (1972) Reading for the 'seventies, *in* Melnik, A. and Merrit, J. (eds) *Reading: Today and Tomorrow*. London: London University Press.

Moynihan, D.P. and Mosteller, F. (eds) (1972) *On Equality of Educational Opportunity*. New York: Random House.

Myers, D. (ed.) (1973) *The Failure of Educational Reform in Canada*. Toronto: McClelland and Stewart Ltd.

Natanson, J. and Prost, A. (1973) *La Révolution scolaire*. Paris: Editions ouvrières.

OECD (1967) *Social Objectives in Educational Planning*.

Ortega y Gasset, J. (1957) *Revolt of the Masses*. New York: Norton.

Orwell, G. (1970) *The Collected Essays, Journalism and Letters of George Orwell*, Vol.3. Harmondsworth: Penguin Books.

Orzack, L.H. (1959) Work as a 'central life interest' of professionals. *Social Problems*, Vol.7, No.2 (Fall).

Parekh, B. (ed.) (1975) *The Concept of Socialism*. London: Croom Helm.

Parker, R. (1974) *The Myth of the Middle Class*. New York and London: Harper Colophon Books.

Parker, S. (1971) *The Future of Work and Leisure*. London: Paladin Books.

Parkin, F. (1972) *Class Inequality and Political Disorder*. St Albans: Paladin Books.

Pateman, T. (ed.) (1972) *Counter-Course*. Harmondsworth: Penguin Books.

Pedley, R. (1963) *The Comprehensive School*. Harmondsworth: Penguin Books.

Peters, R.S. (1966) *Ethics and Education*. London: Allen and Unwin.

Piaget, J. (1960) *Language and Thought of the Child*. London: Routledge and Kegan Paul.

Pieper, J. (1964) *Leisure, the Basis of Culture*. New York: Pantheon Books.

Porter, J.A. (1965) *The Vertical Mosaic*. Toronto: University of Toronto Press.

Postman, N. (1971) Telling it like it ain't: an examination of the language of education, *in Alternatives in Education*. Ontario: Ontario Institute for Studies in Education.

Postman, N. (1973) The politics of reading, *in* Keddie, N. (ed.) *Tinker, Tailor ... The Myth of Cultural Deprivation*. Harmondsworth: Penguin Books.

Postman, N. and Weingartner, C. (1969) *Teaching as a Subversive Activity*. New York: Delta.

Quine, W.G. (1974) Polarized cultures in comprehensive schools, *in Research in Education*, No. 12 (November).

Rawls, J. (1971) *A Theory of Justice*. Cambridge, Mass.: Harvard University Press.

Raynor, J. (1969) *The Middle Class*. London: Longmans, Green.

Redfern, H.B. (1976) 'Movement' and Professor Bantock's theory of popular education. *University of Manchester School of Education Gazette*.

Reichenback, H. (1947) *The Elements of Symbolic Logic*. New York: Macmillan.

Reimer, E. (1971) *School is Dead*. Harmondsworth: Penguin Books.

Riesman, D. (1964) *Abundance for What!* London: Chatto and Windus.

Robbins, L. (1949) *An Essay on the Nature and Significance of Economic Science*. London: Macmillan.

Roberts, R. (1973) *The Classic Slum*. Harmondsworth: Penguin Books.

Rubinstein, D. and Stoneman, C. (1970) *Education for Democracy*. Harmondsworth: Penguin Books.

Runciman, W.G. (1969) The three dimensions of social inequality, *in* Béteille, A. (ed.) *Social Inequality*. Harmondsworth: Penguin Books.

Ryle, G. (1949) *The Concept of the Mind*. London: Hutchinson's University Library.

Salaman, G. (1975) Occupations, community and consciousness, *in* Bulmer, M. (ed.) *Working Class Images of Society*. London and Boston: Routledge and Kegan Paul.

Seasholes, B. (1965) Political socialization of Negroes, *in* Lincoln Filene Centre for Citizenship and Public Affairs, *Negro Self Concept*. New York: McGraw-Hill.

Shanks, M. (1961) *The Stagnant Society*. Harmondsworth: Penguin Books.

Shaw, G.B. (1964) *Androcles and the Lion* (preface). Harmondsworth: Penguin Books.

Shorter, E. (1973a) The history of work in the West, *in* Shorter, E. (ed.) *Work and Community in the West*. New York: Harper and Row.

Shorter, E. (1973b) *Work and Community in the West*. New York: Harper and Row.

Silver, H. (ed.) (1973) *Equal Opportunity in Education*. London: Methuen.

Silver, H. (1975) *English Education and the Radicals 1780-1850*. London and Boston: Routledge and Kegan Paul.

Simon, B. (1960, 1974, 1974) *Studies in the History of English Education*. 3 vols. London: Lawrence and Wishart.

Simon, B. (1972) *The Radical Tradition in Education in Britain*. London: Lawrence and Wishart.

Skidelski, R. (1969) *English Progressive Schools*. Harmondsworth: Penguin Books.

Skilbeck, M. and Harris, A. (eds) (1976) *Culture, Ideology and Knowledge*. Milton Keynes: Open University Press.

Smith, N.B. (1972) Reading: an international challenge, *in* Melnik, A. and Merritt, J. (eds) *Reading: Today and Tomorrow*. London: London University Press.

Steiner, G. (1973) After the book? *in* Disch, R. (ed.) *The Future of Literacy*. Englewood Cliffs, NJ: Prentice-Hall.

Stenhouse, L. (1967) *Culture and Education*. New York: Weybright and Talley.

Strong, R. (1972) The nature of reading, *in* Melnik, A. and Merrit, J. (eds) *Reading: Today and Tomorrow*. London: London University Press.

Tawney, R.H. (1973) Secondary education for all, *in* Silver, H. (ed.) *Equal Opportunity in Education*. London: Methuen.

Tawney, R.H. (1974) *Equality*. London: Allen and Unwin.

Taylor, G. and Ayres, N. (1973) Born and bred unequal, *in* Silver, H. (ed.) *Equal Opportunity in Education*. London: Methuen.

Taylor, W. (1969) *Society and the Education of Teachers*. London: Faber and Faber.

Thompson, E.P. (1961) Review of *The Long Revolution*. *New Left Review*, No. 9.

Thompson, E.P. (1968) *The Making of the English Working Class*. Harmondsworth: Penguin Books.

Thompson, J.F. (1973) *Foundations of Vocational Education*. Englewood Cliffs, NJ: Prentice-Hall.

Tumin, M.M. (1967) *Social Stratification*. Engelwood Cliffs, NJ: Prentice-Hall.

Utley, T.E. (1975) Concepts of equality, *in* Vaizey, J. (ed.) *Whatever Happened to Equality?* London: BBC.

Vaizey, J. (ed.) (1975) *Whatever Happened to Equality?* London: BBC.

Veblen, T. (1970) *The Theory of the Leisure Class*. London: Allen and Unwin.

Walsh, W. (1966) *The Use of Imagination*. Harmondsworth: Penguin Books.

Warner, D.H. (1972) A conversation, *in* Melnik, A. and Merritt, J. (eds) *Reading: Today and Tomorrow*. London: London University Press.

Weir, M. (ed.) (1976) *Job Satisfaction*. London: Fontana Books.

Wellek, R. (1973) The attack on literature, *in* Disch, R. (ed.) *The Future of Literacy*. Englewood Cliffs, NJ: Prentice-Hall.

Westergaard, J. (1972) Sociology: the myth of classlessness, *in* Blackburn, R. (ed.) *Ideology in Social Science*. London: Fontana Books.

Westergaard, J. (1975) Radical class consciousness: a comment, *in* Bulmer, M. (ed.) *Working Class Images of Society*. London and Boston: Routledge and Kegan Paul.

Westergaard, J. and Little, A. (1964) Trends in social class differentials in educational opportunity. *British Journal of Sociology*, Vol. XIV.

White, J.D. (1973) *Towards a Compulsory Curriculum*. London and Boston: Routledge and Kegan Paul.

Whitehead, A.N. (1955) *The Aims of Education*. London: Williams and Norgate.

Wilensky, H. (1961-2) Labour and leisure: intellectual traditions. *Industrial Relations*, Vol. 1.

Williams, R. (1961a) *Culture and Society*. Harmondsworth: Penguin Books.

Williams, R. (1961b) *The Long Revolution*. London: Chatto and Windus.

Williams, R. (1962) *Communications*. Harmondsworth: Penguin Books.

Williams, R. (1973) Base and superstructure in Marxist cultural theory. *New Left Review*, No. 82.

Williams, R. (1975) You're a Marxist, aren't you? *in* Parekh, B. (ed.) *The Concept of Socialism*. London: Croom Helm.

Wilson, B. (ed.) (1975a) *Education, Equality and Society*. London: Allen and Unwin.

Wilson, B. (1975b) Introduction, *in* Wilson, B. (ed.), as above.

Wilson, J. (1966) *Equality*. London: Hutchinson.

Young, M. (1970) *Rise of the Meritocracy*. Harmondsworth: Penguin.

Young, M.F.D. (ed.) (1971a) *Knowledge and Control*. London: Collier-Macmillan.

Young, M.F.D. (1971b) An approach to the study of curricula as socially organized knowledge, *in* Young, M.F.D. (ed.), as above.

Index